Solacium

by
SJ de Lagarde

2nd edition, March 2018

'A good and fascinating read, suspenseful, even if, before reading Solacium one would not expect to be passionate about the subject. The characters, sub-characters, plots and sub-plots are carefully and fascinating thought out and intertwined. A good read.Buy it!'

Saaskia Aark-Bennett, author of Dodging Joe

'As a professor of literature, this book appealed to me for its incredible narratology qualities and its impeccable style. Both are so rare in young authors and debut novels. The intertwined storylines make for a thrilling read that goes by very fast, and the characters are extraordinary while still being very easy to relate to... and of course the theme is incredibly powerful and very carefully, lovingly absorbed by the narrative. The author was able to grasp the complexity and intensity of the disease and still offer an engaging, compelling story. I really recommend it, it will be worth your reading time.'

Carole Llewellyn, author of Une Ombre Chacun

'One of the best books I've ever read!!! Reading this intriguing and compelling novel gave me goosebumps. This book took me out of my comfort zone, left me speechless,and crumpled my brain like a piece of paper. It is like anything I've read before. This novel deserves more attention.'

Books of Cat, book blogger

'It was one of the most intriguing books I've read lately!! It was a pretty deep book that kind of makes you think. And brings light to kind of what a person suffering from Schizophrenia goes through, and what aspects of it would also affect their family. I enjoyed this book quite a bit, AND THAT ENDING!!! Oh my goodness! I wouldn't have guessed that ending in a million years!'

A.Bibliophiles.Book.Blog, book blogger

'Could not put it down! Rarely do I come across a book that has such an impact on me. As someone who works in the field of mental health, I was so happy to come across a book that tackles the real issues surrounding mental health including the stigma. Based on a true story, Solacium gives us the allows us to enter into the mind of someone struggling with mental illness.'

Ayesha, book blogger

'Brilliant read. Read in 2 days so testament to it being a gripping and fascinating story. Completely escaped into the unfolding of events and the characters still linger in my mind. Deep, dark book with a beautiful feel for friendship and raw love. Very much looking forward to the next novel '

Laura Ziderman

'Thoroughly recommend! Absolutely beautifully written. Could not put this book down and can't recommend highly enough. The detail that SJ goes into, truly brings the characters to life. Can't wait to read what she writes next.'

Amazon Customer

'MUST READ! Fantastic read- gripped from the first to the last page. Beautifully written, characters well developed and the story compelling. Highly recommend. Can't wait for the next book!'

Missymoo79

'Gripping account of youth, love and mental illness. Heartwarming and heartbreaking story of youth, love and the torment of mental illness. Beautifully written first novel by a promising author. I thoroughly enjoyed and highly recommend it'

Miss P Garrido

'A gripping story from the very beginning - part love story, part tragic descent into psychosis. This is one of those novels that you tell yourself you simply must stop reading and go to sleep as soon as you get to the end of the chapter...and then stay up all night because you can't stop!'

MonsterV

Dedication

To my childhood friend Z for without him this book would have never been a story. Thank you for the memories and the insights.

To my darling husband J for his unrelenting patience and wise counsel.

To all my friends and family who have been so supportive and who volunteered to read and give their valuable feedback. A part of you all is in this book.

And last but not least THANK YOU to you my reader for giving Solacium a go and letting me draw you into this story.

xx

SJ de Lagarde

PROLOGUE

Berlin, October 2010 - 24 hours after the incident

'My name is Jay, and I'm a good person', he kept repeating to himself as he stepped out of the police van. The daylight hit him with such brightness, he was thankful to hide under his hood. The first thing he noticed was the sound. It was deafening. People were screaming and shouting. He closed his eyes in a desperate attempt to shut out the harsh light and the screams as he wished himself elsewhere. As he took a few hesitant steps forward he felt cold sweat trickling down between his broad shoulder blades. He walked slowly like a pig to the slaughterhouse, like a dead man walking.

Again he repeated the sentence in his head 'My name is Jay, and I'm a good person'. Slowly he looked up at the sea of screaming people crowding in on him, pushing each other out of the way to get a closer look. Their evil eyes wide open, they wanted to peel his skin off with their claws and feast on his limbs. He tried to take a step back, but a strong arm held him tightly into place.

A microphone was thrust in his face, striking his cheek. Jay flinched, tightly clenching his jaw. A journalist fired questions at him but he couldn't understand a word that was said. The man's mouth opened and closed, white bubbles of spittle forming at the corners. Jay's head shrunk further into the hood of his blue jumper as the hand that held his arm jerked him to one side. His long fringe hung low down his face. He closed his eyes in a desperate attempt to escape.

Someone else wrangled free from the media scrum, pushed past the police cordons, held up a camera and started eagerly shooting him from all angles. He could hear the TV anchor urgently addressing his audience, only registering snippets of the reported story. *Blood spatters on three-meter high ceilings. A human tragedy. A monster on a bloody rampage. A family forever destroyed.* The camera flashes blinded him and Jay bared his teeth in an awkward grimace before a police officer drove the photographer back beyond the cordoned-off area. Jay bowed his head in shame. His beard touched his chest. He was glad they hadn't made him shave this morning. These days he rarely looked in the mirror but when he did he liked how the fuzzy dark brown hair blurred his face and hid his bloated features.

He rubbed the palms of his hands together, they were sweaty and numb. Slowly he felt his vision slip out of focus. He clenched his big calloused hands into fists and repeated quietly 'My name is Jay'. Over and over again. 'I'm 30 years old and I'm a good...' The man tightened the grip on his arm until it hurt and shouted in his ear to shut up and walk straight ahead. Reality narrowed and Jay felt the cold, steely grip of fear clawing its way up his numbing arms. His heartbeat accelerated and he could feel his pulse throbbing on the inside of his wrists.

'Who does this? What kind of an animal does this? That psycho needs to be locked up for life!', someone screamed.

Suddenly he couldn't feel his feet anymore and he realised he had stopped walking. The symptoms were familiar to him. It always started with the same symptoms. Soon his mind would fog up and his vision blur until he was unable to move a muscle, he would start hyperventilating, the headache would come and then he would hear it. He tried to control his breathing and ignore the raucous crowd by staring intently at his dirty trainers. He exhaled slowly and noticed a shoelace had come undone. The thought of simply bending down to tie it crossed his mind but he couldn't. The cold steel of the handcuffs dug into his wrists.

Staring down the barrel of the camera, the TV anchor continued breathlessly reporting on the scoop of a lifetime. *The victim had to be identified by his dental records. They had to drag the hysterical wife from the crime scene.*

Jay gritted his teeth. The urge to turn around and run away as fast as he could was overwhelming. To run away from the crowd, the noise, the policemen and the tall, dark building he was being led to. As if hearing his thoughts, the square-shouldered policeman next to him grunted menacingly and tightened his grip on Jay's arm. Suddenly Jay heard a familiar voice whispering his name insistently. He shuddered in terror.

Jay. Psst. Jay. It's me.

Not now.

You need me. I know what to do. I can get you out of here. Let yourself fall on the floor and bang your head against that sidewalk. You must do it.

No.

Hit your head against the edge until it bleeds. You must do it now. Do it. Until your skull cracks open and your brain pours out onto the concrete. You have no choice.

He shook his head.

No.

The voice giggled devilishly and hissed disapprovingly.

You know you must do it. There is no way out. A fatal injury is your last chance to escape.

No.

As he looked up in despair, he scanned the crowd and all the faces blurred into one sweaty ugly mass. He wanted to scream. And then he stopped. His eyes locked on her. The skinny blonde girl in the floaty white dress. She stood motionless amidst the commotion, her long white blonde hair framing her pale, delicate face. A beam of light burning through the dark fog. She held her head up high, elegantly cocked to one side. Accentuated by the bruised dark circles beneath them, her eyes were black with sadness and her lips moved silently.

He shuffled past her, pushed and shoved by the policemen at his side. She calmly looked up and stared at him with piercing eyes. She looked straight into his soul with such conviction that the voice in his head retreated back into its furthest corner. She smiled a melancholic smile. Silently she pressed the palms of her hands together in prayer and mouthed 'I'm with you. Always'. Although silent, the words resonated in his head like the bells of a church. He took a deep breath, bracing himself, and the two policemen grabbed his arms and dragged him towards the large wooden doors of the building. The sign next to the entrance read: Criminal Court of Justice.

Part one - An endless summer
Sophie Liebtreu

***

'You know how the time flies
Only yesterday was the time of our lives
We were born and raised in a summer haze
Bound by the surprise of our glory days'

Someone like you,
Adele

***

CHAPTER 1

Berlin, December 2010 - 2 months after the incident

The antibiotics Sophie Liebtreu-Mackenzie was taking were strong enough to clear out the green mucus that festered under her eye sockets, but with a blocked nose and inactive taste buds, food tasted like cardboard. After carefully navigating through the conversational minefield that was the family dinner, Sophie was relieved to retreat to the living room. Wrapping herself in her favourite wool cardigan, she curled up on the red leather sofa and watched her daughter Juliet sleeping soundly in her travel cot. At two months, Juliet was growing into a cute dark-haired baby with green inquisitive eyes and now that Sophie and her husband Martin Mackenzie had survived the chaotic first weeks of parenthood, they had finally started to settle into a more regular routine.

It had taken Sophie a while to convince herself and her husband to escape the daily London grind and spend their daughter's first Christmas with her family in Berlin. Earlier that day, as the plane touched down at Berlin Tegel airport and the terminal building drew closer, Sophie had thought of her parents waiting at arrivals and silently pledged that this year, there wouldn't be any rows. For once they would all get along. She would nod her head in consent to her mother's never-ending flood of well-meaning advice on how kids should only be fed organic, locally-sourced products. She would pat her brother Sam silently on the shoulder and not lecture him on how he should apply for business school rather than wasting his talent working in a coffee shop. She was not going to say anything heinous to her sister Anna, no sarcastic comments about her fear of everything and no derogatory comments about her never-ending wallflower status. Not this time. Finally, she was hoping her child would awaken the grandfather in her father.

She looked at her daughter, suddenly overwhelmed with the desire to squeeze her and shower her with kisses. *My little dove of peace.* Juliet's first Christmas was going to be harmonious and peaceful, Sophie vowed.

Her sister Anna quietly slid next to her on the sofa. She was four years younger, the middle child and radically different from her older sister. As much as Sophie appeared outgoing and confident, Anna was quiet and introverted.

'So what are our plans for tomorrow night?' Sophie casually enquired as her brother Sam slumped on the other side to her with a glass of red wine.

Her mother Vera looked up from her iPad, removed her reading glasses and smiled.

'Well, your father and I being creatures of habit, we've booked our usual table at Freddy's for their Christmas party.'

Sam groaned and rolled his eyes, mocking their parents' predictable Christmas dinner, but Sophie nodded. Freddy's was a welcome change from the usual sugar-coated Christmases with too many 'jingle bells' and 'ho ho hos'. Sophie preferred spending the evening in the same, rock-themed restaurant as every year to sitting at home and witnessing John Liebtreu, her father, retreat into his study to systematically down beer after beer, only to reappear, blind drunk and swearing.

With a rock band entertaining the guests the evening was inevitably a success, and usually ended with Sophie's father drunk, dancing uncoordinatedly – but in a better mood than if he had stayed at home. Sophie's husband Martin nodded in approval. The rather straight-laced Scottish investment banker she had married a year before she got pregnant with their first child had come to appreciate the slightly different take on traditional Christmas. He would laugh at Sophie's mother's eccentric sparkly outfits and keep a watchful eye on her father.

'That's a fabulous idea – it'll be fun! Who else is coming?' Sophie hoped her voice hit the right tone of cheerfulness.

The party was usually joined by a group of her parents' friends, including Henry Adler, her father's best friend. Henry was a handsome and gentle man in his early 60s and a regular guest at her parents' dinner parties. Suddenly nervous, Sophie bit her lip. Was his son Jay going to be there? Jay was her childhood best friend. They had made it a habit to meet up whenever she was in Berlin, but since she got married she had only seen him once. *That one time in Kreuzberg,* she swallowed hard at the uncomfortable memory. Up until the age of 18, they had spent every Christmas together. But it was different now... She hadn't seen or heard from him since their last encounter, after she had found out that she was pregnant.

When she eventually decided to email him after the birth of her daughter, her emails were not replied to, her voice messages ignored and while she was anxious to check on him, she also worried to find out he didn't feel the same about her. She wondered if she would introduce him to her daughter.

'Is Jay coming too?'

Sophie's question hung in the room unanswered for what seemed an eternity. When her mother finally lifted her head, her face had turned pale and her features twisted into a mask of sadness. Her mouth twitched nervously as she tried to speak, but the words seemed to fail her. Sophie's heartbeat accelerated instantly.

'What's wrong?' she whispered.

'Oh Sophie, we didn't know how to tell you this. We need to talk to you about Jay. We have some bad news,' she finally croaked, her eyes welling up.

The last time Sophie had met Jay he had been in a fragile – but stable – state and he had promised her he was going to seek help. That was nine months ago. Her mind raced as she tried to remain calm but her hands started tingling, and she flinched nervously at the touch of her brother's hand on her arm. Her mother glanced over to her husband John who seemed to shrink into his armchair. He looked ill at ease, being the bearer of bad news was a role that didn't suit him.

'Jay was involved in an incident,' Sophie thought she heard her father say. He tried to remain matter-of-fact, but Sophie could sense the raw emotions he was trying to mask.

'Is he ...dead?' she whispered, lightheaded with dread and her eyes wide with anxiety.

'No he didn't die. He... he was involved in an incident.'

Her brain was trying to absorb the information and simultaneously analyse the body language of both her parents. Everything around her slowly shifted off kilter. The room started spinning. She felt drunk and nauseous, her fingers digging deep into the red leather of the sofa.

Incident...incident...incident...

Her father's words still ringing in her ears, she noticed how they all suddenly stared down at their feet. Eventually, he started to speak, his voice low and hesitant. Every word was a grenade exploding in her head, each one blowing a crater of aching emptiness into her soul.

When her father finished talking, a single tear rolled down his rugged cheek and disappeared into his beard. An uncomfortable silence froze the room. Sophie's thoughts rolled around in her head, aimlessly and uselessly, like dice without eyes.

My best friend Jay. My first kiss. The man I thought I knew. So gentle. So talented. A killer? Oh Jay, what have you done?

Somewhere in the house the automatic boiler timer switched itself on with a hum, breaking the leaden silence and pulling Sophie back into the living room. Her daughter Juliet started crying and automatically, Sophie got up, her limbs stiff and her mind numb.

***

Berlin, June 1994 - 16 years before the incident

Irritated, Sophie Liebtreu pushed her maths course book to one side and stared at the ringing phone with narrowed eyes, willing it to stop. She knew it was her mother calling, wanting her to be sociable and come down to greet the guests. It was late on Sunday morning and Sophie's parents were organising a summer brunch barbecue. Usually she didn't mind spending time with her family on these occasions – they tended to behave better when their friends were around. But since she had a mountain of homework to finish, Sophie didn't feel like hanging around the barbecue helping her dad flip sausages. Maths was usually her forte, but she had been buried in her books since sunrise and was getting nowhere. Chewing the tip of her pen, she gazed out the window, admiring the flawless morning sky and noticing the kids next door playing football in their garden, all in ugly matching shell suits. They looked dorky, and Sophie dreaded her mother inviting them to join the barbecue.

Worried they would spot her in the window, she quickly turned back to her books. All those abstract rules, she understood them, and she could make the connection to the real world. She took pleasure in discovering what made these calculations relevant and what they meant in her day-to-day life. In a reality where she feared her father's next violent outburst she liked retreating into the safe world of numbers. Her exam was on Wednesday. Although she loved the subject and her teacher even more, at the rate she was memorising the formulae, she would never be ready to secure her usual A+.

The phone was still ringing and with a sigh she reached for the handset. 'Vera?' She tried not to sound too exasperated.

'Sophie, please come down. Everyone is here; the barbecue is ready and I want you to greet our guests.'

'But Vera, I'm still studying.' Her mother hated being called "mother", and so Sophie and her siblings had been banned from using what she considered an offensive word. They only ever addressed their mother by her first name.

'I have that maths exam next week, and I need to get through these exercises'. With the phone in one hand and the receiver in the other Sophie paced around, kicking clothes around her messy bedroom.

'I'm sure you'll be okay, just come down and eat something. You need to eat, you've lost weight again. You've been holed up in your room since Friday. The weather is gorgeous, and you're as pale as a ghost. You need a bit of sunshine. Come on!' her mother urged her.

'I'm not hungry' Sophie mumbled. She stopped in front of the mirror and looked at the skinny girl staring back at her. Looking at her protruding ribs, she conceded her mother was right; she had lost weight. She was pale and her white skin only highlighted the angry blemish that sprouted on her chin. Self-consciously she picked at it, feeling ugly. She tugged her favourite blue t-shirt over her mid-riff and smiled at the memory of her best friend Camelia convincing her to shoplift it, adamant second-hand shops didn't have security cameras and that she shouldn't be such a coward. Camelia stole stuff all the time. So often and so successfully, that she had been able to set up a little business and happily sold t-shirts and dresses out of her school bag to her classmates during lunch break. Sophie smoothed the t-shirt against her flat stomach.

The adrenaline rush had been so powerful when she had slipped it in her bag that the t-shirt became Sophie's most prized possession, a trophy and a symbol of her brazen attitude.

'Ok mum, I'll come down and say hello but only a few minutes then I'll get back to my room', she muttered reluctantly.

'Nonsense, you'll stay long enough to help me chop some vegetables for the side dishes. Besides Henry is here with his son Jay and I want you to meet him. You'll see he's about your age, and he's lovely. He's quite creative; he really is a talented young man. You could learn something from him.'

There it was again. Her mother would always drop thinly-veiled hints into the conversation in the hope her daughter would develop some artistic skills. Much to the disappointment of her mother, a successful artist who regularly exhibited her paintings at art galleries across the country, Sophie didn't have an artistic bone in her body.

'Ok then, come down now and I expect your widest smile', her mother chirped down the phone and hung up.

Sophie looked at herself again, picked up some concealer from the floor and proceeded to camouflage the spot under a thick layer of makeup. It wasn't working out so well; it looked bigger now, and she cursed under her breath. She quickly ran a comb through her white-blonde hair and slipped on her dirty skateboard shoes before bounding down two flights of stairs to join her mother in the kitchen. Her mother's dandelion hair floated around her head like a copper halo and Sophie cringed at the sight of the outlandish bright kaftan she was wearing. *Why can't she just be a bit more... conventional.*

Busy chopping tomatoes on the large wooden dining table, her mother was chatting animatedly to Henry, her husband's best friend. Other guests loitered around the kitchen, smoking and drinking gin and tonics. Sophie waved a quick hello to Henry; he wore his usual cartoonish red braces which made her chuckle. Her father had great respect for his childhood friend and as far as Sophie understood he was the CEO of a publishing company. Sophie didn't quite understand what kind of job that was supposed to be but she got that Henry was a very wealthy man who was somehow friends with her dad. Sitting next to him was his son. His head bowed; he was busy drawing. She noticed the expensive-looking pens scattered across the table. Copics.

Sophie recognised the brand, she had a box of those on her desk. The best felt-tip pens a graphic designer can buy in Germany according to the ad. After one particularly violent outburst, her father, by way of an apology for bruising her, had bought her the box, willing her to explore her creative side. But the pens just reminded her of the black eye she had sported for a week, and had remained untouched in the box on her desk.

Jay looked up from his sketchbook and stared with wide eyes at the skinny white-haired girl standing awkwardly in front of him. Her heart skipped a beat. His eyes were a beautiful emerald green, flecked with gold and framed with thick dark eyelashes. His stare had such a hypnotising intensity that she froze, unable to move a muscle.

'Sophie, meet Jay. Jay this is Sophie, my eldest daughter. You're both about the same age and I believe you two will get along marvellously', her mother beamed. Sophie caught herself thinking how much she hated it when her mother did that fake smile with raised eyebrows. It made her look like an actress, over-dramatic and insincere.

Sophie smiled tentatively, hoping her blushing face would go unnoticed but the boy continued to look at her non-plussed, further fanning the fire in her cheeks. Finally and ever so slowly he acknowledged her presence and gave her the slightest of nods, before returning to his drawing.

Wow you're a bit arrogant, aren't you? Feeling embarrassed and flustered by his blatant indifference, Sophie decided he was way too aloof to be of any interest to her. Evidently, she had better things to do. Her mother, however seemed to have other plans for her.

'Sophie I thought after lunch you guys could all go to the swimming pool for the afternoon. Jay can borrow the spare bike. The weather is fab, they're announcing 32C', she whispered out of earshot.

'Do I have to? Mum...Vera, I really have to study this afternoon. It's a complicated topic...' she pleaded with her mother. She glanced nervously over at a disinterested Jay, who didn't bother to look up from his drawing. She didn't feel like babysitting a spoilt rich kid, even if he had the most amazing eyes she had ever seen.

Her mother shot her that look, the nervous look of a beaten animal Sophie loathed and dreaded in equal measure. It meant: "Don't make this an issue to take up with your dad". Knowing it was a lost battle and that peacekeeping was the better option, Sophie shrugged her shoulders and slunk sullenly out onto the terrace.

Feeling her skin prickle in the heat of the morning sun and breathing in the hearty smell of the barbecue, she conceded the swimming pool seemed like a good idea. When her father spotted her standing idly, he shouted the sausages were ready, and the table needed dressing. Sophie hurried inside to execute his order immediately. Her father was an impatient man.

She ran into her younger brother Sam, a cheeky six-year-old with a mop of blonde hair that her mother insisted on cutting herself. The only reason it didn't look terrible was because he was irresistibly cute. He smiled a white-toothed grin at his big sister and her heart glowed with pride. Without the shadow of a doubt, she would happily always stand in the line of fire to protect her darling brother. She wasn't sure if she would do the same for her sister Anna, but so far she had never had to. Her sister was the quiet type and lived in a world of her own, withdrawn from reality, a fragile wallflower immersed in a world of music.

Anna played the piano at school and every time discord flared up in the household she would vanish and retreat to her room to listen to Chopin's Nocturnes on her tape recorder. For fear of drawing attention to herself she would crawl under her duvet, and keep the volume so low she had to press her ear against the stereo so hard it left grid marks on her skin. Sophie often wondered whether her father remembered he had a third child.

Sophie asked her siblings to get their swimming gear, and when Anna whispered whether she should pack a towel for Jay, they both discreetly peered over at the boy dressed in black. There was something odd about the way he just sat at the table, his head still bowed, in silence, except for the squeaking of the pen on paper. Sophie wasn't sure what to make of him.

While her sister vanished to finish packing and with her brother helping their father, Sophie walked over to the table and summoned the courage to tap Jay lightly on the shoulder. He flinched and looked up squinting in the bright sunlight. She sat down next to him and pointed at the drawing 'What are you drawing?' He shrugged and answered with a soft voice:

'Thoughts.'

'Thoughts? Well, they look pretty complicated.'

He smiled, and Sophie smiled back at him. She liked how his eyes lit up and she swore she felt the air warm up around them. Slightly uneasy with their closeness, she observed him from the corner of her eye as he continued filling out the snaking tentacles he called his 'Thoughts'. *There is something about the way he holds his pen. So delicately, as if it's a living thing and he is worried he might hurt it.*

He brusquely turned to her with a defiant look in his eyes and Sophie felt her cheeks burn again as she quickly looked away.

'Hey Jay, come here'. There was a sharpness to his father's voice that Sophie recognised, and they both stiffened and moved apart instinctively. Without looking back Jay walked off into the garden and when Sophie came back from the kitchen with a basket of freshly-cut bread, she witnessed Jay's dad slipping his son a few banknotes, which he folded neatly in his trouser pocket.

After lunch, they packed their rucksacks, promised their parents to come home no later than 6pm and set off for the local swimming pool.

'Soph will we get some ice-cream?' her brother shouted excitedly, peddling his bike next to hers.

'Mom didn't give me enough money'. She hadn't bothered to ask her father knowing the answer would have been a variation on the theme of 'ice-creams are full of artificial colourings which give you cancer'. Everything gave everybody cancer, or at least that's what her father chose to believe. Sam pulled a face to hide his disappointment but before he could drive off into the woods, Jay fished the money his father had given him out of his pocket and whispered that he had enough to buy ice cream for all of them. Sophie's heart glowed a little brighter as she caught Jay's light smile.

In the shade of the huge oak trees, the air was refreshingly cool, and they settled into a leisurely pace.

'Sorry about my mum when she introduced us earlier. She can be so overly dramatic sometimes. Most of the time actually. It's like she lives in her own world. It's so embarrassing.' Sophie huffed apologetically and narrowly dodged a fallen branch to avoid crashing her bike into Jay's. Frowning and deep in thought, it seemed he didn't notice. She carried on talking, desperate to engage him in a conversation.

'It's hard to live under the same roof as the parents. They can be so annoying.' She bit her lip at the understatement. More often than not it was a nightmare at home. Sometimes, late at night, rocked by insomnia she would fantasise about running away again. What prevented her was the fear of the punishment she knew would receive if caught. Last time, the belt had left indelible marks on her thighs.

'Sometimes I wish they'd get a divorce'... *So I can get rid of him,* she finished the sentence in her head.

'Believe me you don't want your parents to get a divorce. All you become is an unwanted burden that gets shifted from one household to the other over weekends,' he said in a calm voice.

Sophie held her breath; *his parents are divorced,* now it was her turn to concentrate on the road ahead in silence, his words resonating with her – *an unwanted burden.*

Anna and Sam had stopped by the side of the path and were gesticulating animatedly. Sophie dropped her bike to the floor and followed them into the bushes. Sam stopped and pointed at something furry covered in leaves. Eyes wide with excitement he whispered: 'Look Sophie! It's a dead rabbit! What do you think happened to it?'

From what Sophie could see it was indeed a dead rabbit. Its head had been half eaten by something bigger. Her brother picked up a stick and started prodding it only to be pushed aside by Anna, who scowled him for trying to touch it. Sam stomped away and kicked up a few fallen leaves with an angry foot. Anna and Sophie carefully bent down to take a closer look, curious, neither having seen a dead rabbit before. Half of its skull had been ripped open by a bloodthirsty predator, but its open eye was staring at them as if to say "help, get me out of here". Fresh blood was still oozing out of the head wound, as if they had disturbed the predator's killing just minutes ago. It was creepy, and Sophie shuddered as she gently pulled her sister up, wondering whether they'd have to bury it.

A shout broke the silence of the forest. As they turned around Jay towered above them, holding a big rock over his head. With a swift swing he crashed it onto the dead animal. Its bones crushed under the weight of the rock. Black blood spattered onto Sophie's trousers. Her sister gasped in horror. Her brother hid behind a tree. All eyes were on Jay as he just stood there, motionless, his arms hanging at his sides, staring at the rock he had just thrown. Then he turned around to face Sophie. She swallowed uneasily at the sight of the look in his eyes.

'What did you do that for?' Sophie whispered.

'It told me it was suffering and wanted a quick mercy death', he breathed back.

'But...it was already dead...', she continued with wide eyes . 'There was no need to ... crush it to a bloody pulp'. *It told him it was suffering.* He shrugged his shoulders and walked over to pick up his bike from the floor.

They rode in silence the rest of the way to the swimming pool, each of them trying to erase the images of the crushed, dead rabbit out of their heads. Sam broke the uncomfortable silence with an excited scream: 'We are here!' They locked their bikes in the stands and queued for what seemed like an eternity before entering the busy outdoor pool.

Back at her parent's house later that afternoon, Sophie checked her freckled completion in the mirror of the hallway. The skin of her face felt tight and she wished she had applied more sun-cream. As she looked to the side, she noticed Jay in the reflection of the mirror. He was standing a bit further down the hallway clutching his rucksack, ready to go home, studying one of her mother's paintings on the wall. He's quite tall for his age, thought Sophie, as she discreetly took him in. They'd had a fun afternoon at the pool, mostly spent jumping off various diving boards, cutting shapes mid-air and dive-bombing into the cool water.

When Sophie tilted her head to one side, she could still hear her ears gurgling with water. Her hair smelled of chlorine and had developed a slightly green tinge after reacting to the chemicals.

She smiled as she recalled how her brother's eyes lit up when Jay handed him his ice-cream. Sophie made her brother promise not to tell their father, and Sam had sworn he wouldn't, until the minute they arrived at home he blurted it out. As the deluge of cancer comments washed over them, Jay had stepped in and politely explained he hadn't realised it would be such a problem and apologised. John had reluctantly calmed down. With a rap on his daughter's head he had let them all go.

Thankfully her brother hadn't mentioned the dead rabbit and Jay's strange behaviour. Sophie shuddered. She looked over to him again and her heart jumped at the sight of him standing right behind her, staring at her silently with intense eyes.

'Jeez you scared me,' she giggled and blushed. He had studied her in the mirror for a few minutes before he pointed at her face.

'Looks like you caught the sun. You're quite red,' he said matter-of-factly.

'Errrm yeah'

His comment embarrassed her even more. Her face was red and shiny, her hair entangled and greenish, the spot on her chin was flaring up and her eyes blood-shot from all the chlorine. She quickly turned away, but he caught her arm and leaned forward to whisper in her ear.

'I had fun today. I like your freckles, they're cute. Don't mention the rabbit to my dad.'

She unexpectedly felt a strange heat pooling in the pit of her stomach. *That's what they mean by butterflies in your stomach.* Not knowing how to reply, she leaned in to give him an awkward peck on the cheek. He froze and looked at her with raised eyebrows. Now it was his turn to blush. He mumbled something Sophie couldn't quite catch and walked off to join his dad, who was saying his goodbyes to her parents. Jay politely shook their hands and waved her brother and sister a nonchalant goodbye. As he walked out the door Sophie expected him to turn around one last time to look at her. To her disappointment he didn't.

After their Mercedes had left the driveway, she stood in the kitchen for a while, feeling slightly disoriented. How strange this afternoon had been, she thought as she stared at Jay's drawing of his 'Thoughts' that he had left behind. A labyrinth of intertwining shapes in reds and dark blues. This boy, just a few months younger than her, who seemed so shy and calm. This boy who was so unsettlingly handsome and kind. She uncapped a pen and started doodling on a blank page.

This boy who had laughed wholeheartedly when her brother tripped her up by the swimming pool, and she had landed flat in the water. This boy who had crushed a dead rabbit with a rock. She shook her head and wondered what had caused him to react so violently. She looked up as her father entered the kitchen, and she quickly lowered her gaze at the doodles and hastily crossed out the hearts she had drawn. She wondered if she would be seeing Jay again anytime soon, but as she looked into her father's moody face, she refrained from asking him.

CHAPTER 2

Berlin, December 2010 - 2 months after the incident

'Jay? Hi, it's me Sophie. How are you doing?"

She could barely hold the receiver because her hand was shaking so much. The words toppled out of her mouth like dominoes and nervously she pressed her lips together into a fine line. She didn't want him to know that this phone call was the hardest one she had ever had to make and that it took all the courage she could muster. She willed herself to calm her racing heart but couldn't help pacing anxiously around her parents' bathroom. She had locked herself in but was certain her mother was glued to the door, listening intently, not wanting to miss a word of the conversation.

'Sophie?' His voice sounded just the same as it always did, soft and a little cautious as if perpetually braced for bad news. Maybe this whole story isn't true, she told herself. She desperately clung to the hope that her parents were mistaken, that it had never happened. But deep down she knew. He had committed an irreversible crime and nothing would bring back the man she used to know.

'Sophie? Is it you? Is that really you ... Soph I'm so happy you called.'

He was breathless with excitement and the joy in his voice brought tears to her eyes. Her heart flooded with guilt. *I should've called him sooner.*

'I found out what happened. Only just now. My parents just told me. I'm sorry I didn't call sooner... How are you?'

I'm not sure I want to know the answer to that question, she thought as soon as the words had left her mouth.

'I'm ok I guess. It's tough in here, but I'm ok. So you found out where I am?'

Jay was sectioned in the maximum-security wing of a mental hospital called the Solacium Klinik, a few miles west of Berlin. Sophie had a vague memory of her Latin classes back in school and thought that naming an asylum 'Comfort' was a poor attempt to fool the public into thinking this was a place of healing rather than a prison. After much internal debate, she reluctantly asked Jay's father to give her the phone number, but she had kept it in the depth of her handbag for three days before mustering the courage to call her childhood friend. It had taken her two attempts to get through to him – the first time she hung up, as the fear had rendered her speechless.

'Errm yes I found out. How is it in there?' she asked.

Isn't the answer obvious? She bit her lip and silently cursed her tactlessness. *I'm not very good at this.* Although she had rehearsed what she was going to say over and over again in her head, she didn't factor in her nervousness making her mind go blank, and ask all the wrong questions. But then again, what else was she going to say to him? *What do you ask a man in his situation?* The line clicked, reminding her the conversation was recorded. She resisted the sudden urge to hang up on him.

'Well Sophie...' he dragged out his answer purposefully. 'It is a mental institution. It's kind of full of crazy people.'

His sarcastic tone surprised her so much that she burst into giggles. A lighthearted laugh echoed down the line and the sense of relief that washed over her was overwhelming. She realised that not only had he not lost the sharp wit she had always loved him for, more importantly he seemed still capable of feeling some sort of human emotion.

'So I guess you fit right in then, huh?'

She wondered where the conversation was going. There were a million questions she was itching to ask, but the fear of the terrifying truth paralysed her. It was difficult to sound out how he truly felt underneath the lightheartedness and sarcasm. He was locked in the kind of place that required a phone security check for every outside caller, including personal detail verification, passport identification and recorded phone conversations. He couldn't possibly joke about his situation unless... he had truly lost his mind. His father had warned her that, pumped with anti-psychotic drugs, Jay had previously grunted incoherently down the phone, like an animal, primal and uncontrolled. That he had howled in terror while hammering his fists against the plexiglass walls of the phone booth. That two wardens had to hand and foot cuff him and that wearing a straightjacket was a necessary safety precaution. Sophie couldn't quite ascertain his current mental state, but she was relieved that he had instantly recognised her voice and seemed to be able to hold a more or less normal conversation.

'I guess so.' He softly chuckled. 'So how are you doing? I heard you had a baby, congratulations!'

'Errr...thank...you....' the words stuck in her throat and for a split second she considered talking about her daughter. After all he was locked up in a safe place and he was not going to be of any harm to anyone for years. Despite everything that had happened, he was still her friend. Her best friend.

Suddenly she noticed his breathing had quickened. There was something utterly terrifying about that sound. As she felt her hands become clammy, she resisted the urge to hang up. Her lion heart whispered words of caution; *don't tell him about Juliet, not yet.* One day he would be released and she would worry about introducing Jay to her then but for now, she needed to ensure her daughter was safe from harm.

***

Ibiza, July 1995 - 15 years before the incident

The smell of burnt charcoal floated in the warm air. It was late afternoon and Sophie lay sprawled out on a deckchair in the garden, her bare legs stretched out in the evening sun. It's been a good holiday so far, she thought. It was quiet at this end of the garden. She dozed in the soothing heat of the sunset, unaware of the mosquitoes clustering and floating above the lavender bushes. Soon after sunset they would be moving closer to the house, hungry for human blood. Three weeks of Ibiza sunshine had turned Sophie's usually alabaster skin a lovely shade of gold, even though the little bloodsuckers had left angry red blemishes on her calves the night before. She scratched the itch nonchalantly.

'You have sweet blood, and that's because you eat too much red meat', Sophie's mother would say. She was a vegetarian and expected everyone around her to be as well. Sophie sighed contentedly, ignoring a slight nagging feeling that she should help set the dinner table. Lazy from a day at the beach, she preferred reading the book she had picked up from her father's holiday book collection. Thomas Harris' Red Dragon. It was scary and gory. She loved it. The plot revolved around a psychopathic serial killer who murdered young women by inserting mirror shards in their eyes. Sophie was just getting to the part where he was making plans for his next victim.

'Sophie!' a voice screamed from behind the deck chair, making her jump and the book fall to the floor. Her brother Sam smiled at her and Sophie greeted him with her best annoyed-to-be-disturbed look. His deep tan contrasted against his wiry dark blond hair and Sophie secretly wished she too had inherited her father's dark complexion. While it took her three weeks to achieve a mere glow, her little brother was a deep shade of bronze within three days. His sun-bleached hair was getting too long behind the ears. Gone were the days of the bowl cut, now her mother refused to cut his hair all together.

'But I want him to look like a rock star!' she would exclaim in excitement. Their father had resorted to cutting the boy's hair now, with mixed results judging by the rebellious mismatched kinks and curls escaping from behind his ears. Sam was still wearing his swim shorts, and his bare feet looked like they hadn't been washed since he returned from the beach.

'Mum... I mean Vera,' he quickly corrected himself 'sent me. It's dinner time, everyone's already sitting down... I'd hurry. Dad's grilled lamb cutlets.'

After he said this Sophie noticed the sweet smell of the lamb with a hint of rosemary. Her stomach briefly flipped with nausea.

'Ok, I'll race you to the table!' she shouted, ignoring the familiar anxiety dinner time conjured, and got off her deckchair. Her brother turned on his heel and ran off, laughing excitedly down the garden path, dashing past the lavender bushes to the barbecue patio. When they got there the rest of the party were already helping themselves to salads, antipasti, bread and couscous. Careful to slide into their seats unnoticed, Sam and Sophie joined the others at the kid's end of the table. Their father shuffled past them, two bottles of wine in each hand which he planted on the table with a satisfied grin on his tanned face. Their sister Anna looked up and smiled a shy smile. She looked pretty with her waist long sun-kissed brown hair, wearing a cute blue liberty-print sundress. She pushed the chair out next to her for Sophie to sit down, but Sophie ignored her to go and sit next to Jay. Turning around to seek him out by the buffet, she missed the disappointed look in her sister's eyes.

At the other end of the table Jay's dad, Henry, was talking animatedly with Sophie's mother. Vera looked radiant in her long colourful kaftan. Her wild bright red hair curled past her shoulders down her back; she was leaning in, giving Henry her undivided attention. Across the table Jay's aunt Sonia was chatting with Sophie's father, their neighbour Stefan von Kempen and his wife Mariana. Apart from the gorgeous raven-haired Mariana, who was in her late twenties, they were all in their early forties and enjoyed wine-fuelled evenings outdoors, talking about politics, house prices and how capitalism was going to ruin the world. Typically the type of conversations that bored Sophie to tears. The neighbours had brought their two children along; Tim, who was around Anna's age and his little brother Jack who was a year younger than Sam.

Jay and Sophie were quietly debating their after-dinner plans, considering either a midnight swim in their neighbour's pool or sneaking into the evening variety show of the nearby hotel, normally reserved for paying guests. As she pushed her food around from side of the plate to the other, pretending to eat, Sophie's ears suddenly pricked up as she picked up the word 'murder' in the adults' conversation. She shushed the others, and they collectively held their breath to eavesdrop on their parents' conversation.

'It's been for sale a while now, but nobody wants to buy it,' her father John said.

'No wonder,' mused Henry. 'Considering what happened in that house, it wouldn't surprise me if it remained empty for another 30 years.'

Sophie looked over at Jay. Both of them frowned at the same thought, *what happened in that house?*

'Although I hear apparently it isn't actually empty. The gardener told me he saw lights flickering in one of the first-floor rooms the other night. Considering the property has been cut off from the electricity mains, it must have been a candle or a flashlight. What we don't want is a bunch of rogue campers hanging around the house, or worse, drug addicts. Especially with all these reports of burglaries in the area.'

Henry seemed concerned and poured himself and Vera another glass of red wine. Her grey eyes shone as she folded her hands under her chin.

'What's the asking price for the property? They can't put it too high now can they?' Stefan asked, looking keen. His expression differed from that of his wife, who sat next to him like a prisoner on a bench, not making much effort to hide her bored expression as she poured herself another shot of tequila.

'I think it's about 40 million pesetas, which is a good price. I'm not sure how big the property is in terms of square meters, but it's big. Three floors, with a large balcony on the first floor and a roof top terrace with stunning views of the bay… there must be at least ten bedrooms. And don't forget the land, it must have at least four hectares of usable land. It could be worth triple if not more if you did it up nicely.' Ever the businessman, her father gave his verdict.

'Yes but, even if the price and the location are attractive, you wouldn't want to live there would you? I mean it's bad karma. If the walls could talk, they'd have a gruesome tale to tell.'

Her mother slurred her words slightly and looked around the table with hooded eyes and wine-stained lips. Her father shook his head in disagreement, patronisingly patting her outstretched hand. He was the pragmatic business-minded one as opposed to her mother, who tended to live in a world of her own and made most of her decisions based on superstition.

'Why?' Sophie blurted out, her curiosity getting the better of her. 'Why would you not want to live there? What happened in the house? A murder?'

Silence spread across the table, and the adults looked across with a dazed look on their faces as if they had only just then realised their children were sitting at the other end of the table. The sun had set, and the dark of the night was unfolding like a blanket. John got up from the table and lit the candles in the Moroccan storm lights.

'Something terrible happened in that house. You don't want to know; you're all way too young to hear about this, especially you two Sam and Jack.'

The youngest at the table both looked at each other and shrugged their shoulders with an offended look on their faces and shouted in unison:

'No we're not!'

'Please tell us the story dad, pleeeeeeease,' Sam pleaded.

'Come on dad!' Sophie was now desperate to hear the story.

Finally, John shrugged his shoulders and said with a wry smile on his face:

'Ok, you asked for it. Don't say I didn't warn you if you get nightmares.'

Sophie's father grabbed one of the candles on the table and placed it slowly down in front of him. The candle light lit up his face and his features shone like a grotesque mask. Basking in the attention, and with the children perched on the edge of their seats, he started his tale.

'A long, long time ago, a salesman travelled all the way from Saudi Arabia to this island to open up a pottery business. The pots he was selling were of such exquisite craftsmanship that his business flourished, and he soon was able to afford to buy the villa of his dreams. The villa behind our house. His wife and his three kids travelled all the way to Ibiza with all their belongings and settled into the new house. For many years, they lived happily, until one day...on a dark and stormy autumn night... he went mad.'

John paused for effect. They all leaned in closer and lapped up the tension. Sophie's heart suddenly skipped a beat as a warm hand gently squeezed hers under the table. Discreetly she turned to her right and shot a glimpse at Jay who was biting his lip and frowning, staring straight ahead. Nervously, she took a quick look around the table, but no one paid any attention to her flustered cheeks as her fingers entwined around his. A warm breeze was rustling through the leaves of the fig trees and made the candle lights flicker. Her father lowered his voice, narrowed his eyes and continued the story.

'That night a storm was raging. It was raining heavily and above the noise of the thunder the neighbours suddenly heard terrifying screams coming from the house. Upon arrival, the police found the salesman sitting on the stairs with an axe in his hands. He had killed his wife. And his three kids were found dead too. They say he was mad.

Since then the house has been empty, but legend has it that on stormy nights the lights can be seen flickering on the first floor. They say the house is haunted with the ghosts of the wife and her three kids.'

Her brother looked terrified. Anna reached out to give him a comforting hug.

'That's enough now!' Their mother Vera knocked over her glass of wine while trying to reach across the table to tap her husband on the arm.

'It's just a story, and we're not even sure this is exactly what happened, it might not even be true. So don't worry too much about it,' she said, shaking her head, ignoring her husband.

Jay let go of Sophie's hand and her skin instantly went cold, missing his warm touch.

Jay's father quipped that however gruesome the murder, the property was still a good deal and rebuilding it into a luxury retirement home would be every pensioner's dream come true. While the conversation moved onto stair lifts and heated swimming pools with wheelchair access, the image of the salesman sitting on the stairs, a bloody axe in his hands, stuck in Sophie's head. Her imagination started running wild. It reminded her of the book she was reading with its psychopathic serial killer. Lost in thought, she swatted a mosquito on her arm and rubbed the bloody trace it left, wondering what could have driven the man to such insanity that he killed his entire family. She had to find out.

After dessert the kids were dismissed from the table, leaving the parents to their steady descent into drunkenness. A fat pink moon had risen above the fig trees, lighting the way back to the house. While Tim and Anna walked ahead with the two younger ones in tow, Sophie, her cheeks burning with excitement, tugged on Jay's shirt to slow his pace.

'Hey, I have an idea for tonight, you know that villa? We should totally check it out,' she whispered, her eyes shining with mischief.

'The haunted house you mean? I'm not sure Sophie,' Jay hesitated. 'What if the story is true?' Much to her disappointment he didn't sound very enthusiastic.

'Even better, it will make it scarier.' Sophie wasn't prepared to let go. 'I'm sure we have a torch somewhere in the shed we can borrow. Come on let's do it, it'll be exciting.'

'...and what about the ghosts?' He stopped walking and stared at the dusty ground.

'You're kidding right? There are no ghosts; it's a good story that's all. Don't be such a wuss'. She smiled provocatively while elbowing him into the cactus bush. He chuckled, avoiding the menacing needles.

'Look, we won't be able to get close to the house anyway. They built a wall all around the property, and we can't get past the entrance gate. I saw they sealed it with a huge padlock.'

'I don't care, we'll follow the wall and see if there is anywhere we can climb over it.'

'What are you two whispering about?' Tim and Anna stood right behind them and once Sophie reluctantly explained her plan to break into the haunted house they didn't want to hear about going to bed. Both Sam and Jack couldn't contain their excitement and ran off to the shed to get the torches while the others swapped their flip-flops for some sturdier trainers. In the pale moonlight, they stealthily walked up the sandy road towards the main gate of the villa until they reached the tall iron gate.

Jay had been right; the gate was padlocked. Even though it looked like it was a hundred years old, rattling didn't move it one inch.

Looking up the towering spikes, they quickly dismissed the idea of climbing the gate as it was too high. Her plan thwarted; Sophie kicked a root in frustration, with no other effect than a painful one-legged dance. Meanwhile, Jay disappeared into the bushes following the path alongside the wall. The others quickly followed his lead, and after a few hundred meters Anna stopped and pointed at something in the dark. Once Sophie's eyes had adjusted to the darkness, she saw what her sister had discovered; there was a hole in the fence large enough for an adult to crawl through.

They crept quietly through the wild olive grove, careful not to trip on the many broken branches littering the dusty ground. The two boys had fallen silent after Sophie shushed them for giggling too loudly. After all, this was breaking and entering. Rebellious as she was, she knew this was a criminal offence. Further up the hill the villa towered darkly above the trees.

It was very much the imposing ten-bedroomed house their parents had described at dinner. A traditional Finca, one of the ubiquitous farmhouses on the island of Ibiza, probably over a hundred years old, with a tall grain tower connecting the south wing to the front of the house. The paint was peeling off the once white walls, and the roots of many trees had found their way through the concrete and burst through the walls. All the windows and doors had been boarded up with large weather-washed wooden planks. They walked up the steep hill through thorny bushes. Thorns yanked at their t-shirts and scratched their bare legs as they helped the little ones cross the bushes onto to the path that led up to the main entrance of the house.

'We won't be able to enter through here' Sophie whispered, tapping on the large beams that sealed the entrance. 'We'll need to find another way to get in'. She looked up and wondered whether they could try to climb up to the balcony on the first floor, but looking at her little brother bent over, inspecting his scraped knees she conceded it would be too dangerous for the younger ones and swiftly dismissed the idea.

Jay nodded in agreement and silently signalled at them to follow him down the side of the house. A small dark shape lurked on the wall. A lizard-like animal with webbed feet observed the group as they passed the boarded-up bay windows. Their feet crunched through a bed of glass shards, sparkling like diamonds in the moonshine.

They entered a courtyard and discovered a narrow side-window, its panes hanging off its hinges like broken wings. The ground was littered with glass, but the window was large enough to climb through. They cautiously peered inside and could see nothing but darkness.

'Ok, who's coming with me?' Sophie whispered, feeling brave. The boys jumped up and down with their fingers raised, screeching 'Me, me, me!'

'Be quiet!' She shushed them nervously, reaching out for their hands.

They pushed themselves up the ledge and held onto the rickety window frame, careful not to cut their hands on the shards of glass sticking out of the brittle wood. It was cold in the house and so dark they couldn't see their hands in front of their eyes. While outside the night was full of the sound of chirping crickets, inside it was dead silent. An oppressing silence that was only disturbed by glass shards crunching under the soles of their trainers. Not knowing what to do next, they stood rooted to the spot for a while, waiting for their eyes to adjust to the darkness. Tim fumbled with the torches.

A strange damp smell hung in the air, a mixture of rotting wood and something more sinister – like decomposing rat carcasses. Someone next to her shuffled anxiously in the darkness and grabbed her hand. It was her sister. Finally, Tim managed to switch on the torch but in his eagerness to give it to Jay, he let it slip to the floor with a loud clang. Gasps erupted all around, and they all moved closer to grab each other's hands. The torch's bright beam cut through the darkness and highlighted a dirty black and white tiled floor, covered in dead cockroaches and flies, broken furniture and rotting curtains. Directing the light beam up, Sophie could make out large damp patches blistering across the peeling walls like a terminal case of leprosy.

The faint sound of water droplets hitting a metal surface echoed from across the room. They silently formed a queue, and as they advanced deep into the house, the entry window faded and was finally swallowed up by the darkness. They got to the kitchen to find water leaking from the old-fashioned tap onto rusty pots and pans that filled the huge ceramic sink. The sink had been overflowing for some time, and the putrid water ran down the front onto the kitchen floor. The light beam chased shadows into dark corners. As they slowly edged their way to the staircase, careful not to slip, Sophie's heart started racing. This was the staircase where they had found the murderer. She imagined him sitting motionless on the steps with a bloody axe in his hands; his head bowed, wet black hair slapped across his face. Wet with blood. His long white tunic blood spattered. Blood slowly sliding off the blade and dripping on the floor. Blip blip blip. The same sound as the water drops in the kitchen sink. Sophie shook her head vigorously to dispel the terrifying thought.

This isn't real. It's all in my head. She had to regain control, as the older sister she couldn't allow herself to panic and scare everyone else. Suddenly she sucked in her breath. There was a shadow right by the staircase. A shadow the size of a tall man.

She stopped dead in her tracks and caused everyone else behind her to bundle into each other. A round of shush's echoed in the room.

'What is it?' Anna whispered alarmed.

'That... shadow over there', Sophie's voice sounded shaky and faint. *Oh my god. Did the shadow just move? Something or... someone is standing right there in front of us.*

Everyone was huddling around her now, and she slowly raised the torch towards the shadow with a shaking hand. They were staring at a tall old-fashioned coat stand. *Nothing to be scared about. Just an old coat stand. Thank god. Ok, now get a grip*, Sophie urged herself. *It's an empty house, the only living thing we might stumble on would be a cockroach.*

With Sophie taking the lead, they continued walking up the narrow winding marble staircase. Faint moonlight bathed the place in an eerie light, and when they stepped through an arched door frame they entered a spacious room with a balcony overlooking the olive grove, and a view further down the hill towards the bay and the sea. The floor was littered with empty tin cans and beer bottles. They navigated carefully between the rubbish. When Sophie shone the torch around the room, angry graffiti screamed at them in big dripping letters from the dirty walls. 'Anarchy!' 'Marijuana, beer and heroin' 'We're here to stay!' signed 'Hijo de Putas'. Sons of bitches.

A shiver crept up her spine as Sophie spotted a dirty mattress on the floor, a pile of clothes next to a rucksack and a storm light. It dawned on her this place wasn't haunted, somebody actually lived here – they had just walked into a squatter's bedroom. Judging by the writing on the wall they weren't the sort of people who'd be happy to be disturbed.

There was a sleeping bag on the mattress, and before she could make out whether there was a human shape inside it, Jay shouted 'Sophie! Watch out!' Adrenaline shot through her like a lightning bolt and in a flash she ran back to the door stumbling over empty cans. She fell into Jay's arms dizzy with fear. The flashlight fell on the floor and broke. Instantly everything went pitch black. Everyone clung to one another. One of the boys started sobbing with fear.

'Run!' Jay urged them. 'Sophie, take Anna and Tim, run! Downstairs! Now!' They stumbled down the stairs in seconds, slipping and tripping over each other on the way down, crashing into the coat stand at the bottom of the staircase. Scrambling back to their feet, they ran back through the kitchen into the main room. Sophie was breathless with fear, running as fast as she could in the darkness, blindly dragging her sister by her elbow towards the exit window, hearing Tim's ragged breath right behind her. She pushed her sister up onto the window ledge, and Anna landed on the other side with a thud.

'Where's Jay? And Sam and Jack?' she panted peering through the broken window into the dark.

Seconds later Jay came running towards her with her brother in his left arm and Jack flung over his shoulder. They jumped to safety and grabbing the younger boys by their hands they ran out of the courtyard, closely followed by the others, down the path, into the thorny bushes and through the olive grove. They slid through the hole in the fence, ran down the sandy path towards their villa and only stopped, still panting, when they reached the safety of the gate, closing it with a bang.

They sat down on the stairs to the house, catching their breath.

'Are we safe now?' her brother Sam asked as he wiped is nose with the back of his hand.

'Yes of course we're safe, it wasn't dangerous ok? We just disturbed someone sleeping, that's all. No big deal' she answered confidently, determined to downplay what happened, suddenly conscious that her father would fly into a fit of rage if he were to find out what they had done.

'Now show me your knees.' Bar a few bruises and scrapes on their arms and legs, they had got away with just a scare. Sophie made them line up and swear solemnly, right hand raised, no fingers or toes crossed, that none of them was to mention tonight's escapade to their parents.

'Not a peep. This is our secret. If you say anything we'll be grounded for the rest of the holiday and there'll be no more trips to the neighbour's swimming pool or the hotel up the road. You understand that?' All nodded a silent yes.

'Ok good, now you better go wash your hands and faces and climb into your beds while the parents are still at the barbecue, ok?' Sophie ordered, ruffling her brother's dusty hair. He smiled obediently and then ran off towards the house with his sister in tow. Once alone, Sophie sat down next to a silent Jay. His head in his hands, he had not said a word since they got back. When she gently touched his shoulder to check on him, he flinched and looked up in a daze.

'Are you ok?' Sophie whispered hesitantly, recoiling under his penetrating gaze. 'You look like...' *you've seen a ghost,* she thought '...you're not feeling well.'

He blinked, put a quick hand through his hair and rubbed his temples.

'I'm ok'. His breathing was still fast, but his voice sounded disaffected and calm.

'Do you want to talk about what happened in the house just now?' She wanted to know what he'd seen and what prompted him to sound the alarm. Her left hand ached. She noticed she had cut herself on the broken window frame. Dismissing it as a minor injury, she wiped the blood on her denim shorts.

'Didn't you hear the voices?' He whispered. *The voices?* She looked up from the blood-stains on her shorts and raised an eyebrow at him.

'What voices? You heard voices in there?' she enquired.

'I heard whispers. Someone was threatening to harm us. I started hearing them when we walked in, and they got clearer and louder as we walked upstairs. It was scary.'

Oh god, she thought, *there was actually someone there. How close had we been to getting caught by some crazed drug addict?* She felt a pang of guilt as she thought about her scared little brother. It had been her idea to go into the house. If it hadn't been for Jay, who knows what might have happened. He shook his head and got up.

'I don't think it was a drug addict I heard. I think it was the ghosts; they tried to warn me'... he pointed at her 'warn us.'

Suddenly he smiled lightly, extended a hand at her and said: 'Never mind. Come with me, let's go swimming.'

She reluctantly held out her bloodied hand and wondered if he was joking or if he actually believed in ghosts.

When they got to the neighbouring villa, they stopped by the pool-house to put on their swimming gear. The pool lights were still switched on. The water glowed an inviting aquamarine. The terracotta tiles still radiated the heat from the day's sunshine, warming the soles of their feet. A balmy wind rustled through the fragrant pine trees. A concert of a million chirping crickets was in full swing. They sat down and dangled their feet in the soothing blue water. Sophie couldn't let go of her friend's claim to have heard voices in the house. Trying to remember the exact sequence of events, she couldn't confirm whether the bulge in the sleeping bag had moved... But she was certain she hadn't heard any voices.

Jay didn't look like he was wasting any more thoughts on the night's events; he gently kicked the water, smiling mischievously. Sophie took the bait and splashed him back. Soon they started kicking water at each other, their laughs echoing in the silence of the night until Sophie lost her balance and tumbled into the pool. The water was cool. She opened her eyes and turned under water to look up at the surface. Jay's blurry shadow towered over her. She loved being under water. The sounds were muffled, the light soft and that sense of weightlessness felt like absolute freedom. Her lungs tightened and with a kick of the feet she broke the surface as Jay slowly lowered himself down into the water next to her.

Jay was tall for his age and while the water reached up to Sophie's chin, he was standing comfortably. His arm warmed against hers, and being so close changed the atmosphere from playful silliness to something a bit more charged. Her heart was now beating so frenetically she was convinced he could hear it. Fighting the urge to say something derogatory to break the tension, she bit her lip. The desire to kiss him was overwhelming.

He looked at her shyly and whispered: 'If you want you can kiss me…I mean, you don't have to…but it would be…'

Her heart somersaulted and her skin tingled in anticipation. She closed her eyes and lifted her lips to his.

'…nice' he exhaled.

Sitting on the steps to their parents' villa with their t-shirts dripping onto the warm stone flooring, they looked out over the garden in silence. Every now and then the cool night breeze carried merry bursts of laughter from their parents, who were still finishing dinner at the back of the garden. Mosquitoes were humming softly around them. Jay sat a few meters away from Sophie and stared at something invisible in the dark. He shuffled his feet awkwardly. A tinge of disappointment tugged at her heart. *Why won't he sit next to me and hold my hand?*

Finally, Jay broke the uncomfortable silence: 'That was my first kiss', he said quietly, stubbornly avoiding eye contact.

'Ah well, no big deal. I kissed someone before'. She bit her lip and immediately regretted saying the words. *I don't even know why I said that. To make me sound more mature – or maybe to punish him for not sitting closer?*

'So how good was I?' He looked up with a lopsided grin.

'Not bad. But I think you will need a lot of training', she retorted, making him laugh out in surprise. He stood up, stared some more at the darkness, hands on hips, and then walked over and gave her a brusque kiss on the cheek. His hair was still wet. Cool water droplets sprinkled her face. 'Goodnight' he chuckled. She watched him slowly walk off into the darkness.

'Goodnight' she answered quietly, missing him already and impatient for sunrise. 'I look forward to spending the rest of our holiday together…' she whispered to herself.

CHAPTER 3

London, January 2011 - 3 months after the incident

'Solacium Klinik, West Wing G7', said a bored female voice as she picked up the phone.

'Hello, this is Sophie Liebtreu-Mackenzie. Could you connect me to Mr Jay Adler please'.

Sophie tried her best to sound confident, but her trembling voice gave away how nervous she was. Their last call had been surprisingly upbeat, but she knew that didn't mean all was fine with him. According to his father, Jay regularly suffered mood swings as the doctors adjusted his drug dosage. He would slip into bouts of depression so severe that he refused to get out of bed. He would lie there staring at the ceiling for hours on end. Sophie was shocked at the trial-and-error approach the psychiatrists were taking. They seemed unwilling to acknowledge that, despite the horrific crime he had committed, Jay was still a human being, not their guinea pig.

After verifying Sophie's identity, the voice confirmed with a curt 'Hold please'. Forgetting to put the phone on mute, the warden shuffled away from her desk, opened a door and barked with a tone that commanded obedience, 'Mr Adler, phone call! Now.' Silence. She shouted again for Mr Adler to get off his lazy backside and for someone to take the restraints off and drag him to the phone booth immediately. A wave of anger rushed through Sophie as she overheard what seemed a typical exchange between the wardens and their 'patients'. *How dare she speak to him like that.* Before she could think of anything suitable to say, she heard a clicking noise on the line and the female warden enquired: 'Miss? Are you still there? Yes? This could take a few moments. Please hold'.

The line went dead. Sophie started nervously picking at her fingernails, they're so short, she thought, *I really ought to kick this habit.*

It was a good 10 minutes before the line clicked again, and someone breathed heavily down the phone.

'Hi Jay, it's me Sophie.' The breathing stopped, and there was an eerie silence at the other end of the line.

'Sophie?' he sounded slightly baffled 'Oh hi.'

This time round there wasn't any enthusiasm in his voice. Trying her best to ignore the stab of disappointment in her heart, she asked him how he had been and what he was up to. His answers were short and mumbled. Eventually, he sighed and said:

'I'm sorry, I just woke up. I'm not really ready to have a proper conversation yet.' Sophie glanced at her watch and noted it was 10am in London and 11am his time, quite late for a weekday in an asylum where wake-up calls resounded through the cells at 7am.

'I know the feeling. I'm pretty much useless before my first a cup of coffee. Not even able to string a half-decent sentence together without a good shot of espresso!' she joked. His soft laugh warmed her heart. How she loved that laugh! It always made her think of summer, and she smiled, suddenly confident in the knowledge that no matter how drugged up he was, their bond hadn't broken.

'It's those goddamn drugs they're giving me. They make me so groggy; all I can do is lie in bed and count the cracks in the ceiling.' His speech was slurred. 'Where are you? In Berlin?' he asked, his voice laced with hope.

'No, I'm back in London', she answered almost apologetically. Sophie was at work and had locked herself in one of the meeting rooms of an open plan office, discreetly answering the nods of her colleagues who passed by the glass-door. She thought how surreal the situation was. *If they knew who I'm talking to!* Ignoring the hustle and bustle on the trading desks, she stepped closer to the window. It was a glorious winter's day with a flawlessly blue sky. The sun shone a bright light down on the city. She leaned her forehead against the cold glass and her breath steamed up a view of St Paul's cathedral as she spoke.

'It's a beautiful day today. I wish you could see what I see now.'

'I can't see what the weather is like today. I don't have a window in my cell.' He sighed. A windowless cell. Sophie felt a shiver creep up her spine.

***

Berlin, July 1996 - 14 years before the incident

Sophie hurried nervously around the supermarket, dragging the trolley back to the spirits section, frantically wondering what she had forgotten.

'Sophie, chill out. We won't be running out of alcohol, I promise'. Reluctantly Sophie slowed her pace. Dennis was right; they had stocked up with enough beers to entertain the fifty or so friends she had invited to celebrate her 18th birthday, and it was about time to check out and drive to the venue.

Just when she thought she was never going to find a suitable place to hold her party, at the last minute her boyfriend Dennis had pulled some strings and found the perfect location: a forgotten oasis in the outskirts of Berlin, a privately-owned swimming club by Tegeler See, whose owner was an old friend of Dennis's father.

'Don't worry Shorty...' Unaware that she hated this nickname he had for her, he continued, 'the party will be amazing, believe me. The guys will set up the sound system and it's gonna blow your mind. We're bringing the turntables and massive speakers. The neighbours had better go hide! It will be legendary.'

She could visualise it – it would be like an MTV beach party, her friends in swimwear pumping their arms in the air to heavy hip-hop beats. *Let's hope the neighbours don't call the police*, she thought.

As they exited the car park, the boot clanking with bottles, she looked over to her boyfriend. He looked cool, she thought, with his army cap pushed deep over his eyebrows. Unlike most of the boys in her class, his three-day stubble was effortless. However convenient it was to have a boyfriend with a car, it irked her to rely on him to drive somewhere. She vowed that after the party, every penny saved would go towards funding driving lessons.

Sophie wondered if she loved him. He was attractive in a tough-guy kind of way – all broad shoulders, dark hair and big clumsy hands. Sure, she fancied him, but was that enough? She looked out of the car window pensively as the car gathered speed and the buildings blurred by. The 18th of July turned out to be a lovely sunny day. But would tonight be the night? Dennis was two years older than her and had a bit of a reputation. She knew his patience was only limited – if she wanted to keep him she would have to give in to his advances. The truth was she was terrified at the idea of sex.

'What are you thinking about Shorty? Are you worrying again?' he smiled, taking one hand off the steering wheel to pinch her thigh. She brushed his hand away and blushed.

'Yeah, uh, I'm just a bit nervous – it's my first big party. If it's not awesome, people will talk –
it'll be embarrassing'. Sophie winced at the thought but Dennis laughed reassuringly.

They parked the car and got out. Each balancing a crate of bottles on their shoulders, they walked carefully down the narrow dirt path in the direction of the lake. Besides the faint humming of flies in the warm air, it was surprisingly quiet. The lake shimmered peacefully behind the pine trees. At the boathouse, Sophie's father was busy lighting the campfire. When Dennis came over to shake John's hand, he suspiciously eyed him up and pointedly ignored his outstretched hand. An awkward moment passed. Sophie was keen to spare Dennis her father's steely stare and they both returned to the car to pick up the remaining crates.

A rosy-cheeked Vera emerged from the boathouse, broom in hand, to greet her daughter. She proudly pointed at a huge pile of marshmallows in a bowl: 'I found a shop that sold organic marshmallows. Isn't that unbelievable? Organic marshmallows!' she shook her head bemused. Sophie laughed; she loved her mother but she was sometimes a bit strange. Her obsession with organic food was embarrassing, especially when she launched into one of her monologues about E-numbers giving you cancer – a thought her husband had planted in her head. The outcome of this was that Sophie and her siblings were deprived of sweets, ice-cream and most other tasty snacks.

'Vera, I hope you're not planning to lecture my friends about organic food, and tell them to become vegetarians again. It's so embarrassing.'

Her mother looked at her with a mocking look on her face and moaned:

'Don't be such a teenager, you should be proud your parents aren't boring and conformists like all the others. We might be a bit different but hey, we know better!' She winked at Sophie and spread out her two fingers into a peace sign. 'Peace and love honey, don't forget!'

Sophie rolled her eyes. Sometimes she wished her mother would be more like her friends' parents, who wore normal clothes and had nine-to-five jobs. As an artist, her mother was ultra sensitive, her moods volatile as mercury. On good days she would be the life and soul of any party, but when the dark days came, she would lock herself up in her studio among her canvases, sit on the sofa and stare at the wall. Lost in the depths of depression, she couldn't always be there for her children. It was often up to Sophie to look after her siblings.

It didn't help that her father seemed oblivious to his wife's state of mind, or chose to ignore it and turned to alcohol instead. Sophie sighed and started unwrapping the tea lights, placing them next to the ashtrays on the tables.

She was busy ramming flares into the dusty ground when she heard the first guests coming down the path. Two skinny girls with shiny waist-long hair hurried along the shore giggling excitedly.

'This is awesome!' they shrieked in unison and pointed at the small wooden boats moored at the end of the pier. 'Are these boats for real, I mean can we use them? That's so cool!' they shouted.

Sophie shielded her eyes against the late afternoon sun and smiled at the sight of her two best friends Camelia and Justine. They were loud, funny and when all three of them were together they felt invincible. Sophie gave them a quick peck on the cheek, happy to have them close.

A sunset sky bathed the lake in soft pink light; wafts of blue smoke floated out on the silvery surface of the water. When they switched on the fairy lights, the place looked magical. The campfire was roaring. Dennis and his friends enthusiastically speared sausages to roast over the tall flames. After a few technical hitches, the sound system was working, the loudspeakers were hooked up, and some relaxed Bob Marley beats were drumming in the background.

Sophie's brother Sam and her sister Anna were playing cards at the table next to a group of girls from school, all busy giggling and smoking filter cigarettes. Making sure her guests were catered for, Sophie smoothed a kink in the white table linen and picked up a beer bottle from the tin bath tub. She was way too excited to eat even a bite from the freshly-roasted sausage Dennis shoved in her face. After a few sips of beer she finally relaxed a bit. More guests were arriving, smiling and bearing gifts, and it finally felt like the beginning of a great night.

Her friend Nils walked up to her with a mischievous glint in his eyes.

'How are you party girl?' he asked as he pushed a shot glass in her hand.

'It's vodka,' he whispered with a conspiring smile, pointing at a bottle hidden inside his jeans jacket. Worried her father could see them, she quickly gulped down the vile-tasting alcohol. Her eyes watered. As she coughed and spluttered Nils continued, trying hard not to laugh at her red face:

'This is an amazing place, you know I live just around the corner and didn't even know it existed. Apparently there are some pretty big fish in the lake, I can't wait to take the boats to water.'

She laughed and through the blur of her teary eyes she spotted her latest guest walking towards her, a big bouquet of flowers in his arms. The young man standing in front of her was wearing paint-spattered trainers, faded jeans and an army green jumper.

'Jay!' She shouted in delight and leaped forward to hug him. 'You came!' She hadn't seen him in a while and he had grown taller, his shoulders broader. He looked very handsome; her stomach flipped as he smiled down at her, his arm around her waist.

'Happy birthday' he mumbled and shoved the flowers in her arms. 'I know flowers are kind of lame, but my mum insisted,' he shrugged apologetically.

'Yeah flowers are so old-school' she smiled as she inhaled the gorgeous perfume of white lilies, hyacinths and tulips. 'You're such a gentleman', she joked as she poured water into a watering can and carefully arranged the flowers. Jay grabbed a beer from the improvised ice-box, as he cracked open the bottle Sophie frowned at him.

'Since when do you drink beer?' she teased.

'It's none of your business really now is it?' he answered, avoiding her stare.

She jabbed a finger softly at his chest. 'Jay, you're too young to drink. If my dad catches us, I'll be in trouble. Big time.'

'Why would it be your fault?' He looked mildly annoyed, gently pushing her finger away.

'It's my party and I'm meant to be responsible for my guests and stuff. Can't have you throwing up all over the place can I? Anyway, the only reason we're allowed alcohol tonight is because my dad cannot survive the evening without beer... Otherwise we'd all be on the lemonade.'

With under-eighteens in the picture, her father had made it clear that while beer was ok at the party, spirits were banned. If any guests were found drinking anything else he would not hesitate to shut the party down. Sophie knew that with his police record, he wasn't going to take any chances. Thinking of Nils' clandestine vodka supply, she was as nervous as she was excited to break the rules.

Jay rolled his eyes at her, 'I'm not a kid anymore, I'll be 18 in a couple of months. I can hold my drink.'

'Okaaaaay fine then. So who did you come with tonight?' she asked mockingly.

'My mum' he smirked.

'I see' she stifled a giggle 'You're not a kid anymore and you come with your mum to my party huh?'

'Aren't your parents here too?' He said petulantly as he flipped the beer cap in his fingers and snapped it over the sticky kitchen counter. They held eye contact until Sophie burst into laughter, and Jay's reluctant smile turned into a wide grin.

'Never mind the flowers; I have another present for you'. He shrugged off his backpack, took out a few spray-paint cans and rummaged through the bag. Sophie picked up one of the cans; they were the kind her father would use to fix the paint job on his car. *What was Jay doing with so many of those in his backpack?*

'Jay? What are these for?' she asked with a raised eyebrow, picking up the next can, labelled "sunset lilac". 'You have a lilac car that needs a new paint job? What do you need these for?'

Jay snatched the can out of her hand and shoved it back into the bag.

'Errm yeah, I use them for spray painting. Not a car though, I...err...' He looked down at his hands. 'I spray walls.'

'Do you mean graffiti?' The guys in her class used to brag about going out on the town in the dead of the night, their backpacks rattling with spray cans, to scout out a wall on which to leave their mark. They always went for the most inaccessible spots, such as highway bridges and the top of buildings. Some of them boasted about being train sprayers and would take photos of themselves, hiding behind ski masks, proudly standing next to colourful renditions of their sprayer acronyms. One particularly popular place was the Hauptbahnhof, Berlin's central train station. Sophie would pass tons of their graffiti on her way to school.

'Mmmm yeah,' Jay nodded, avoiding looking at her. 'Look, just don't tell my mother about this. I kind of shoplifted these.'

'Oh ok. So do you actually go out at night to paint?' She found that quite exciting. At school she had never dared approach the graffiti-boys, who treated everyone outside their clique with great indifference.

'Well, yes my friend Frank and I go out at night looking for good spots. I'm just starting out so most of it is just scribbles, but there's a rush to going out there. A risk of getting caught. The thrill is quite addictive. If you want I'll show you where we've been.'

Sophie smiled encouragingly, *he's so cute*. A far cry from the boys at her school, he didn't make her feel gauche and awkward like they did. Jay reached out and handed her a small blue envelope, her name written across it in a sleek black font. She flipped it open and pulled out a cassette tape.

'I hope you like it; these are some of my favourite tunes. I think it will remind you of our holidays in Ibiza. It's quite chilled out.' He shuffled his feet and took another swig of beer. Sophie's throat tightened, this had obviously taken him a while to compile. She was touched.

'Thank you', she whispered eventually, not knowing what else to say.

'You're welcome,' he shrugged and turned away.

At that moment, a voice shrieked 'Sophie!' and her friend Camelia grabbed her arm.

'What are you doing hiding in the kitchen, isn't this your party? You just have to see this, Dennis is DJing, his fat friend is breakdancing!' Camelia dragged Sophie outside and out of Jay's sight. Sophie put the tape in the back-pocket of her jeans. With a last glance back at the handsome boy; she ran over to join the crowd gathering around the dancers.

Midnight came and went. The party was in full swing. In the small club-house, people were dancing, a deep hip-hop bass booming, and a group of them had decided to get out the boats. As they fished around for missing oars, Sophie walked over to the barbecue, trying to remember where her friend Nils had stashed the liquor. She passed a small group sitting next to the huge campfire, laughing and roasting marshmallows – her mother's organic marshmallows. Sophie chuckled to herself.

After crouching around the bushes for a bit, blindly fumbling around roots and rocks, she finally found Nils' secret stash. Unable to read any labels in the dark she just picked up as many bottles as she could stuff under her jacket.

Suddenly she heard voices nearby. Her ears pricked up as she recognised the sing-song tone of her mother's voice. Creeping closer, she spotted her mother sipping a glass wine by the fire, intently listening to someone in the dark.

'I do worry about him becoming anti-social', the voice with a Canadian accent said. 'I know teenagers go through a new rebellious phase every week but I sense there's something wrong with him. He never talks to anyone. I don't think he has many friends. He's always wearing those shabby hoodies. I bought him loads of designer outfits – the sort most kids would die for – and what does he do? He wears this tatty old sweatshirt covered in paint stains. I feel embarrassed when I pick him up from school. I can just guess what the other mums are thinking.'

Sophie's mother whispered an inaudible response and the woman spoke again:

'Yes I know, but that's not all. I think he's up to no good. The other day I looked in the rucksack he was hiding under his bed, and it was full of spray-paint cans. What's he doing with those? He said it was for a school project, but I don't believe him. He's such a bad liar.'

The angry voice paused, and Sophie realised this was Elizabeth talking, Jay's mother. A painful cramp worked its way up Sophie's ankle but curious to hear more, she ignored it and shifted as close as she could without getting noticed.

She's still picking him up from school? At seventeen? Incredulous, Sophie thought about how her mother had left her to her own devices from an early age. *Talk about claustrophobic parenting! Poor Jay.*

'I wouldn't mind so much if he were doing well at school but his grades have dropped. Lately, he's been hanging out a lot with this kid, Frank. I can't put my finger on anything in particular, but I know something is up. I don't like seeing them together. Frank is a bad influence. He smokes. Cigarettes and probably worse. Jay is only a kid for heaven sakes; he should be concentrating on his homework. No doubt he's bright, but he's just so...' she exhaled loudly in exasperation. '...Slow. Lazy. Impressionable. He drives me and Caspar insane.'

Caspar von Schoenefeldt, Jay's stepfather, was a renowned plastic surgeon. Sophie remembered Jay opening up one day on holiday, and telling her how his mother had been having an affair with Caspar for years. One day during a heated row, Jay, unable to keep the secret that oppressed him for so long, had blurted out to his father that when she was supposedly "at tennis with her girlfriends", Elizabeth was in fact secretly seeing this man. After many fights and many reconciliations, his parents finally decided to separate for good. All this was much to Jay's horror. Having revealed the secret that split them up, Jay had always harboured the hope that he could bring them back together. Although Jay had maintained a veneer of indifference when he told the story, his voice eventually broke when he whispered that he had ruined his parent's marriage. Sophie wanted to comfort him and tell him all this wasn't his fault, but her well-meant words had fallen on deaf ears. Nothing seemed to reach him. For the rest of the day he had just sat on the beach staring at the waves, ignoring her pining looks.

Suddenly the cramp in her leg became unbearable. She was brought back to the present situation, uncomfortably hidden in the bush. Deciding she had heard enough; she skulked back towards the pier clutching the spirit bottles close to her chest. She wondered about what she had just overheard. Jay was doing badly at school and apparently had no friends. Elizabeth's tone had been quite harsh. *Slow, lazy, impressionable.* Sophie didn't think any of these attributes described her friend. Instinctively she disliked the woman who struck her as a high-maintenance, spa-visiting, prosecco-sipping Stepford wife. The kind of woman who left her husband for an obscenely rich celebrity, who moved her straight into his ten-bedroom villa in the posh suburbs of Berlin. No doubt she had found him to be a great catch.

Sophie ran down the lantern-lined path to the pier where her friends were getting ready to board the boats. She handed the liquor bottles to Dennis and noticed that everybody had stripped down to their swimming gear. While her friend Justine showed off her perfect curves in the smallest of bikinis, Sophie, with a body resembling more that of a twelve-year-old boy than an eighteen-year-old girl, decided to keep her shirt on.

The boats floated away from the pier and drifted out into the darkness of the lake. The oars slowly pushed through water black as ink and they inched further towards the centre of the lake. The mood was ebullient; joints were lit and people swigged from the bottles that were passed around. The insouciance was infectious. Looking at the burning stars above, Sophie felt that she was part of something bigger. Bigger than her fears, her loneliness and her dark thoughts. She was young, and she was the future. Today was the first day of the rest of her life; she was going to move out and start a new life, move to France, study psychology and make new friends. It was all ahead of her, and she knew it. As she looked around the boat, she paused and seeing all of her friends' smiling faces in the soft glow of the candles, her heart swelled – a lump rose in her throat; she wanted to hug them all. *I could die right now, and it would be OK because this moment is worthy of a lifetime.*

After graduation, they would all go their separate ways to embark on different lives. It was sad in a way to lose her friends, but the lure of freedom and the desire to escape the clutches of her controlling father was more powerful than any urge to stay with her friends. Sophie took another sip from the bottle she was handed. The tequila burnt all the way down her throat to her stomach, warming her up from the inside.

Suddenly she realised she hadn't seen Jay since the start of the evening. He wasn't on any of the boats. With a tinge of guilt, she wondered who he'd been spending the evening with. He didn't know anybody and Sophie doubted he had spent the evening with his mother. Sophie slowly scanned the lake. The shoreline blurred into the distance, and the weeping willow blended into the night. The boat-house shone like a far-away lighthouse. The wind carried the bass of the music and the occasional burst of laughter across the black water. A hooded silhouette sat at the end of the pier, its legs dangling over the water. Smoke curled above its head, and the faint glimmer of a cigarette hovered above his chest. The silhouette cut a lonely figure, she thought to herself.

Suddenly the boat rocked, knocking her into Nils' arms. The bottles were almost emptied, and the mood had lifted to become boisterous. Her friends started ramming the neighbouring boats with their oars, shrieking pirate 'harr harr harr's. In an increasingly drunken haze, everyone started pushing each other off the boats. Next to her, Justine lurched into the lake with a squeal of delight. Water splashed up and soaked Sophie's shirt. Feeling invincible, Sophie took another gulp of tequila and tossed the empty bottle into the boat before diving head first into the cool water. The drunk dizziness faded instantly as she broke the surface. Swimming around finding her bearings, she looked over to see that her friends had moored the boats to the floating platform and started a raucous diving competition.

She headed towards them, but after a few strokes, a sharp pain shot up her leg. Struggling for air and trying to hold her head above water, she started to panic as the cramp spread up to her thigh. She tried to turn on her back and massage the cramp out of it, but as she tried she felt her right foot tense up too. Within seconds both of her legs had turned as rigid as logs. An attempt to scream for help failed and died in a muffled gurgle. Water started filling her mouth. Slowly, helplessly, she sunk towards the darkness at the bottom of the lake. *I'm going to die. On my 18th birthday. A virgin.* As she closed her eyes, her final breath bubbled towards the surface and everything turned black.

Suddenly two strong hands grabbed her tightly and dragged her limp body back to the surface.

A slap struck her cheek. 'Sophie, wake up!' The voice was muffled and seemed to come from far away. She willed her eyes to open, but her eyelids were too heavy and swollen to lift. Instead, she tried to move her legs. They ached and felt as stiff as wood and refused to move. Her head spun. She was teetering on the edge of consciousness, afraid to fall back into the darkness. Someone was pressing down on her chest with all his weight. Upon release, the air burned into her lungs. Again, and again. Finally, she rolled to the side and started coughing uncontrollably, bringing up foul-tasting water. Her body was shaking as she was hugged with a towel and a strangled voice urgently whispered in her ear: 'Sophie, stay with me. Come on, open your eyes.'

Soft grass brushed against the soles of her feet, and she breathed in the clean washing powder smell of his t-shirt. Slowly she managed to open her eyes and blinked at a world that was all out-of-focus. As she regained her vision, Jay hunched over her with a worried look on his face. When she started sobbing, he gingerly pulled her up in his arms and held her for a moment.

'What happened?' she asked with quivering lips, as the numbness in her legs slowly faded.

Jay didn't answer and instead passed her jeans and a jumper. She unbuttoned her clammy shirt with stiff fingers and welcomed the dry clothes. His jumper was too big for her and smelled of paint and tobacco, but it was soft on her skin.

'I nearly drowned, didn't I?' she asked quietly. He nodded with a concerned look in his eyes. Her head swirled as they listened to the screams and laughter echoing in the night. *Didn't anybody notice?* She wondered. They were sitting a few meters behind the pier, under the weeping willow.

'You saw me struggling in the water and jumped in to save me?' she guessed.

He remained silent and nodded again, staring at the ground. Until then, she hadn't noticed that his jeans were wet. Trying to get over the dizziness, she breathed a sigh that made her lungs whistle in protest.

'Are you ok? You look a bit faint', he asked, finally speaking again.

'I'm not sure. I just don't know what happened out there. All of a sudden I couldn't move my legs anymore'. She shuddered remembering the feeling of helplessness and the sheer horror of sinking below the surface.

'You probably had a bit too much to drink' he suggested 'and too little to eat'. He looked at her skinny body. She bowed her head in shame, but Sophie knew he was right, not only did she have too much alcohol, but she didn't get to eat much during the day. A bowl of cereals that morning and probably not more than a bite of sausage and a forkful of salad for dinner. The dark demons of anorexia were never too far away, and somehow she knew that her friend was aware of the everyday battle she fought to sustain her body.

'You're right' she conceded reluctantly 'I haven't eaten much today. With all the party organisation, I just didn't find time to eat.'

She tied her long wet hair into a ponytail. 'I can't eat when I get nervous; the mere thought of food makes me nauseous.'

She was so used to lying about her being fine that even admitting that she wasn't to herself was a novelty, never mind speaking it out loud. His hand felt warm in hers, and her anxiety melted away. She couldn't quite explain it, but when he was around it was as though a lightbulb switched on, shining bright and clear.

'You saved my life Jay,' she whispered looking into his eyes. He brushed her comment aside with a shrug as if to say, 'I had no choice'.

'Oh my god, imagine – I could have died on my birthday. Dead on my 18th, a virgin'. As soon as she said the word she regretted it leaving her mouth, and her cheeks reddened instantly.

'Oh... I thought you and your...errm...boyfriend would have had... you know', he looked over to the platform. Dennis was probably still there. Suddenly a disappointing thought popped into Sophie's head. *Shouldn't he have noticed I wasn't there anymore?* Clearly he hadn't. She could have drowned, and he hadn't noticed. Her throat ached, and hot tears prickled in her eyes, threatening to overflow.

'No, we haven't yet. I kind of thought tonight would be a special night. But he's too busy partying; he didn't even notice I'd gone.' A single tear slid down her cheek. Jay looked pained as he awkwardly wiped it away with his thumb.

'I think...' he hesitated. 'I think you shouldn't be with this guy, he's not good for you'. He shook his head and Sophie sensed his anger rising. 'I watched you two tonight, and he's not giving you the attention you deserve. He should be by your side looking out for you; he should have given you time to sit down and eat something. I saw him dancing with other girls, laughing and joking and having a great time. A boyfriend doesn't do that', he hissed through gritted teeth. 'If I were your boyfriend, I would have eyes only for you. He doesn't deserve you, and you shouldn't be with him...' His dark eyes glowered intensely.

'Jay... wait, what?... What are you saying?' She was lost for words, never having heard him speak so passionately.

'You should be with...', he breathed in, '...you should be with me.'

Her mouth dropped open.

'I love you', he said softly.

She looked at him in total disbelief.

'Jay. ..I didn't know. ...I don't know what to say'. Slowly it dawned on her that he must have followed her all night to have witnessed her with Dennis. She looked at him sitting next to her with his arms folded around his knees, frowning into the distance.

'I don't think this is going to work, Jay. Dennis is my boyfriend and even if sometimes I'm not sure about him… it doesn't mean I can be with you. I know you saved my life, and I don't even know how to start thanking you for that, but I don't think I'm the right person for you. You need to be with someone else.'

His face hardened. He ran his hand slowly through his damp hair. When he turned to her the disappointment was etched in his eyes, but he replied calmly:

'It's ok Sophie. I didn't expect you to break up with him, but you should know that he's not the one for you.'

She leaned over, put her arms around his neck and kissed him gently on the cheek 'Ok. Look, we can still be friends, right? Boyfriends and girlfriends come and go, but friends are forever. I promise you Jay we will be friends for many, many years. Whatever happens. When we're old, like, you know, 40 or something, we will still be friends and call each other up and chat. I promise.'
He smiled lightly.

'Let's hope so, I don't want to lose you. Ok, enough now with the melodrama. Let's get back to the party and find something to eat. You'll feel better once you've had a steak sandwich!' He jumped up and held out his hand. Sophie got up gingerly, still a little unsteady on her feet and grateful for his help. She waited for him to put his arm around her waist and together they slowly walked up the hill back to the club-house.

Later that night, as she inched away from Dennis, who was softly snoring into his pillow, she looked out of the window. Soon the first rays of sun would be shining through the curtains, a new day as an 18-year-old. What a strange night it had been. Reflecting on her brush with death, her thoughts turned inevitably to her rescuer. How lucky she had been that he was there. Suddenly the image of the lonely figure sitting at the end of the pier smoking a cigarette flashed up in her mind. That hooded silhouette. So close yet so withdrawn. *Jay*. He had sat there, all the time looking out for her. Sophie tried to remember the rest of the evening before the lake incident. The more she thought about it, the more she could visualise him in the background, blending in with her friends, observing her from a distance, never taking his eyes off her. She wasn't sure whether she should be flattered or slightly unnerved being watched by a silent bystander. Dawn was breaking outside. The sky was turning purple.

Jay had selflessly jumped to her rescue – the mere thought made her heart shrink. 'I love you' he had said. No one had said that to her before, not even Dennis. She had turned Jay away and thinking about it broke her heart. Where was he now? Maybe he was thinking of her. She could not forget his final words. He whispered 'Just don't do it. Not tonight. Not with him'. And she hadn't.

CHAPTER 4

London, February 2011 - 4 months after the incident

Her phone beeped next to the keyboard and Sophie stopped typing to glance at the flashing display: 'On my way, see you 20:30 at the Gaucho, x'. Although it reminded her a bit of going on a blind-date, she was looking forward to meeting Timothy von Kempen tonight. Eighteen years since they had last seen each other. She couldn't help but wonder how he would look now.

After a quick message to her husband asking whether he had managed to pick up their daughter from nursery on time, she walked out of the office building into the cold winter evening. She shivered and buried her neck deeper into the high collar of her winter coat.

She had become a stressed working mum, juggling her career with taking care of a baby. Most of the time, she tried not to break down into tears in the back of a black cab, anxious to make it on time to the nursery – constantly torn between the love for her child and the passion she had for her job. She walked briskly into the foggy backstreets of the city, her white breath steaming in the freezing air, and she wondered what Tim would make of her. What would Tim remember from all the holidays they had spent together? What did he think of what happened with Jay?

They met at the bar, and they hugged each other awkwardly, like work colleagues bumping into each other at the weekend. He was as handsome as she remembered him but oddly, he didn't seem to have changed that much since she last saw him, all those years ago. He laughed when she pointed it out. 'I know, the other day I was at a newsagent and the owner ID'd me before letting me buy a box of matches', he chuckled. He had an affable twinkle in his eyes and a real throaty laugh she liked.

They sat down for dinner and after they ordered the conversation started flowing naturally. It turned out he had carved out a successful career for himself as a model. He had done catwalk shows in all the fashion capitals of the world. Sophie could see how his delicate, slightly androgynous looks, with high cheekbones and chiseled jawline gave him a feline, predatory air that would photograph well.

'Did you hear about Jay?' He was slightly taken aback by her brusque change of subject. He averted his eyes and played with the last bit of steak on his plate.

'Yes, I heard'. he looked up, and his eyes shone in the candlelight. 'It's sad', he whispered and suddenly frowned. 'Actually it's not sad. You know, I discussed this with my boyfriend the other day and...actually... It's awful. It's worse than that. It's just... disgusting', he spat scornfully. Her fork stopped midway to her mouth. She was shocked at his unexpected acerbic tone.

'How could he do that to his family? He had everything going for him. The model looks, intelligence and talent – and on top of that rich parents who gave him everything he wanted. I know his folks very well. His mom Elizabeth and... Caspar. He's a decent guy...' he wiped his mouth with a trembling hand correcting himself '...was...'

Tim looked at her with dark eyes, and his mouth twisted in anger. 'Jay's bedroom was always stuffed with the latest gadgets any teenager would have killed for'... He choked at his poor choice of words. 'I mean... the latest video games, TV, VCR, you name it he had it. One evening I stayed over for dinner, and I remember he mentioned he liked the idea of taking up drumming. A couple of weeks later when I went back there was a brand new drum set in his basement studio.' Tim was cross, and Sophie could see his point. It was easy to believe that Jay was spoilt rotten by his parents, particularly following their divorce. But Sophie knew the gifts all came at a hefty emotional price-tag. They were tokens of guilt for a lack of parental love.

'At the time I was quite jealous of him, weren't you?' Sophie smiled sadly. 'But all these gifts, they masked something sinister. The Jay I know wasn't at all interested in the boy-toys, the expensive clothes and the five-star holidays. He just wanted to find an outlet for his feelings, something to soothe his anxieties, to quench the feeling of guilt that nagged him since he split up his parents. He wanted to be an artist. Making music and painting gave him solace from the pressure he got from his parents. I think he felt they were trying to bribe him with gifts to make him follow in their footsteps. He was meant to take over his dad's business: the shops, the warehouses, the whole structure. He should have become the succeeding CEO. But...'

'...but that didn't quite work out as planned. That selfish monster ruined a whole family', Tim was still seething. Sophie shook her head, her eyes stinging. When the waitress interrupted them for more drinks, she nodded eagerly. Tim looked at her, suddenly aware of her distress. She stared at the remains of her steak on the plate, and a lonely tear rolled down her burning cheeks into the corner of her mouth. She quickly downed the rest of her cocktail. *Where's that bloody waitress? I need another drink.*

'I'm sorry Sophie', Tim reached over the table and took her hand in his. 'I didn't mean to upset you. I know you and Jay, you shared something special didn't you? A bond I never quite understood. We all looked up to you two; you were such a great pair. Beautiful, cool and just so grown up. I was in awe, little scrawny teenager that I was', he laughed. 'Do you remember that time we all went to Formentera and then that thing with the Ferry happened? Talking about missing the boat…'

Sophie rubbed her eyes and smiled tentatively at the memories of them holidaying together. It was nice someone remembered them from the glory days of the endless summers they had spent together – thinking the world was at their feet.

***

Formentera, August 1997 - 13 years before the incident

The sun shone brightly, and Sophie slowly scanned the horizon, her hair blowing in the wind. Nothing but water as far as her eyes could see. Endless turquoise waters sprinkled with small flecks of white where the waves broke the smooth surface. Sporadic waves, each a short burst of opportunity and then disappearing again in the uniform mass of the sea.

What am I going to do with my life? She wondered and looked out on the Mediterranean sea for inspiration, hoping to find the answer lying somewhere between two crests of a wave. Now she had finished school, would she go to university to study fashion like her friend Justine, or would she work in a bar and backpack across Asia like Camelia. Another wave rose, crested and vanished into the ocean beyond the earth's curve, silently unfolding and folding into the sea like the thoughts in her head.

Sophie was envious of her friends' ability to plan out their ambitions for the next five years, while she struggled to make up her mind. *Perhaps I'd like to go to art school?* she mused, thinking how this would please her mother.

A sense of hopelessness washed through her at the weight of her life-determining decision, and she swayed on her feet as her hand reached out to grip to the railing. Her stomach rumbled, reminding her she hadn't had breakfast that morning. A seagull flew by, shrieking loudly, and elegantly perched itself on the top of the blue and white stripped deck chair next to her. It turned its white and grey feathered head and stared at her with beady eyes, squawking loudly and ruffling its feathers impatiently. It seemed to be questioning her: 'What now with your life?' Creepy bird, she thought and as she stepped forward and shooed it away angrily, a soft chuckle reached her ear. Sophie turned away from the disgruntled seagull, who hopped off the deck chair in a huff. Jay slid off one of the covered rescue boats and walked towards her, a large smile illuminating his face.

'Here you are. Chasing birds. Do you need some help? It doesn't look impressed with your kicking skills,' he smirked. Her anger melted at the sight of him. He looked tanned and relaxed in his white t-shirt, army supply shorts and tattered trainers. Her stomach tightened.

Ever since he had confessed his love for her after saving her life at her birthday party, he had been avoiding her. Even now they were back on the island for the summer, he was even quieter than usual and spent hours scribbling in his notebook with eyebrows knitted in concentration. Most of the time he looked distant and cross.

So cross that every time she plucked up the courage to go and talk to him, she changed her mind at the last minute and decided to stay put. Sophie feared rejection, or, worse perhaps, indifference. First she was crushed, but then she had no other choice but to frustratingly admit that after she had told him they would only ever be 'just friends', he had taken her at her word.

'Where were you hiding? I looked for you earlier, weren't we supposed to have breakfast with the others?' she asked, nudging him gently in the ribs. Her hand was itching to reach out for his. Jay raised an eyebrow and inched away from her. *Oh shit I need to stop trying to touch him all the time, it's embarrassing.* The thought alone flushed her cheeks, and she quickly looked away, pretending to be particularly interested in the flaking paint on the railing.

'I was watching you. What were you searching for? What's out there in the sea?' He stepped closer and folded his arms next to hers over the railing. She could feel the warmth of his skin next to hers and it raised the fine hairs in the nape of her neck. She gulped and followed his gaze to the endless Mediterranean sea. A misty coastline appeared on the horizon.

'That's Formentera… looks like we will arrive soon.' She feigned indifference, but her voice trailed off suddenly strangled.

Jay moved and their skin touched. A wave of desire rushed through her whole body. *He is so close.* She wondered what would happen if she turned her head towards him. *Would he kiss me?* Her heart skipped a beat and, unable to move, she stubbornly continued staring at the sea. The thought of kissing him didn't leave any room for rational thought. Her whole being gravitated towards him, locked in irresistible attraction. She wanted his lips pressed against hers, and she held her breath, closed her eyes and slowly turned to him. One, two, …three…

Suddenly Jay lifted his arm abruptly and shoved her to the side. Sophie tripped and tottered against the railing, just about managing to hold on to the side and regain balance. Confused and shocked at the sudden change of mood, she looked up to see her father stomping up the deck, looking furious. Her heart sank.

'Where the hell have you two been?' he thundered. 'We've been looking for you everywhere. We're all finishing breakfast downstairs. The ferry will arrive in less than 20 minutes – you need to be ready to disembark with food in your bellies. This is the last chance you'll get to eat until lunch time.'

Jay smiled politely and nodded, but her father looked him up and down with clenched jaws, decided to ignore him and glowered at his daughter instead. Sophie mumbled a half-hearted apology which he dismissed with an irritated hiss, and she trotted sullenly behind him to the ferry's breakfast buffet.

As she sat down at the table, she picked at her rubbery croissant and tried to ignore the exasperated stares from her mother across the table. As always she had managed to anger her father and put her mother on edge. *Thank god he didn't catch us kissing*. Guilty and deflated, she hung her head to hide her burning cheeks in her wind-tousled hair.

Half an hour later they disembarked from the smallest port she had ever seen. It was a sandy beach, with a pier that regulated traffic twice daily between the small island of Formentera and its bigger sister island Ibiza. A group of chain-smoking fishermen in dark linen shirts were having coffees and white wine, discussing their morning catch. Sophie walked down the jetty, clutching her rucksack in one arm and tightly holding her brother's hand, and watched on as a fishing net was hauled in. The net split open and a silver flow of freshly caught fish loudly spluttered out on the pavement. The fishermen yelled orders at each other in coarse-sounding Spanish punctuated by throaty laughs and coughs. Hurriedly hosing down their catch, they then proceeded to kill the fish with one blow to the head. Flung into large plastic crates, the fish were ready to be shipped to the local market where short fat women in large straw hats and black dresses would praise their freshness to islanders and tourists alike.

Her brother Sam tugged at her sleeve and pointed at one of the bigger crates, his eyes wide in amazement.

'Look!' he whispered, frozen with awe. 'Look at that fish. It's huge.'

On a bed of salty smelling seaweed, a shark stared at her with its dead eye. A menacing row of sharp white teeth shone in its open mouth. The deadly predator was about two meters long. Its smooth grey skin glistened in the sun. It was dangerously beautiful, and Sophie couldn't take her eyes off it. Its wet gills seemed to still bristle in the sea breeze. Even in death it looked triumphant. I wish I was as strong and fearless as that shark, she thought.

It was her sister Anna who broke the spell and dragged them away from the fish to a small car rental office where their father had gone to pick up the keys for their car.

'Ok everyone, this is how we are going to do it' her father's loud voice boomed above her and brought her back from her shark reverie. Her mother Vera and her friend Mariana von Kempen stopped chatting and walked over, followed by her husband Stefan and his two kids Tim and Jack. Jay stood next to his dad and looked bored. Sophie discreetly tried to get his attention, but he ignored her. She felt a pang of disappointment. Did he not sense that she had intended to kiss him before her father had interrupted them?

'We have rented two cars for today's island exploration', her father continued, pleased to have a captive audience. 'And two motorbikes. The last ferry departs at six promptly, so we need to be here no later than 5:30pm. Don't forget that the tanks for the cars and bikes need to be refilled when you hand in your keys. Jay and Henry are taking the motorbikes.'

Sophie climbed into the car with the rest of her family and looked out the window to see Jay expertly starting the engine, nonchalantly fastening the black helmet on his head, revving up the machine and disappearing down the dirt track behind the car park. Sophie couldn't help but feel impressed and a little bit envious. *Where did he learn to do that?* She wondered if her father would ever let her ride a motorbike.

They drove away from the tiny port and up to the north of Formentera. The mild air smelled of pine trees and sea salt. The sun shone brightly on the beautiful and sparsely-populated island.

Oranges and lemons brightened up the dark foliage of the trees lining the road. They passed a couple of small villages and here and there in the green hills Sophie could make out the pale pink roofs of tucked away retreats. Formenteran women were gathering in the fields to pick ripe olives from silver-leafed trees.

Sophie woke up as the car was coming to a halt. She rubbed her eyes. Wondering how long she had slept, she stepped gingerly out of the car and stared straight down a precipice. The cliff abruptly fell into the sea below, and she was instantly gripped by overwhelming vertigo. Her legs turned to jelly. She slowly edged her way along the side of the car to get to the front, trying to dodge a cactus bush the size of a grown man. Its thorns pierced through her t-shirt and scratched her bare legs. She cursed loudly and her father who was unloading the boot, shot her an exasperated look and reprimanded her:

'Don't swear, Sophie. I know you think you're all grown up now and that the family laws don't apply to you anymore. But let me tell you that as long as you're living under my roof, my rules still apply. You'll wipe that arrogant expression off your face before I do. I also expect you to look after your brother and sister and help your mother', he spat.

He is using me like I'm his au pair. Convenient for him when all he does is get drunk and then fall asleep on his sun lounger. Hot anger welled up in her and it took all her willpower to bite her tongue and not answer back. She resigned herself to nod and keep her mouth shut, but couldn't resist shooting him a glowering look.

Her father would always take out his frustrations on her. Mostly ignoring her brother or her sister, he would always go for Sophie first and then her mother. But while Vera bowed to his every whim and mood, excusing his violent behaviour because he was the breadwinner of the family, Sophie was finding it increasingly tempting to fight back. She wanted to defy his narrow-minded views on her future and defend her attitude, which he generally qualified as belonging to a sullen teenager.

'Where have you been?' he'd growl, his eyes narrow and bloodshot. 'Do you know what time it is?' He'd sit in the dark of the living room, his hand clutching his watch, growing angrier with every minute she was late coming home. She'd apologise weakly but he'd ignore her, suddenly jumping up in a surge of rage. 'How dare you defy my orders' he'd scream, his hand raised.

Deep down she knew the time had come to stand up for herself and refuse to be beaten any longer. Soon she would leave to go studying. It was just a matter of time. As she picked up the beach bags her father had tossed at her feet and followed him down the narrow winding path to the beach, she knew she was battle ready.

Later that afternoon they all had lunch by the beach at a small family-owned restaurant with a palm-thatched rooftop. Glad to escape the glare of the midday sun, Sophie sipped on her lemonade, picking at the remainder of fresh fish in lemon sauce, as her bare feet played in the sand. The kids were all sitting together at the end of the table, debating which ice-cream flavour tasted better. Sophie was only half listening, instead trying to concentrate on the adult conversation. The wine had been flowing freely since the beginning of the meal – the table was replenished with pale pink rose and beer at regular intervals.

'Maybe we shouldn't drink so much, remember we are still supposed to drive back to the port tonight to get on the last ferry back to Ibiza', said her mother, sounding only mildly concerned.

'When is the last ferry?' asked Jay's father Henry.

'At six.' Vera answered, coyly playing with her serviette. Sophie sometimes wondered if her mother was attracted to Henry. Sophie thought he looked like an older version of his son and unlike her choleric father, he was funny and sharp-witted.

'Six? That only leaves us a few hours' Henry quickly checked his watch 'What a shame. It's quite enjoyable out here. Look at these clear turquoise waters, if you'd plant a few palm trees on either side of the beach you'd think you were in the Caribbean.'

'And the wine isn't too bad either' Mariana interjected in her loud, husky voice. She shook her black mane and lit up another cigarette. She was very beautiful in a wild, untamed way. Long, tangled, ebony hair, dark eyes framed by big eyebrows and she only ever wore black or white. She drank and smoked too much and shouted her opinions in a heavy eastern European accent. She had a very good body for a 30-something year old, and Sophie always felt uncomfortable in her presence as she often witnessed Mariana's attempts to tease Jay. *Was it teasing or inappropriate flirting?* She wasn't sure, but the woman's cougar behaviour put Sophie on edge.

'We're getting old. Look at us.' Henry swerved an unsteady arm across the table. 'We used to party every night, until sunrise. And look at us, now we're middle aged we've become so...'

'Boring?' Vera laughed out loud.

'Yes indeed I think there's an element of truth in this'. When Henry smiled, the resemblance with Jay was uncanny.

Mariana shook her head eagerly and poured herself another glass of wine.

'Yes I keep saying this to this old fart here' pointing at her husband Stefan. 'That we need more adventure in our lives. Do something a bit more out of the ordinary. Be a bit more...'

'Spontaneous?' Vera giggled, the wine had emboldened her . Sophie's father stared silently into his wine glass. He looked drunk. Sophie's stomach knotted up instinctively, knowing the look in his eyes and that she had to be on her guard. Drinking made him unpredictable and aggressive, and she would undoubtedly be in the firing line.

'Yeah spontaneous. That's the word'. Henry sipped his gin and tonic, with a mischievous glint in his eyes.

'How about we miss that boat tonight and just stay here?' He straightened up in his chair and smiled provocatively at the rest of the table.

'Stay here? You're not serious! At this time of the day we'll never find a hotel,' Sophie's father slurred with a mocking tone.

'So what? We could just stay on the beach and sleep on our beach towels.' Henry ignored the aggressive tone and smiled at the rest of the table.

'Yeah right', he scoffed and took a drag of his cigarette. Sophie wished he would stop smoking so much, but being built like an ox he didn't seem to worry much about his health.

'Hey, wouldn't it be cool to stay on the beach tonight?' Jay whispered conspiringly as he pushed his dessert over to Sophie. 'Here have some of mine, I don't like strawberry ice cream.'

That's a lie. Why is he always trying to feed me? Am I too skinny? She felt like asking him, but she smiled instead, happy he was talking to her. Deep in her heart she knew she was and hated it. She wanted to be tall and strong. Not the skinny wispy weakling she was.

'It would probably be the coolest thing we would ever do with our parents… But I think they need a little help. We need to get them a bit more drunk and then convince them this is their plan.' Her heart beat a little faster at the idea of spending the night with Jay on the beach.

'I think they'll take care of the first bit by themselves, look at all those wine bottles on the table. They're sorted for the afternoon, and they might just be too drunk to notice the time.'

Jay was right. After they finished lunch, Sophie, Jay and the kids left the parents at the table to open yet another bottle of wine and headed back to the deserted beach. They walked along the water line for a bit in the heat of the afternoon sun. The little ones started a game of football, and Jay grabbed Sophie by the arm and dragged her away onto the path leading to the deserted car park.

'Come with me, I have to show you something', he said, smiling at her. Her heart was beating fast as she skipped over rocks and seaweed, trying to keep up with him. In the shadows of the pine trees, she spotted his motorbike, and she turned to Jay, her face a question mark. He motioned her to wait, fumbled in his shorts and fished out the keys. He held out his hand for her to take them.

'What?'

'Go on, take them.'

'I can't! I've never done this before' She clasped her hand on her mouth.

'I'll teach you, it's not hard.'

She felt a surge of adrenaline rush through her and couldn't help but jump up and down in excitement.

'Ok. Let's do this. What do I do first?'

Jay pushed the motorbike off its stand and rolled it to the middle of the sandy path. It looked heavy and big and dangerous. He handed her a helmet and when she put it on, he pulled her towards him to fasten the clasp under her chin. He stood so close that she could see her reflection in his pupils. He knocked the helmet and laughed, 'Ok off you go now and try not to kill us'.

She slid onto the seat in front of him, well aware of his arms on either side holding onto the steering and his torso against her back. He ignited the engine and revved the motor. The sound exploded in her ears, and she noticed her hands were shaking when he lifted her right hand to press it firmly against the accelerator. She yanked the handle backwards; the engine roared and the bike jumped forward in a cloud of sand and dust.

They were on the road, and she felt like they were going a million miles per hour. Pine trees, bushes, cars and people were flying past in a blur. She wanted to laugh and whoop out loud; it was exhilarating. She suddenly noticed Jay had slung his arms around her waist, and she was driving the bike on her own. Sophie felt powerful and strong. *I love this,* her heart sang.

They rode for a while, away from the beach and inland, along small deserted country roads and dusty dirt tracks up to the top of the highest point of the island until they reached the red and white lighthouse. Jay stabilised the bike and Sophie hopped off, grinning from ear to ear. She removed the helmet and shook out her tangled hair.

'Jay, that was amazing!' she cried, her eyes shining with enthusiasm.

'I know. I love the feeling of freedom and speed. It's addictive, isn't it?'

'Yes!' She jumped into his arms, and he spun her around laughing. She shrieked in delight, and they stumbled against the wall of the lighthouse. Feeling lightheaded and breathing rapidly, she locked eyes with him, and the mood suddenly changed. He pressed himself against her; one arm folded against the wall and with his other hand he grabbed her shoulder. His hand was slightly shaking and the intimacy of the gesture froze her to the spot. With his face up close, she noticed the ever so slight shadow of a two-day stubble and the specks of white sand on his tanned skin. She looked up into his eyes, unsure of what would happen next. He frowned at her and his grip on her shoulder intensified to the point she bit her lip to not wince.

'I … I want to kiss you', he breathed as he slid his hand on the nape of her neck, drew her closer and kissed her softly on the corner of her mouth.

Sophie closed her eyes holding her breath. Pressed against the wall of the lighthouse in the golden glow of the setting sun, she kissed him back with all the hunger of her repressed feelings.

When they eventually let go of each other, the sky had turned a pretty shade of pink and Sophie smiled, feeling deliriously happy.

Until she checked her watch and gasped in horror.

'Oh my god. Oh my god. Oh my god' she shouted in panic. It was past five. Way past five.

'Fuck. The ferry!'

They jumped on the bike and sped back to the beach. As they arrived in the car park Sophie's mother awaited them, anxiously pacing in front of their car. Guilt hit Sophie like a ton of bricks. She was in trouble, and she knew it. She jumped off as soon as Jay stopped the bike and ran over to her mother who stopped her in her tracks.

'Sophie! Where in god's name were you two? We've been looking for you everywhere. I can't believe you thought it was a good idea to disappear at this time. We've missed the ferry. You better watch out; your dad is furious.'

The familiar mix of helpless fear and instinctive aggressiveness knotted her stomach.

As she saw her father running up the path, breathing heavily and with crazy eyes, she shifted into flight or fight mode. He grabbed her violently by the arm and shook her, banging her skinny body against the car. He started shouting, spit flying into her face, reminding her that, as the oldest kid of the group, she was responsible for watching over the little ones. Apparently her brother Sam had fallen over and scratched his knee, and when he had walked back to the restaurant he had found their parents getting ready to go back to the port. Once they couldn't find them by the beach, they sent out a search party but Jay and Sophie were nowhere to be found. Now the last ferry had left the island, they were stuck until the next morning with no place to spend the night. Her father was seething and yelled at her for turning up so late. Anger welled up in her like bubbling lava and, throwing caution to the wind, she shouted back:

'I am 19 now and I shouldn't have to ask if I want to go somewhere. You are treating me like a child.'

'I treat you as I think you deserve to be treated. When you're on holidays with the family you obey the rules of the family', he bellowed back, his hands trembling in anger. 'Your selfish behaviour has landed us in a fucking embarrassing situation. Where are we going to sleep tonight? Hmm? You tell me miss smart ass!'

'Don't make such a fuss. The others said they were quite happy to stay out on the beach tonight, you said it over lunch', Sophie looked desperately over to her mother for support. But Vera looked away and said quietly 'It was a joke Sophie. We never intended to do this really'.

'You will not talk back to me like that' Sophie's father hissed, dangerously tightening his grip around her arm. But Sophie felt she had passed the point of no return. She was too angry to control her long pent-up feelings.

'I fucking talk back to you if I want to. You can't stop me. You're drunk, and you should be ashamed of yourself, you would've probably killed us all driving around as drunk as you are', she screamed at him jutting out her jaw provocatively.

She didn't see it coming. She only heard Jay's shouting and her mother's whimpering when the blow hit her face with a loud smack. She stumbled backwards and crashed against the boot of the car. Her left ear was ringing. Black dots blurred her vision. She lost her balance and slid onto the dusty floor. Her father towered above her menacingly, his fist still raised. His eyes were mad as he launched into her again. Sophie cowered on the floor, instinctively lifting her arms to protect her head. She screamed in anticipation of the next blow. Which never came. Slowly she lowered her shaking arms and peered up. Jay had pushed her father aside and held him at arms length. Vera had ushered the kids into the car. Sophie scrambled to her feet, put back on a shoe she had lost in the fall, and, with one last look at her father's angry, distorted face, she ran off towards the beach.

She ran and ran until her lungs burned. She slid and stumbled in the sand, hot tears streaming down her face. She only slowed down when it got too dark to see. Leaving behind the lights of the restaurant, she climbed up the rocks at the far end of the beach. The waves crashed below, and she sat down in a nook on top of the cliff overlooking the darkness. Protected from the wind, she curled into a ball and sobbed hysterically until her shaking body relaxed, and she eventually fell asleep.

She woke up to the sound of Jay's voice insistently calling out her name. Her limbs stiff and aching, she slowly rose from her foetal position and answered with a croaky voice. The light of his torch bounced off the rocks. As he climbed up, he found her shivering in the dark and rushed to put his arms around her in a consoling embrace. He held her head as tears of relief rolled down her cheeks. His arms were warm, and his skin smelled of sun-cream.

They sat down on the edge of the cliff and watched on as the moon rose above the hills. As the moon grew fatter Jay's features became clearer and he looked concerned as he bowed over her and inspected her left eye. It felt sore and swollen. He let out a frustrated sigh and without saying a word, pulled out a first-aid kit he had found in one of the cars.

'Hold it there, this will reduce the swelling', he ordered. She felt the soothing effect of the cold compress almost immediately as she held it against her bruised skin. While Sophie tried not to flinch, Jay proceeded to delicately apply cream around the swollen eye socket.

Then he pressed two painkillers in the palm of her hand and ordered her to wash them down with some whisky. She took the bottle and took a big gulp of the eye-watering spirit. The alcohol warmed her instantly, and her head started spinning.

'Where did you find that?' she wondered.

'They're all back in the bar. They plan to sleep on sun loungers by the beach and with no blankets apart from wet beach towels – they're drinking to keep warm. They're doing a pretty good job. I somehow doubt they'll notice one of the bottles disappearing from their table' he chuckled.

Her stomach suddenly growled with hunger. Jay smiled and pulled out a gorgeous smelling takeaway pack from his rucksack.

'Ta-da: Lamb stew with potatoes, homemade. A traditional Formentarian recipe or so the old cook told me. I thought you could do with something decent. It might be a bit cold though. I walked for a while before I found you', he said nervously.

'I can't believe you did all this' she mumbled with a full mouth as she greedily tucked in. She devoured the meal in seconds and whooped when Jay delved once again into his magic rucksack, this time pulling out an apple tart wrapped in plastic. 'You're amazing', she said.

Jay didn't reply and stared intently at the black sea, a thunderous expression shadowing his face.

'What is it?' she whispered anxiously, but she wasn't sure whether she wanted to know what had happened after she ran off.

'I'm sorry. I shouldn't have asked you to come with me. It was my fault, and I should've stepped in sooner. I should have protected you'. The anger filtered through his low voice. He took a sip from the whisky bottle and handed it to Sophie.

She shook her head and took the bottle.

'It's not your fault; we were both on the bike, I agreed to go with you.'

'Your dad is an asshole. He shouldn't have hit you. No one should be allowed to hit their kid' he said in a solemn voice.

'I know, but to be fair I provoked him. It's not like I couldn't have avoided it. I was mad, and it escalated. It's no big deal.'

She bit her lip and touched the bruised edge of her eye. It was painful, and she took another sip from the bottle, coughed and slowly lowered herself onto her back her arms crossed behind her head. Looking at the starry midnight sky, with a full stomach and Jay so close, she felt much better.

Jay said nothing for a while and then asked:

'This is not the first time this has happened, am I right?'

Her first impulse was to deny the allegation he made but then she resigned herself to saying:

'Yes... this has happened before'. She didn't know what else to say. She didn't want to talk about it. Instead she took another sip from the bottle to forget this whole thing had happened and wished herself back to the lighthouse, moments before she looked at her watch.

As if reading her thoughts, Jay lay down next to her without saying a word. He pulled her towards him. Her head rested on his chest while he gently stroked her hair. She inched her head closer to his and seconds later they found each other's lips. He kissed her with such infinite tenderness, she held her breath so as not to disturb the stillness of the moment. Her body melted against his, and his hand closed around hers. Their kisses grew more passionate and her stomach knotted with desire. He held her face with both hands and kissed her hard, his ragged breath against her hot skin. Her hands slid under his t-shirt and traced along his smooth back. She kissed his neck and tasted the sea salt on his skin.

There was something equally desperate and erotic about this moment, waves crashing below them, the starry night sky unfolding above them, like they had stopped existing as individuals and shared a destiny frozen in this exact moment of abandonment. She wanted to be with him. He was the one, and she knew with every fibre of her being. He kissed her because he loved her, and she knew that was true from the way he had looked at her, a ferocious protective expression in his eyes. And when he gently pulled her t-shirt over her head and unhooked her bikini top, she didn't pull away. His tentative touch explored her body and she shivered with excitement. It felt right.

She trembled in anticipation as she helped him out of his clothes. He held her tightly and his skin was warm and smooth against hers. 'I want you', he whispered urgently in her ear. Feeling hot and dizzy, she nodded, and he carefully rolled on top of her and slowly parted her legs. She gasped as he entered her; and he froze for moment searching for her approval. She gave him a brief smile.

Waves of desire rushed through her body. Her arms slung around his neck, she wanted to hold him closer, his body becoming one with hers, as if somehow his closeness was giving her soul a shelter from the hurt and she wanted to never let him go. He was hers, and he was going to protect her. Their breathing quickened; both trapped in a whirlwind they had never experienced with anyone else before. Although Sophie had experienced orgasms through experimental masturbation before, the one brought on by the man she loved was so powerful the world around her shattered into nothingness and this time her tears were celebrating a life-changing moment.

As they sat side by side, gazing at the line where the sea touched the sky, he wrapped his arm around her waist and studied her face with a look that was equally one of wonder and uncertainty.

'Where do we go from here?' he whispered, and she while she didn't know the answer to his question she knew that regardless of time and location, an unbreakable bond would forever keep them close.

CHAPTER 5

London, March 2011 - 5 months after the incident

'Kate, can you please cancel my business trip to Zurich. It's not worth going now the conference has been postponed.'

Her assistant looked at her, clearly annoyed. The plans had changed again. Sophie mouthed a silent sorry and Kate shook her head, tutted disapprovingly but grabbed the phone to proceed cancelling the flight and hotel.

It didn't really bother Sophie to change plans at the last minute. Her daughter had the flu, and when faced with the choice to either nurse her 5-months old back to health or hang around a dull three-day conference about emerging market investing, Sophie knew which option she preferred. But she was careful not to say that out loud. After returning from maternity leave a few months ago, she still felt like she had to prove to her colleagues that she was back, in charge and committed to the job.

She had made it to vice president at a large American financial institution and looked after high net worth client relations across Europe. Most of the time she enjoyed her work as a private banker but there were days when she struggled. Today was one those days. With a sick daughter banned from nursery, she had to juggle work commitments with looking after her. Luckily her devoted husband Martin was a great help and had taken the morning off work to look after the baby while she rushed around the office pretending everything was ok.

She was marking up the presentation she was proofreading when her phone rang. Slightly irritated to be disturbed, she picked up the receiver. 'Sophie Liebtreu-Mackenzie, how can I help?' she answered automatically, noticing that the number on the display started with 0049. A call from Germany.

'Are you Sophie Liebtreu?' A woman with a strong German accent asked amidst the noisy background of what turned out to be a newsroom.

'Yes that's me. How can I help?' she answered impatiently. She was used to receiving dozens of calls a day from her clients across Europe. Clamping the receiver between her jaw and shoulder, she rummaged around her busy desk searching for a pen and a post-it, ready to take down trading instructions.

'Sophie Liebtreu, are you familiar with the Adler case? I have a few questions I'd like you to answer.' Sophie froze. The pen dropped onto the desk in slow motion as the words echoed in her head. *The Adler case. Oh god.* She felt the blood drain from her face.

'You do know Jay Adler don't you?' Automatically she answered 'Yes', and instantly regretted it.

'The verdict of his conviction has been announced today. He got 20 years in a psychiatric clinic. Do you think his sentence is justified? How do you feel about the news?'

Sophie blanked. Sweat started running slowly down her spine.

'Who is this? Where are you calling from?' she managed to ask through clenched jaws.

'I'm Ingrid Bachman, news reporter at Bild-Zeitung. I report on the Adler case. My sources say that you were intimate with the defendant. How intimate were you? Is it fair to say you were his long-term girlfriend?'

Sophie swallowed with difficulty, and she felt her palms getting clammy. The Bild-Zeitung was Germany's widest circulated broadsheet. A tabloid newspaper that revelled in scandalous news stories. If it boosted circulation figures the paper had no qualms about bending the truth to sensationalise stories and was regularly attacked for slander. Not that its four-million readership cared much about the authenticity of its news stories, it was the most read newspaper in Germany.

'How did you get my number?' Sophie finally whispered as the blood rushed back to her cheeks. She was all too aware of the curious stares from her colleagues looking up over their cubicles. She turned her back to them and desperately tried to regain her composure.

'My sources are well-informed' snapped the reporter impatiently, and continued firing questions at her. 'What happened on the night of his incarceration? Were you there? Would you describe him as a monster?'

Sophie wiped the sweat off her brow and took a deep breath.

'Ingrid Bachman, I will not answer any of your questions. I will not provide you with comment in any shape or form. You are not to contact me again. Goodbye.'

She slammed the receiver back on its base with a shaky hand. The stares of her colleagues burned in the back of her head, and she tried to ignore them as she stubbornly looked at her computer screens. The graphs and charts started to blur as her eyes filled with hot tears. 20 years the reporter had said. *20 years. Locked up, in a psychiatric unit.*

Did she think he was a monster, the woman had asked. Sophie didn't know what to think. Her head spun, and she shakily got up to walk over to the office kitchen. Out of her colleagues' sight, she ran her hands under the tap and dabbed her temples with cold water. She took a couple of deep breaths, poured herself a glass of water and looked out at the London skyline. *20 years.* Jay would be in his fifties before he was free again.

***

Ibiza, August 1998 - 12 years before the incident

'So where do you think we can score some then?' Frank asked in a low voice, scanning the bay of San Antonio with knitted eyebrows as if to spot a forgotten smugglers bag full of drugs floating amidst the waves. Sophie shrugged, wiped the sand off her fingers and took a sip of her beer.

'I don't know; it's not like I have a weed-dealer detector.' she snapped.

The warm evening breeze carried a soft lounge beat as Ibiza's party lovers gathered on Cafe del Mar's beach stretch for the daily sunset ritual. Sophie side-glanced over to Frank. She wasn't quite sure what to make of Jay's best friend. Was he a nice guy who pretended to be an asshole or was he really just an asshole? she wondered as she inched away from him. He had a habit of sitting irritatingly close to her, so close that she could smell his body odour. Everything about him got on her nerves. His white nylon baseball t-shirt that was way too big for his skinny frame. The pair of slouchy worn out jeans with a waist slung way too low. *For god sakes who wears jeans with half their ass hanging out? That trend came and died.* His name was Frank Stahl and Sophie didn't like him.

His skin was so white it was translucent. Even after he had been on the island for a week, he still looked a sickly pale hue. No wonder, as he never sat in the sun and preferred staying indoors whenever he could, playing video games. Which suited Sophie fine – it meant she could finally be alone with Jay.

Jay. She had caught a glimpse of him earlier that evening as he slammed the cab door shut, staring straight ahead, his neck stiff and his eyes dark with resignation. It wasn't so much that she wondered where he was going to dinner with his dad, but rather what they had to discuss so privately. 'I'll meet you at the bar later' he had whispered in her ear and his hot breath had raised the hairs on her neck. Their relationship was a strange one. They had been intimate, but they weren't a couple. On many levels they were close like best friends but he seemed to always keep her at arms-length. It was as if he had built invisible walls to guard himself. It left her hurt and frustrated, until she came to terms with the fact that, although never enough, being friends was all that they would ever be.

'You said you knew a weed guy' Frank moaned interrupting her thoughts. Every time she looked at the young man, she saw nothing else but the offensive blackheads on his nose, and it would make her skin crawl. Luckily he hid under a large baseball cap, which he never took off, even when he went for a swim. She disliked the way he always tried too hard to impress her, and when she wouldn't react to his pathetic advances, he would resort to making snarky comments at her.

He was looking at her with washed-out blue eyes, still waiting for an answer. She resisted the temptation to snap at him again and instead patiently answered:

'I don't know to be honest. Last year I met this guy in the M bar. His name was Dave. English. And he knew this dealer guy who sold me some weed.'

She had met Dave the previous summer at the trendy M bar in San Antoni. He was a big burly East-London type who worked the clubbing scene over the summer and saw no harm in selling a bit of weed on the side.

'Would you recognise him if you saw him?'

Frank's eyes darted from left to right while he drummed his fingers on his knee.

'Not sure. He was tanned, with a shaven head and this tattoo on his shoulder. I don't remember of what though, maybe a swallow? He was older, like 25 or something.'

She looked around at the people sitting on the beach. That description could have applied to almost every guy there. *Don't they all look the same in their tank tops and aviator sunglasses.* Laughing loudly, the lads on holiday swigged from San Miguel bottles, smoked Embassy's and hugged big-bosomed girls. The girls wore miniskirts so short they didn't leave much to the imagination. Sophie observed them sitting on the rocks across the bay. Black silhouettes against the setting sun.

Frank crouched down next to her and sucked on his beer, looking defeated. He had been moaning all day about being on the planet's most famous party-island without any drugs, and how this holiday had turned out to be quite lame. Having spent so many summer holidays on the island, she had never found it 'lame'. They sat in silence for a while until she couldn't bear the awkwardness of his sulky presence any longer. She mumbled an excuse of needing the bathroom and wandered off.

The music had changed from upbeat house to slow hypnotic beats. People moved closer to the shoreline and quietened down, listening to the music while slowly getting drunk. The floor was littered with empty sangria jugs and beer bottles.

Sophie walked up to the bar and paused to admire the rich decor of the Cafe del Mar. The walls and the ceiling were hand-painted and looked like a psychedelic version of the Sistine chapel. The DJ stood behind the turntables in the elevated DJ booth. His head cocked to one side, he was intently listening to the sound in his headphones. He waved as she walked past him, and Sophie smiled back coyly, not sure if he meant to wave at her or the tall slender brunette standing behind her. The poster on the wall behind him read "Jose Padilla, resident DJ at Cafe del Mar. The undisputed creator of ambient chill-out music".

Pushing her way past the noisy crowd, she ordered another beer at the bar, retreated to a quieter corner, and weighed her options. Finding weed tonight was going to be a challenge. When she met David the year before he worked as a bouncer at Privilege, one of Ibiza's most infamous clubs, but with no number to call him on, the chance she would bump into him tonight was next to none.

Everyone else here was on holiday as she was. The sweet smell of weed permanently hung in the air but Sophie couldn't make out who was smoking it. And besides what was she going to do? Just walk over to some random guy and ask him where he got his gear from? She shook her head. That wasn't going to work. She took a sip from her beer when suddenly someone tapped her on the shoulder. Lowering her beer on the bar, she looked at a short guy smiling at her. He was wearing a shiny blazer over a v-necked t-shirt which instantly put her off. That and the greasy slicked back hair and the gold chain around his neck.

'Hi, my name is Mark, where are you from?' he asked, holding out his hand for her to shake. A question she wouldn't have to ask him as his accent instantly gave him away. He couldn't be more French if he'd tried.

'Hi', she said reluctantly, ignoring his outstretched hand and clutching her beer while discreetly scoping out an escape route.

'Ok, mysterious woman, let me guess then if you won't tell', he insisted with a wink.

Oh god, yeah go on then give it a try. He guessed Norway, and she didn't care to correct him. It was her waist-length platinum blonde hair and her Scandinavian accent that gave it away, he laughed. *He is only wrong by a few thousand kilometres on the map.* They continued exchanging platitudes about how long she had been on the island and when she was flying back. Sophie, Jay and Frank had arrived a week ago, and Jay's father had given them the keys to his villa for another two weeks.

'Oh, lucky you, I'm flying home tomorrow.'

Yeah, lucky me indeed, she thought and assumed the man was probably looking for someone with whom to spend his last night on the island. She yawned into her beer, bearing the painfully stilted conversation and preparing her excuses to leave, when he pushed a business card into the palm of her hand.

'I know this will sound like a cheesy chat up line but let me assure you it isn't'. She tentatively looked at the card and turned to him nonplussed.

'I'm a model scout for this agency you might have heard of: Elite?'

She slowly shook her head. *Maybe I've heard of the name before.*

'Well, I'm looking for girls your age and your frame for catwalk jobs. Take my number and give me a call. Lancôme is looking for models just like you. I'd like to organise some test shots with you. See how you do, and we can take it from there.'

She laughed out loud in disbelief. He sounded genuine but when she looked down at her skinny legs, boyish hips and small breasts, she found it hard to believe he'd just offered her a model job. People had always commented negatively on her appearance and for years she had been bullied at school for looking lanky and gauche. Shouts of 'the anorexic albino' had followed her throughout college. Her father's voice echoed in the back of her mind. *Sophie listen, unfortunately you are not gifted with great beauty, so do yourself a favour and do not rely on your appearance to get you through in life. Be smart instead. It's your best option.*

Her ex-boyfriend Dennis had once asked her if given the money, would she choose a breast enlargement or a nose job – or perhaps both – he had chuckled. His comments stung way beyond the short time they had spent together. She shook her head to dispel the painful memory of their ugly breakup.

She twisted the man's business card between her fingers. Mark de Lanelles. Elite. A number. The address. Paris. She wondered how easy it would be to print a batch of fake business cards and hand them out to random gullible girls. Ibiza was probably the largest possible hunting ground, and she felt like congratulating this little man on the creativity of his pick-up technique when suddenly she spotted something peeking out of his jeans pocket.

'Are those rizzlas? Does that mean you smoke... err you know...' she pointed at the long blue cigarette paper strip.

'Pot?' he laughed and Sophie nodded.

'Yeah, I do. You want some?' he asked as he pulled a pack of cigarettes out of his pocket. They walked down the beach to a more secluded spot, and they sat down on the rocks as he started to expertly skin up a spliff. He burnt the hashish lump with his lighter until it softened at the edges, and crumbled it into his palm. He had Sophie hold a cigarette while he quickly rolled a filter he ripped off the inside of the cigarette pack. Carefully, he split the cigarette and sprinkled the tobacco in the mix he had prepared. He licked the sticky side of the paper and quickly rolled the whole into a perfect cone.

He handed it to her with his lighter and smiled: 'Ladies first'. She hesitated for a second. *Was this safe?* Throwing caution to the wind, she lit up the spliff and carefully drew in the heavy sweet tasting smoke. Its effect was near instant. Her eyelids drooped, and her hands felt heavy. Her heart was bouncing against her ribcage and her mouth dried up. She wanted to remain in control – after all this man was a stranger, she had to remain on her guard, but suddenly she was tickled by an irresistible urge to giggle.

'You seriously think I could be a model?' she chuckled. 'Something wrong with your eyes, but it's a good pick-up line, I'll give you that. I bet all the girls fall for it! Thank you for the spliff, but I really need to go back to my friends. See you around.'

'Call me if you change your mind', he said hopefully.

Sophie smiled briefly by way of apology and stumbled back to the bar, lightheaded and a bit unsteady on her feet, as if her mind was wading through melted marshmallows.

As she frayed her way through the sunset worshippers, her hand found the lump of Moroccan hash in her pocket and she rolled it between her fingertips, wondering if she should be feeling guilty for stealing it. But she dismissed the feeling as quickly as it came. The sod had deserved it. She tottered along the shoreline amidst the increasingly drunken crowds until she finally spotted Frank's lanky frame hunkered down on the beach, gazing out at the sea.

Sophie sat down next to him. Both of them silently observed the darkening skies. The sun shone blood red through the thin grey veil of clouds above the horizon. The morning star tentatively glimmered above them as if asking the sun's permission to make its nightly appearance. The music had simmered down to slow beats. Ignoring the crowd around her, Sophie submerged herself in the ethereal beauty of the sunset. The sinking sun dipped into the golden waters as every onlooker held their breath. A collective sigh marked the end of the day and the beginning of another night of hedonistic partying. A wave of applause erupted from the far end of the beach and washed over to their side to die at the opposite corner of the bay.

The music changed, and as it got darker, a merry group of extravagantly dressed performers emerged from the sea and ploughed through the crowd. Busty, bikini-clad girls, adorned with large angel wings, blew kisses at the crowd and handed out flyers for the night's party. Dwarfs dressed as jesters on stilts juggled with glitter balls. Fire-eaters showed off their muscly torsos and blew flames into the night sky. A stunning girl in a silver bikini with comically long false eyelashes and a huge blonde afro handed Sophie a flyer, grinning invitingly, her eyes wide and her pupils dilated.

Sophie studied the flyer. A pool party at Es Paradis club. She looked up, and the girl in the silver bikini had morphed into a dwarf who held up a sign saying 'Your sins are my sins'. An overpowering gasoline smell hung low in the unbearably hot air. Panic welled up in her. *Wow, I'm acting weird. I'm stoned!* Her head was spinning as she stumbled backwards away from the screaming crowd. A familiar hand grabbed her shoulder, and she relaxed as the feeling of panic subsided. She turned around and said:

'Finally you're here. I thought you'd changed your mind and left me babysitting your friend all night!'

Jay hugged her nonchalantly, and she breathed in the faint smell of his perfume on the collar of his polo shirt. He held her at arm's length and studied her face.

'You ok? You seemed a bit lost in the crowd.'

'No, I'm fine. No big deal. Let's find Frank. He was just here behind me, a minute ago'. They walked along the water for a bit. Frank seemed to have got lost in the crowd, and they decided to go back to the bar for some beers.

'So, how was dinner with your dad?' She looked at him expectantly, as he pushed a stumbling drunk guy out of the way to reach for two beer bottles on the counter.

'It was alright'. As usual he wasn't giving anything away. He had a tendency to clam up when she asked about his dad. She never knew what they talked about together. It sounded serious. Sophie didn't think she'd ever had dinner on her own with her father. Although intrigued she knew Jay well enough to realise it was pointless to keep digging.

'Cool' she acknowledged, her hand in her pocket, rolling the lump between her fingers. *Maybe a hit of this will loosen him up. But later. We have all night.*

'What about you, how was the evening with Frank?' he asked. There was a faint intensity to his voice that made her wonder if he was jealous.

'Errm yeah, well I'm not going to lie. It was a bit of a challenge. He isn't the most talkative of people, so the conversation wasn't exactly on fire', she downplayed.

'I see' he tried to conceal it but, by the way his lips curled ever so slightly into a tentative smile, Sophie detected a hint of relief.

'I don't think I actually like Frank very much. He is so...' *Awkward, weird, dumb, annoying?* She didn't know how to describe him, and the words stuck in her throat when she spotted Frank's pale face appear behind Jay's shoulder. She blushed violently and quickly grabbed her beer to hide her embarrassment, hoping Frank hadn't heard her.

Apparently he hadn't and Sophie silently thanked the rowdy group of British men downing tequila shots just next to them. Their howling and japing drowned out any snippet of conversation they subsequently tried to have. They opted to leave the sunset beach and instead amble to the centre of town.

Jay and Sophie joked as they strolled, her arm hooked in his, down the dark narrow side-streets leading to the harbour.

On the way, they stopped at a corner shop to buy lemons, a small bag of salt, a bottle of tequila and some San Miguel beer. The main street to the harbour, which they'd nicknamed Mad Cow Disease Street, was heaving with holiday-makers pouring out of bars, loud and rowdy, singing and falling over each other. Girls were wearing the tiniest of skirts and cropped tops showing off too much flesh. Guys with gel-spiked hairstyles and identical cheap shirts, roamed in packs of five or six, their faces reddened from the sun, drunk on cheap alcohol. Sophie skipped over one of the many puddles of vomit on the sidewalk and caught a snippet of conversation:

'Pphwoaarrr...did you see that bird with the massive tits', roared the pink-shirted drunk in a thick Mancunian accent, excitedly swinging his pint while trying to turn his mate's attention to the well-endowed brunette stood next to him.

'Huuuhhh?' his identical mate looked as green as his shirt as he tried eyeing up the brunette, cross-eyed and staggering. His eyes widened as he took in her large breasts squeezing out of her latex boob tube. He took a step towards her, struggled to get her attention, suddenly heaved and spattered the remains of his evening meal down her legs and onto her diamante-strap sandals. Pasta by the looks of it. The girl howled in disgust.

An involuntary witness of the depravity displayed, Sophie giggled loudly and hooked her arm deeper into Jay's. *Thank god we're not like them.* It was only early evening and already the tourists were wreaking havoc. Mad Cow Street claimed its first victims. As she slid past a tightly-entwined couple, licking each other's faces off, she wondered how many more scenes of debauchery they would have to endure before the night was through.

Once they got to the harbour, the sticky heat ebbed off. They welcomed the cool sea breeze on their faces. Strolling along the dike, they watched taxi boats aligning, spilling out a new load of party-eager thrill-seekers. The air was electric, with a promise of endless hedonistic fun. Jay, Frank and Sophie took off their shoes and walked down the beach until they found a stack of sun-loungers chained to a palm tree. Sitting on top with their feet dangling in the darkness, the lights of the bars twinkling in the distance, they listened to the distant sounds of waves and the screams and shouts of the revellers.

While Frank cracked open the bottle of tequila, Jay fished out his Swiss army knife and carefully cut the lemons in equal slices.

'Guys, we don't have any glasses' Sophie remarked.

'Don't worry we don't need them. Unless you are worried you'll catch something? No one's got herpes, right?' Frank made an unattractive snorting noise. Sophie wasn't looking forward to sharing the bottle with him but Jay laughed and winked at her as he dug into his pockets. With a flourish he produced three shot glasses.

'Picked them up from one of the tables we passed earlier' he shrugged as he proceeded to clean them out with a dash of tequila.

Sophie sliced the bag of salt open, took a pinch, licked the back of her hand, and sprinkled the salt on the wet patch. The lemon juice ran down her fingers and stung the raw skin around her bitten fingernails. They filled their shot glasses, toasted solemnly 'to a fun night', and licked the salt off the back of their hands. The tequila burned, but the tangy slice of lemon cancelled out its sting.

'Oh god, that stuff tastes vile' Sophie roared.

'Yep and you'd better have another shot right away. It'll take your taste buds out.'

They downed another shot, followed shortly by another, and another one after that, continuing until they emptied the bottle. By now Sophie's throat didn't burn anymore, and the numbing feeling of the alcohol traded places with the soft high of her earlier spliff. They chased down the tequilas with San Miguel beer.

'Guys, let's go and have a look around' said Jay as he climbed down off the sun loungers. He held his arms out to catch Sophie who carefully edged down into his arms.

For a second, she remained motionless in his grip, and as he looked into her eyes she felt a familiar flutter in the pit of her stomach. She was tempted to grab his face and kiss him, but resisting the feeling she detangled herself out of his arms.

They stood outside the enclosure of the swimming pool belonging to one of the posh hotels on the harbour strip. Sophie poked Jay in the ribs expectantly, pointing a finger up at the wall. If Jay helped her up, she reckoned she could climb that wall easily.

'Guys, who fancies a swim?' she whispered, excitedly slurring her words. Jay grinned a conspiring smile. With ease he hoisted her halfway up the wall. As she peeked over to the other side, in the dim light she could make out the dark pit that was the swimming pool. Aside from a few palm trees and empty sun-loungers the place was deserted. Light-footed, Sophie climbed up and smoothly rolled over the edge, only to crash into the lavender bushes on the other side, suppressing a shriek. She carefully crouched behind a nearby cactus and held her breath, but the place remained silent apart from the incessant sound of chirping crickets.

She rubbed her sore bottom and looked up to see Jay's face peering down from the top of the wall. He slid down to land noiselessly on his feet, cat-like, and joined her in the shade of the cactus. There was no one in the flickering light of the hotel lobby entrance. A loud thud behind them made them jump and angrily shush at Frank.

'Jeez he's going to get us caught. He's just standing there, waiting for someone to see him. Can you believe this guy', she whispered angrily.

Jay pinched her softly on the arm.

'It's ok. There's no one here. All the guests are probably drinking at the bar. Seems like they close the pool for the night.'

He was right. The hotel staff had cordoned off the entrance with a small sign saying 'closed for cleaning'. They crept over to the swimming pool, took their trainers off and dipped their toes in the cool water. The night was hot, their t-shirts stuck to their skin, the reflection of the newly-risen moon shone enticingly in the water. Sophie leaned back and looked up at the tapestry of stars burning in the night sky. Her hair had grown so long, it curled back on the tiles behind her. She felt a tug and looked over to Jay gently curling a strand around his fist.

'Your hair has bleached in the sun. It's nearly white now', he observed.

'Mmm... this guy I met earlier tonight thought I was Norwegian', she giggled... 'and he thought I could be a model.'

Jay's eyes widened, which Sophie took as an invitation to continue her story. 'He gave me his business card and said I should give him a call to organise a photo shoot', she smiled and paused for effect. 'In Paris'

She intended this to be funny but when she glanced over, Jay's face had hardened and he looked away. He remained silent for a while. When he finally spoke his underlying tone was angry.

'What did you say to him?' he asked with piercing eyes.

She straightened her back and put her arms protectively around her legs.

'Well, I did think it was a chat-up line. You know, print a few business cards with the words model scout on it and sooner or later you're bound to persuade a girl to give you her number. I thanked him, said I would think about it, and instead had a smoke with him.'

'You smoked with him? What? A spliff? After he chatted you up with this.... fake model business card? Are you out of your mind? How did you know the stuff you smoked was safe? You ... he could have tried to trick you.'

He glowered angrily at her. Embarrassed that he blatantly thought her not attractive enough to be a model, she shrunk her head into her t-shirt. He was right. It wasn't the safest idea to smoke drugs with a complete stranger. But it wasn't a total loss. She grabbed Jay's hand and reached into her pocket to pull out the matchbox-sized piece of hash. Delicately she placed it in the palm of his hand. Jay examined it slowly.

'What the fuck is this?'

'I figured since it was his last night he was never going to smoke all of this himself. I really did him a favour. If it weren't for me the guy would've overslept and missed his plane back to where ever mystery model scouts come from', she smiled innocently.

'You stole this off him?' Jay's voice still had an angry inflection, but he couldn't help but smile a little incredulously. 'You are mad.'

'Not really. As I said I did the guy a favour', she giggled, relieved his annoyance seemed to vanish slowly from his features.

Frank's face lit up when he realised she had procured some much-sought-after hash. He plonked himself next to them. They smoked in silence, passing the joint after a few drags, feet playing in the water, listening to the concert of chirping crickets and breathing in the soft fragrance of the lavender. The full moon had risen and bathed everything in its soft, otherworldly light. They were a million miles away from the circus that was the Mad Cow Street. It was so peaceful by the pool; Sophie idly trailed a hand in the cool water and thought, this is where I want to be. Miles away from home, shitty jobs and my father.

A loud splash woke her from her reverie. She blinked the water off her eyelashes, and Jay's smiling face emerged from the dark waters next to her as he beckoned her over.

'Ssssshh. Are you mad? Don't make so much noise' she giggled.

'Come on' he whispered 'Join me.'

'But...'

'The water isn't cold', he insisted, swimming over to the side of the pool. His bright smile shone in the moonlight.

'I haven't got a swimming suit with me?'

'Who cares, just go in your underwear, I don't mind' he winked at her.

Relieved she'd put on decent panties that day, she decided being braless was not going to deter her. She felt a sudden rush of excitement run through her and feeling liberated, she took off her t-shirt, stripped out of her denim shorts and dove into the pool.

Sophie and Jay tried hard to be quiet but couldn't resist giggling and splashing each other. He managed to grab her foot, and she spluttered and coughed in panic as she sunk into the water. She started hyperventilating while helplessly thrashing the water – a dark wave of panic engulfed her. Jay instantly let go of her leg and swam right up to her, holding a protective arm out.

'Shit, Sophie, are you ok?' he whispered as he guided her back to the shallow end. She buried her face in his neck, breathing loudly.

'Yeah, sorry', she sniffled, trying unsuccessfully to hold in another fit of coughing. 'It's just since that night at the lake, I've kind of developed this fear of water. Well, not actually of swimming in the water, but just when it's dark and I can't see the bottom and being pulled down makes me scared.'

'I'm sorry' he looked crushed. 'I shouldn't have. Just relax. It's ok; I'm here. I'll make sure you're alright', he said, gently stroking her hair. Her eyes closed, she hugged him tightly, her body pressed against his chest. His skin was warm against hers. Her fingers stroked the nape of his neck. He slowly turned his face towards hers. The air was thick with tension and the space between them hummed. It was that electrifying moment just before the kiss, their lips inches from each other. Suddenly the world around them lit up, an explosion of light burned through their closed eyelids. Confused, Sophie opened her eyes. The clear water rippled in the swimming pool and shone bright blue. They gazed at the surface in wonder. It was beautiful.

'What... happened? Did we hit a switch by accident?' she wondered.

'Fuck, fuck, fuck. We got to get out of here quickly', Jay whispered urgently in her ear. In a splash, he pushed her out of the water, and she stumbled backwards to the crumpled heap that were her clothes. She tried to put them on as quickly as she could, but the dry clothes clung to her damp skin. With her wet hair hanging in her face, she stumbled around blindly fumbling for her trainers.

And then she heard them. Her blood froze in her veins. A gruff Spanish voice shouted an unanswered 'Who goes there?' The dogs whined, their claws scratched the concrete. They could see a silhouette of a man struggling to hold onto two Doberman Pinschers on a leash. Her heart was in her throat, and she couldn't move a muscle. The man repeated the question and Jay jumped over to her, thrust her shoes into her hands and shouted at her to run. The dogs howled and barked.

Frank had already picked up his rucksack and was at the far end of the swimming pool frantically waving at them. Sophie ran towards him, barefoot, gripping her shoes tightly, the bare skin of her feet scraping against roots and stones. All of a sudden the howling stopped. The dogs were let off the leash, and their rapid panting got closer and closer. As Sophie finally reached the wall, Frank had just managed to climb onto the pool shed and was already halfway up and out of reach. The dogs' barking rang in her ears as she helplessly looked up to see Frank disappear behind the wall. *Shit. I'm too short, how am I going to get up there.* In frustration, she threw her shoes at him. *Bastard.* Panic gripped her, and her hands felt numb.

Suddenly a pair of strong hands grabbed her and shoved her against the shed with a loud crash. She clung to its fragile roof, her short nails dug deep into the rotten wood. Splinters shot under her skin, the sharp pain driving tears to her eyes. Her bare feet gripped at the wood and inch-by-inch she pushed herself up on the roof. Her whole body was shaking as she paused to look down at the lawn. The growl of the dogs was nearing. And there they were, emerging fiercely from behind the lavender bushes. They slowed down and crept closer. One paw at a time, their black eyes locked onto the intruders' every move.

Poised to pounce and grimacing menacingly, they showed off a row of sharp yellow teeth ready to tear the flesh off their bones.

'Jay, Oh my god, Jay get over here! Hurry up please. They are going to attack. Jay!' In her head she was screaming the words but only a hoarse breathless whisper made it past her dry lips. Jay inched backwards towards the shed. Sweat beaded his brow.

She suddenly screamed as the hounds jumped forward and launched at him. Jay kicked the first one violently in the jaw with his foot, sending the dog flying on its back. As it retreated wincing in pain, Jay turned to the other one, grabbed him by the neck and forced his hands in its jaws. Locked in Jay's steely grip, the dog couldn't close its mouth. It kicked its hind legs angrily, but Jay held on tight. Its eyes rolling wildly in its sockets, the dog wasn't sure how to handle this sudden reverse of fortune. Its paws clawed into Jay's forearms leaving bloody streaks on his skin. A string of drool mixed with blood ran along its neck. Its bloodthirsty growl echoed in Sophie's ears. She shuffled to her feet and nervously looked at the scene unfolding before her eyes. The dog was enormous. Stretched out against Jay's frame, they were almost the same size. She feared for Jay's life.

Suddenly she heard a loud crack, quickly followed by a long whine, ending in a rasped cough. She closed her eyes in horror. When she re-opened them, the dog's body hung lifelessly in Jay's bleeding arms. Sophie gasped in shock. The other dog crept closer, and Jay ditched the limp body towards it onto the grass. In one swift motion he climbed up onto the roof next to her. The dog sniffed at its lifeless partner, and in a last vain attempt of intimidation, jumped up the wall to get at them. More shouts came from the far entrance of the pool and beams of flashlights pierced through the bushes. Jay grabbed Sophie by the arm and dragged her over the wall. They both crashed onto the concrete sidewalk on the other side. Sophie's elbow hit the pavement, and a wave of pain shot through to her shoulder. She had fallen on the shoes she had chucked over the wall earlier. With trembling fingers, she pulled on her trainers as they scrambled awkwardly to their feet and ran down the street. They came to a visibly shaken Frank standing by a lamppost clutching his rucksack.

'Oh fuck! That was... I mean...Fuck. You saved me from getting... Thank you Jay. ' Sophie gasped as she rubbed her numb elbow. Frank suddenly noticed Jay's hands; blood was dripping along his fingers onto the floor.

'Woah dude, you're bleeding? Did that dog bite you?' Jay shook his head. Without a warning Sophie's brain brought up the last image she'd seen before crashing off the wall: the lifeless dog on the lawn. The cracking sound. Then it dawned on her.

'What did you do to that dog?' she screamed at him, near hysterical. 'WHAT THE FUCK DID YOU DO TO THAT DOG?' Jay didn't answer. He looked at his hands with clenched jaws. Blood continued to run slowly down his fingers, dripping onto the pavement.

Slowly he looked up at her. His eyes unfocussed, as if in a trance, he muttered:

'I think I killed it. It needed to die. It was dangerous.'

'What did you do?' she whispered, shaking her head with hot tears stinging her eyes.

'He ripped that bastard's head off. Good riddance I say. That vicious dog would've done the same to us in two seconds flat. Good on you Jay. Good on you. Fucking dog scared the crap out of me' Frank's hands were shaking as he sparked up the spliff he rolled earlier.

After a few drags, he passed it over to Sophie, but she shrugged her shoulders. *No thanks. The situation is surreal enough.* The street was empty. They stood there in the dark, their hair dripping wet, Jay's hands bleeding onto the sidewalk, a dead dog on the other side of the wall… and Frank smoking a spliff.

A nervous giggle escaped her. She clamped a hand on her mouth trying to contain herself. But all of a sudden she burst into laughter. Jay looked at her curiously, until Frank started giggling too. They laughed until their sides hurt and tears streamed down their faces.

Once they regained their composure, Sophie checked Jay's arms. The dog's teeth and claws had torn the flesh but to her relief it wasn't nearly as bad as it first looked. Frank pulled out a flask from his rucksack.

'I thought I'd save this for later. But here you go, use it to clean out the cuts. The alcohol will disinfect it. Wouldn't want you to catch rabies or something nasty like that. Remember we share a room. Don't go all werewolf on me you cave man' he winked at Jay and passed Sophie the bottle. She looked at him doubtfully. He nodded his head and said 'Don't worry, my dad's a doctor'.

As she unscrewed the top, the strong smell of the alcohol made her gag. Whisky. She asked Jay to hold his palms open and slowly poured the amber liquid onto the cuts. Jay's arms tensed up. He hissed with pain as the alcohol bit into his skin. She dabbed the excess alcohol off his hands with the edge of his damp t-shirt. Frank handed her a Kleenex with the instruction to rip it to shreds and use the fine cellulose strips to seal the cuts. 'It will stop the bleeding' he said confidently, and it seemed to work. The shellshocked trio wandered back to the busy party street. After getting some plasters at the 24-hour pharmacy they headed off to the swimming pool party at Es Paradis.

CHAPTER 6

Solacium, April 2011 - 6 months after the incident

'Hello!' She didn't even have to say her name as he recognised her voice right away. Sophie was greeted with a joyful 'Oh hello darling', with just a hint of his trademark sarcasm.

'What's up?' she asked, ignoring the call coming through on the other line. She was at work and conscious of the people on the trading floor in earshot. She snuck off into an empty meeting room.

'Lots, Sophie, lots. The other day we had pizza for lunch', he laughed. 'Yeah and that's about it really. You know nothing changes much in here, same grey routine, day in day out and believe it or not, getting pizza delivered to your room is about as much contact to the outside world we get. Also, it's quite an exciting alternative to the dreary hospital food we usually get. You know what I really miss? I miss going food shopping. I used to love going to the farmer's market. I would go as early as six in the morning, just before sunrise to buy fresh fish and meat. I loved the Mediterranean smell of fresh basil and thyme. And the colourful stalls overflowing with Sicilian lemons and vine tomatoes. The velvety touch of Portobello mushrooms. The sting of coarse sea salt on my tongue and the tangy smell of soft gorgonzola...'

His voice trailed off as he longingly recalled the smaller luxuries of his former life. Its beauty enhanced by its absence. He eventually spoke again, his tone pretending to be cheerful.

'What about you Sophie, what are you up to?'

'Same old. Lots of things really, but I'm not sure you want to hear about it?'

She was equally touched and saddened by her friend's comment. From all the things to long for in a godforsaken mental institution, she didn't think food shopping would be the thing he'd miss most. But as soon as Jay said it, she could understand it. All the smaller things she took for granted were suddenly there for her to reach out for – and out of reach to him. He had been deprived of the freedom of choice.

'I've got time. They serve dinner at six and if someone wants to use the phone booth I'll just pretend not to see them', he chuckled.

'OK, but, are you sure? Doesn't it bother you when I tell you about my life?' Sophie was always worried that by talking too much about the eventful life she led, she would only highlight what her friend was missing out on, making him feel even more bereft of his freedom.

'Isn't that the reason you keep calling? To seek comfort in the knowledge that I'm worse off than you? To brag about your perfect life and everything you get up to?' Sophie could hear the smile in his voice. He was joking.

'I sometimes feel like I should say less as not to make you unhappy.'

'Don't be silly. I love it when you call; you are the most normal person I get to talk to. It comforts me to know there's a world outside these walls, away from psychos and schizos. Besides, when you tell me of your adventures I almost feel I'm there with you.'

Sophie nodded. She understood that and made a habit of sending him a postcard every time she travelled abroad. There was something reassuringly old-fashioned about writing with a fountain pen and licking a stamp. She imagined the headboard above his bed to be full of snapshots from around the globe. Little windows onto the beauty of the world.

'Well, it's the Olympics here in London at the moment. I'm not the most sporty person as you know, but I got tickets to some of the events, and really, really enjoyed it. Makes you think we kind of ruined our chances of ever getting Olympic gold at a relatively early stage in life', she mused.

'Yep, we partied just that little bit too hard; all that potential we threw away for a good rave', he chuckled and continued 'I finished another painting today. It took me a while, you know I'm only allowed to use the therapy room once or twice a week for a few hours, but I managed to finish quite a big canvas for this one. It's for Frank. He seems to think there are still buyers.'

'You're still friends with him?' Sophie had heard from Jay's father that they weren't talking any more.

'Yeah, I know, we had split up for a while, the old cranky couple that we are. But he's still looking after the gallery and he's come to visit me a couple of times since the incident happened. I really appreciate that. It gets very lonely in here. It's pretty good to see some familiar faces from back in the days...' he hesitated, his thoughts trailing back to happier times again.

'Back then, you know, when the possibilities seemed endless, it was all excesses. Sky's the limit. Hugs and kisses and confidence. We had fun – we felt invincible. God we were so arrogant', his voice faltered as he remembered days of hedonism with his best friend. 'And I guess Frank is still my bro, regardless of what happened', he laughed softly.

'So what did you paint?'

'Nothing special. I hope he likes it though. It's a reminder of one of our crazier nights. We were at this friend's house party, playing music, drinking and having a good time. When dawn broke most of the guests crashed out on sofas and mattresses. But me, Frank, and this girl we both liked, Susy I think she was called – we were still up, and we wandered off for a stroll by the riverside. We stopped at this bridge...' he breathed in, picturing the scene, remembering the atmosphere.

'It was going to be another one of those hot summer's days, and we climbed onto one of the bridge's pillars. The sun rose slowly over the river, the light bounced off the skyscrapers like a light show in slow motion. All the choppy waters were flecked with gold. We'd brought a bottle of whisky and we drunk it for breakfast. People passed by; they all looked disapproving, raised eyebrows and all that. They were walking their dogs, going to work, doing their shopping. We reminded them of their lost youth, as they walked along their predictable paths, we just felt... marginal, wild, free. Unhinged and uninhibited'. Suddenly his voice muffled, and Sophie heard a knock.

'Sorry darling. Give me a second'. The muffled sound intensified. 'I'm back. The nurse with the medicine tray just walked past. Right, so now I got my drugs which means I need to finish my story fast.'

Sophie knew what that meant; previous conversations had quickly become one-sided as the drugs acted quickly and made him too sleepy to hold a conversation.

'Go on then. What happened next?'

'Well, we were pretty much wasted. We'd been drinking all night. I looked at the golden waters below. It looked so inviting, like molten soft caramel. I wanted to jump in and be swallowed whole. Suddenly I got up, undressed to my boxers and challenged the other two. Suzy screamed we were fucking crazy and looking down the side of the bridge she was probably right. It must have been a good 15 meters high. Frank accepted the challenge. He must have been just as drunk as me. We crept over to the edge, swigged one last time from the bottle, counted to three backwards and... jumped.'

'No, you are joking, into the Spree? No way! You fools. My god, you could have killed yourself!' Sophie gasped.

'Yes indeed. Drunk as we were, most definitely, but we did it and we got away with it, by the skin of our teeth. When you jump from that height, the water becomes as hard as concrete and I smacked the sole of my feet so hard I couldn't walk for days because of the bruising. Thank god we decided to summersault it to break the speed of the fall, otherwise we would have broken our ankles. The water was bloody cold, and the current so strong I thought we were going to drown like rats. We eventually managed to grip hold of an iron ladder by the dyke and pulled ourselves to safety. I haven't, to this day, found a better hangover cure', he laughed. 'We were crazy kids.'

***

Ibiza, August 1999 - 11 years before the incident

Sophie flipped the flyer in her hands: Espumaaaa! It screamed at her in bright fluorescent letters. Dress code: white. Amnesia's foam parties were legendary, and Jay, Frank and her were looking forward to a night of unleashed hedonism and clubbing until sunrise. Sophie idly wondered how see through her top would get, and she cringed. *Shit, I really should've worn a bikini top.*

'You go' Sophie nudged his shoulder.

'Why me?' he stared at her.

'Because it was your fucking idea in the first place. Come on, don't be such a pussy. You were all talk earlier. Now it's crunch time. You do know that if you don't do it, Jay and I will be taking the piss all night long' she insisted.

'And forever more', Jay chuckled into his San Miguel beer. Frank sighed noisily and apprehensively scanned the bar. It was heaving with glamorous hipsters. Girls clad in skin tight glitter outfits and guys showing off their muscly arms and newly acquired tribal tattoos. It appeared the bar, known as the infamous M Bar, one of the trendier bars on Ibiza, had a Bollywood themed night on and everyone looked as though they'd been dipped in sequins, swathed in brightly-coloured sarongs.

Sophie, Jay and Frank sat at a table under a gigantic palm tree overlooking the open-air dance floor, dressed in plain street wear and nowhere near as glamorous as the other guests. Sophie wore a tiny white t-shirt with a pair of white cut off shorts and scuffed skateboard shoes. The boys weren't exactly dapper either but they had both made an effort to dress in white. While Frank's baseball shirt drowned his skinny frame, Jay's tighter t-shirt showed off his tanned arms.

They had been sitting at the table for a while, their feet resting on their skateboards, passing time before they would head off to the club. They casually sipped on their San Miguels and vodka lemons, their heads bowed together in conspiracy. A pretty girl slid past their table in a flurry of clanging bangles and a waft of sweet smelling patchouli. Frank sneezed loudly and wiped his nose with his long sleeved t-shirt.

'Come on Frank. How long are you going to drag this out for? My beer is nearly finished' Jay exclaimed, and Sophie giggled in agreement.

Frank nervously glanced left and right before looking back at the small shed next to the bar. A waiter swiftly appeared by the door and ducked inside while the door swung shut behind him. A few seconds later the man emerged again, clutching an armload of Grey Goose vodka bottles. He kicked the door shut with his heel and hurriedly walked back to serve up drinks behind the bar. Jay, Sophie and Frank had observed this very same scene a few times during the evening and had quickly noticed the absence of a lock on that door. The shed was stocking all of the bar's alcohol, only a few meters away from them.

'And there is no lock on the door' Frank had insisted earlier, a tad braver than he looked now, nervously fidgeting on his bar stool.

The place was buzzing to the DJ's heavy drum & bass sounds. No one else seemed to have noticed the treasures buried so close. Their plan was to get wasted tonight, and they were thirsty for alcohol. With not much cash to spare on overpriced drinks and the lure of free alcohol so close by, they quickly devised a plan to get their hands on the stash.

A plan they thought very cunning, they just needed one of them to volunteer, and Jay and Sophie had immediately agreed Frank would be the ideal candidate for a stealth operation. He had previously bragged about how him and his mates had once broken into an off-license and stolen hundreds of pounds worth of booze and cigarettes. Looking at him now, dithering about whether or not he should risk it, Sophie lost the little remaining benefit-of-doubt she had for him. *He is a buffoon. All talk and no action.*

'Ok listen, you have to get in there as soon as the waiter comes out and before any of them return. Pick up the bottles...' she instructed as she peeled the label off her beer and took the last sip.

'Yeah' Jay interrupted her, smiling. 'Look out for vodka or tequila. Whisky is fine too. But don't come back with some shit none of us will drink. OK? No Blue Curacao or crap like that'. Sophie nodded in agreement.

'We'll have your back, ok? If somebody comes, we can always create a diversion or something, ok?'

Shaking his head, Frank seemed to have resigned himself to his fate. Under his friend's watchful eyes, he slowly made a move towards the shed. He looked uncomfortable at first but as soon as he got close enough to the door he paused and stumbled forward. He looked pretty drunk from where they were sitting. *That doesn't bode well.* Sophie started worrying that he was going to get caught as soon as he set foot in the door.

'I know what you are thinking... but he isn't that drunk. It's all part of his plan, in case he gets caught he can pretend to be wasted out of his head and in fact looking for the toilets. Give the man some credit, he isn't as dumb as you make him out to be', Jay whispered reproachfully. Sophie remained unconvinced.

The bar was crawling with people queuing to order their drinks. Scantily clad bar girls were rushing to pour rows of shots to leery lads. No one was paying any attention to the young drunk dressed in white, as he stumbled over to the door of the shed. Frank stopped in front of it, quickly looked over to them with a wink and opened the door. Both Jay and Sophie held their breath while Frank slid inside, and the door slammed shut behind him. They looked at each other with raised eyebrows and waited for Frank to return.

The music swelled to a thumping bass, the party crowd started bustling and the mood lifted to new heights. Loud whoops and cheers filled the dance floor. Boys winked at girls. Girls checked out the boys. The warm air smelled of sweat, alcohol and the promise of sex. An atmosphere that made Sophie slightly edgy. *I don't fit in.* Jay stared into the crowd of sweaty dancers with a furrowed brow, his green eyes dark with thoughts she couldn't read. *He doesn't fit in either.*

Apart from joking with her when Frank was around, Jay hadn't spoken to her beyond meaningless superficialities. He was friendly, but she sensed a distance between them. The intimacy they once shared, now years ago, had vanished and was replaced with a casual friendship. She missed their closeness and deep conversations. That morning at the beach, she had caught him looking at her when he thought she was absorbed in her book. His face had instantly sombred when their eyes met. For the rest of the afternoon he had completely shut her out. It wasn't the first time he had done that. But although it had pained her much at the beginning of the holiday, now she was happy when after a few beers he snapped out of his dark mood and engaged with her.

'Hey, what's with the moody look?' she smiled.

He raised a slight-irritated eyebrow, his eyes locked on the group of girls standing next to their table.

'I don't know; this place is just so wrong. Look at all these girls. Look at them! Gyrating around these guys like bitches on heat. They're disgusting. I can see that girl's nipples through her top and that one over there.' He pointed at a petite peroxide blonde in a miniskirt jumping excitedly up and down to the beat. 'If she bends over I could get a good view of her ass.'

Shocked at his crude choice of words and disturbed by the fact that he was paying attention to other girls, she felt a stake of jealousy piercing through her heart. Feigning disinterest at his angry comments, she ripped more beer labels into tiny shreds, and quickly changed the subject.

'Frank has been in there for a while now, what the fuck is he doing? Wasn't he supposed to walk in, pick up a bottle and come back out?' she hissed.

'I'm sure he's alright, he's probably picking out a good one. A 16-year-old Lagavulin would be nice.' He sounded amused, and when she looked up, surprised at his knowledge of fine whiskies, a shadow of a smile passed his lips.

'No but seriously how long has he been locked in there?' she insisted.

Jay checked his watch.

'A few minutes. Don't pa...' the word died in his throat as he slammed his bottle on the table. Sophie flinched and followed his gaze to spot the big burly barman with two empty beer crates in each hand walking towards the shed. Tattoos crawled up his arms to a neck as thick as that of a bull. Sophie's mouth dropped open with a silent 'Oh' as the sour looking barman kicked the door open and disappeared inside the tiny shed.

'Shit' she whispered.

'Holy shit' Her mind raced, Frank was going to get caught red-handed stealing. Skinny as he was, the barman would easily beat the living daylights out of him. *'Shouldn't we step in to help him?'*

Jay tensed up, and Sophie nervously gnawed on her thumbnail as they waited in silence with baited breath, staring at the door, willing for Frank to emerge. The metallic taste of blood filled Sophie's mouth, and a thin rim of blood formed at the base of her fingernail. She brushed her hand against her t-shirt where it stained a red flower of blood on the white fabric. Daylight broke, the sun set, women got pregnant and gave birth, a new president was elected, a war started and ended. An eternity passed before the door opened again with a bang.

Sophie sucked in her breath, expecting Frank to fly out onto the dusty floor. But nothing of the sort happened. The burly barman stepped out, alone, looking slightly flustered, hefting two heavy beer crates on his shoulders. Sweat trickled down his temples as he shuffled back to the crowded bar where one of the bar babes rushed over to help him as he slammed the crates on the floor.

A few seconds later the door creaked open again, slowly this time, just enough for a hunched skinny frame to squeeze through and hurriedly walk over to the exit of the bar. Jay and Sophie exhaled in relief. Two minutes later they had picked up their skateboards and walked over to the exit to find Frank hovering around the entrance of the bar with raised eyebrows, his mouth twitching. They ushered past the muscly doormen and wandered out onto the street and into the night. In the shadow of a wheelie bin, Frank lifted his shirt up and revealed a magnum of premium vodka stuck in the waist of his trousers.

'You did it!' Sophie whooped in delight, forgetting about her earlier doubts and jibes, and she was almost tempted to give him a hug. Almost, but not quite. She wanted to hear his side of the story. Frank nodded, shakily unscrewed the top of the bottle, greedily gulped down a few sips, coughed noisily and passed the bottle to Jay before he started to talk.

'Oh man. Fucking hell. That was intense', Frank took a deep breath.

'What happened? Did you see that guy? He was huge!' Sophie asked.

'I walk in and there I am, inside and it's pitch black. Like there are no windows in that fucking place, and I can't find the fucking switch. So I'm feeling my way around rows of bottles on the shelves. No fucking clue which one is which. I'm like feeling my way around these bottles trying to remember what shape a fucking vodka bottle is when the door opens, and this huge fucking dude walks in. I duck into a pile of I don't know... smelly tablecloths or something... and just when I think he is going to walk over me and I'm going to die I see a cardboard box marked Grey Goose. The guy walks up right next to me, he was so close I could smell his fucking armpits. He picks up his stuff, grunts, and lets out the loudest motherfucking fart you have ever heard in your life and leaves. I thought I was going to die all over again. Fucking bastard', he laughed triumphantly and lit up a cigarette.

Jay bowed down graciously and lifted the bottle in salute.

'Cheers to that bastard for being blind. And cheers to you for being awesome. Let the games begin. Tonight is going to be a good night'. And he downed a large gulp of the stinging alcohol.

They rode along the harbour, a bit wobbly on their skateboards, all the way back to the town centre. As they emptied the bottle, they noisily argued the best way to get to the club. Club Amnesia was on the way to Ibiza town and a few kilometres away from the town centre of San Antonio. They checked the timetable as a club shuttle-bus zipped by, bursting at the seams with all the party-eager people on board. The next bus was not due for another half hour. The taxi option was quickly dismissed when they found out the fare.

Even on skateboards, getting to the club was going to take half of the night. But, vodka-fuelled and merry, everything seemed possible to them. Enthusiastically they rode off in the direction of the highway. The three of them continued to debate how to get there, when Frank suddenly pulled up by the side of the road, walked into the lavender bushes and threw up noisily. A car swerved as Jay walked onto the road and flagged it down. He tapped the driver's window and spoke a few words to the bearded man at the wheel. The Spaniard nodded and waved them over.

Three men in white shirts sat in the back of the Jeep and helped them up onto the benches at the back. The men's English was about as bad as the three friends' Spanish, but somehow the international language of alcohol and high spirits translated into them all heading to the Espuma party at Amnesia, laughing and joking all the while. Sophie left the boys to handle the conversation, pushed her skateboard under her legs and idly scratched a scab on her knee. She was proud of her new deck from Girl Skateboards, she thought the brand name was appropriate. She had taken up skateboarding a few years back, but had never really been able to master it. While the boys tackled aerial tricks on the half-pipe, she was happy when she managed an ollie to mount the pavement, preferring to cruise the roads at a leisurely speed. She stared tipsily up at the night sky fleeting by. Thousands of stars burnt above her head, pine trees were blurring by, the faint lavender perfume in the cool air... *I'm alive, really, truly alive.*

Frank seemed to have recovered from his nausea and was in good spirits again. He was talking animatedly to the shorter of the three Spaniards. They both nodded and when the Spaniard handed him a small box of matches, and Frank fished a few notes out his wallet, Sophie thought he had scored some weed. *Good. A spliff at the end of the night would be awesome.*

After a short ride, the Jeep turned into a rocky road, drove into a dark parking lot, and they all jumped out of the boot. The driver opened the trunk and fished out a few glasses, cracked open a bottle of whisky and poured a round for all. One of them magicked a bag of ice-cubes and a bottle of coke. As Sophie sipped on her fresh whisky coke, the Spaniards started popping open small plastic vials of pills and washing them down with their drinks.

'Ecstasy', Jay whispered in her ear. Sophie froze. She had smoked weed before, but that was as far as her drug experience went. A nervous giggle escaped her mouth. *Ecstasy.* Of course she had heard about the drug, some of the boys at uni were into this stuff. It was their generation's party drug of choice. The generation newspapers had dubbed Generation X. What did the X stand for? She didn't know, probably because they didn't know what to label them. Their generation seemed to gravitate towards hedonism and unaffordable consumerism. They believed the world was their oyster, and they were going to slurp it down with cool white wine. Ignoring the terrible spectre of unemployment looming at the end of their studies, they revelled in dancing to electronic music and getting high on synthetic drugs. Drugs like ecstasy. Which Sophie had never taken before. Jay delicately took her hand and pressed a pill in her palm. She looked at the small pink pill with mixed feelings, consumed with the excitement of the unknown and the fear of what it would do to her. Would she lose control if she swallowed this? There had been news stories about people dying of heart-attacks as nobody knew what lethal cocktail of amphetamines were packed into the innocent looking tablets. Others collapsed and died of dehydration. *Would that happen to us?*

'Are you going to take it?' Jay asked with a glint of mischief in his eyes.

'I don't know, I've never done it before'. As soon as she said the words she realised how uncool she sounded but this was unchartered territory for her.

'Me neither', he looked at his small pink pill and twisted it in between his fingers. Sophie looked back down at hers.

'What is it going to do to us?' she noticed it had a small dove shape imprinted on the back of it.

'It'll make the best party you ever had look like school detention, at least that's what Frank said.'

'Come on guys, what's the hold up', Frank bounded over and punched Jay playfully in the shoulder. 'Are you still playing with those? Come on guys, just pop them – down your whiskies and off we go. Can you feel the vibrations of the beat under your feet? This looks to be one fucking kick-ass party', he laughed excitedly.

The music was coming from the dark, tall building at the back of the parking lot. Droves of club-goers made their way noisily to the entrance and joined the long queue to get in. Everyone was wearing white. Sophie's heart raced with anticipation; she wanted to have a good time tonight. She took one last look at the tiny pill in her hand, glanced over to Jay, breathed in deeply for courage and swallowed it whole with a sip of whisky coke. Jay quickly followed suit, and they exchanged a complicit grin, both a bit unsure of what was going to happen next.

They finished their drinks and on the way to the club, attempted to make conversation with their newly acquired friends, the Spaniards. Sophie was explaining to Jose that they were here on holiday, that their parents had bought a house in the seventies and they would come to Ibiza every year to spend the summer. Her broken Spanish seemed to get better with each sip of whisky. Jose nodded as if he understood what she was garbling about. Encouraged by his enthusiasm, she explained that she was a business school student and currently lived in France. Her friends Frank and Jay both lived in Germany.

Suddenly she stopped mid sentence as a surge of heat coursed through her body. Starting at her feet, it travelled up her toes like an electric current, along her thighs, spread across her stomach and breasts, ignited her hands, arms and neck and finally reached her eyes. Pop. The pupils dilated until her eyes seemed black and for the first time she noticed the glass in her hand. It was a real glass. Not some cheap plastic cup. It was a glass made of glass. The light was bouncing off the sides, and it mirrored like a million tiny diamonds splitting into facets of rainbows. Its otherworldly beauty rendered her speechless.

Without a word, she turned on her heels and walked over to find Jay animatedly talking to Frank. His face lit up when she touched his arm, and a flawless smile spread across his face. She looked at him closely, and his skin was glowing as if he had swallowed a light bulb. His wide eyes were big black pools mirroring her huge smile. He looked irresistibly beautiful. She wanted to stroke his iridescent cheeks and run her fingers through his shiny hair. She slowly lifted a finger to his face and blue electricity crackled when she touched his hot skin. She instantly let go, laughing out loud, and it sounded like the laughter of a child.

The music grew louder as they walked over to the club's entrance. The beat was drawing them in like an irresistible magnetic force pulling them towards its source. As they impatiently stood in line, cradling their skateboards and excitingly hopping from one foot to another, Frank leaned in, and his voice betrayed a sense of concern.

'Guys, I won't have enough money to pay for my entrance. Can you help me out?' Frank had paid for the pills and now looking into their slim wallets, they realised they were a bit short on cash to contribute towards his ticket.

'Ok, we're going to get you in there, don't worry. Sophie and I will come up with a diversion at the entrance and you'll have to slip in unseen.'

Sophie wondered what diversion Jay was thinking of when they arrived at the top of the queue. Two clipboard-clad beauties in micro-shorts and huge platform shoes waved them over, looked them up and down with a patronising raised eyebrow. Apparently satisfied with what they saw, they ushered them to the front desk inside the club. A pink-haired girl sitting behind the desk looked bored and played with her nose ring. She pointed at the skateboards and instructed to put them in the cloakroom. The music was so loud inside, she barked the price of the entrance while digging for plastic wristbands from the box next to her. As Sophie fished out the money from her purse, Jay shouted in her ear 'Faint!'

She looked at him with raised eyebrows. He repeated 'Faint' and winked in Frank's direction. She finally understood, and as she slid the bundle of notes onto the sticky desk, she toppled to the side, closed her eyes and crashed against the hard wood of the floor. The notes scattered on the ground and chaos erupted. Everyone rushed over to either help get her back on her feet or to pick up the money; some quickly stuffing it in their pockets. Jay's angry voice echoed in her head as she continued to fake unconsciousness, shouting for the thieves to hand over the banknotes. The girl behind the desk ordered other guests to get back in line immediately and two big bouncers homed in on the few lads who pocketed the money. Amidst the commotion Frank disappeared inside the club unnoticed.

Once inside a whole world of thumping music, light shows, bikini-clad dancers, palm trees, and swimming pools unfolded before their shining eyes. Sophie scanned the huge hall, taking in the flashing lights, the fluorescent drapes and dry-ice smoke. Thousands and thousands of dancers gathered in the middle of the dome, jerking their arms and legs to the vibrating techno beats. The overwhelming sound engulfed her and seemed to lift and transport her to the epicentre, the pumping heart of the party. The DJ booth sat high above the dance floor and the DJ stood behind a wall of computer screens, decks and mix tables, flipping records nonchalantly in the air while concentrating on the headphones he clamped loosely between his ear and his shoulder. Seemingly oblivious to the hysterical dancing masses below him, he calmly twisted the flashing dials and buttons on the keyboards in front of him. Gigantic speakers grew out of the wall behind him, spread along the curves of the dome like electronic ivy and rained beats on the sea of dancers.

Sophie turned to Jay standing right next to her, still holding her hand as he stared at the DJ with wide eyes. He pointed at him with a huge grin on his face.

'Wow. This is just amazing. This is what I want to be when I grow up', he shouted excitedly.

Sophie laughed. Again it sounded like a child's high-pitched giggle. This drug was doing funny things to her perception. *Fuck I'm wasted.*

'Yes do it. That would be so so cool. And I want to be one of these when I grow up', she giggled, pointing at a group of angel-winged acrobats swinging off trapezes a good five meters above the ground. They seemed to be flying through clouds of smoke, never touching the ground or the ceiling, they elegantly swept through the space above the sea of people.

Hours seemed to have gone by in a flash as they danced, relaxed in the chill-out area, stole drinks off stranger's tables and bought an outrageously expensive bottle of water to keep hydrated. They bumped into familiar-looking people, hugged and made friends forever in what seemed like one breath. Floating inside a perfect bubble of insouciance, freed from the shackles of doubts and insecurities, Jay and Sophie friendship-kissed and burst into laughter as their teeth touched. They managed to lose Frank, only to find him hours later, sleeping on a bean bag under a giant fluorescent mushroom in the chill out area. They poked and shoved him and put a cigarette up his nostril until he woke up spluttering, popped another pill and was off exploring the various rooms of the gigantic place.

Suddenly a siren went off, and as Jay and Sophie rushed back to the main dance floor, the ceiling exploded into a snow-storm with big wet snowflakes descending on the ecstatic crowd. Everybody looked up in amazement, extending their arms to the ceiling as the white mass covered everything in fluffy foam.

Sophie squealed in delight and heaped armfuls of the stuff on Jay, giggling hysterically. The music was drowned out by the cheers of thousands of people lost in a lake of foam. People slid and jumped and dove into waves of the white bubbles. Beach balls bounced off dancers' heads, and inflatable animals surfed the crowds. Foam flakes hung in the air like the cherry blossoms of spring and with foam up to her chin, Sophie waded through the ethereal landscape in slow motion, wondrous and lost.

As the glow of the amphetamines faded like a euphoric memory, her vision blurred with a thumping headache and she started to feel abandoned. *Wasn't this going to stop?* Her wet clothes clung to her skin and all of a sudden she was very conscious that her t-shirt was see-through, and the outline of her nipples was visible through the fabric. A wave of shame overcame her, and she quickly slung her arms around her chest. The foam stung her eyes; she couldn't see anything but white as she pushed through the formless masses, stumbling on a leg, bumping into a torso, slipping and holding onto a wet shirt.

Where is Jay? Panic welled up in her. Her knee hurt and blood trickled down her leg from where she had cut herself on a sharp corner. Her stringy wet hair stuck to her face, and her mascara bled down her cheeks. People pushed and shoved her around like a pinball. *Where is the exit to this hell-hole?* Their mouths open in silent screams and their eyes blackened, the dancers' faces around her seemed distorted and monstrous. No more familiar faces to comfort her.

Her heart raced as she reached the end of the foam pit and ran over to the chill-out area. She frantically looked everywhere, behind every palm tree, by the pool, on the loungers. No Jay. No Frank. She ran upstairs to the VIP area where she got rudely rebuffed to the lower floors. *Jay. Jay.* Her heartbeat screamed. *Jay. Jay. Jay.*

Her feet were drenched in her sodden trainers, and as she flick-flacked back to the dance floor, she desperately tried to peer through the foam, hoping for a familiar face. Nothing. Sophie ran up to the bar, scanned the crowd, tapped strangers on their shoulders, mouthed a confused 'sorry' and scurried off again. No Jay.

Finally, she ran to the bathrooms looking for her friend, and as she opened the door to the men's, she saw him. He had his back turned to her, but she recognised him nevertheless. He was hunched over the sink; his arms wrapped around someone. With his hands gripping the back of a neck, it looked at first as if he was helping someone throwing up. Sophie recoiled against the wall, her words of relief stuck in her throat, when she realised Jay had his arms around a short-haired girl with his hands clamped around her slender neck. The scene unfolded in front of her in slow motion. Jay pulled the girl backwards and grabbing her short-hair tightly, kissed her throat hungrily. He then kissed her open mouth and Sophie could see the girl's pink tongue pushing between his lips.

His free hand slid under her shirt as he ripped the buttons off and pushed her bra down to reveal a large pale breast. In one sweep, he hoisted her up on the sink and pulled up her tiny white denim skirt to reveal a small pair of cotton knickers. He buried his hand in between her legs. Under the cold white light the place looked squalid, toilet paper littered the floor, and the strong stench of urine polluted the damp air. Men were shoving past her to urinate, seemingly oblivious to the scene unfolding in the vicinity. Sophie closed her eyes in disgust, wishing herself elsewhere and suppressing the urge to throw up. *I have to get out of here.* Someone pushed her out of the way and when she opened her eyes, the girl was still there, now struggling under Jay's heavy frame, her small pale hands trying to push him away from her. Panic shone in her eyes like a trapped animal. He ignored her and his hand on his belt, he unbuckled it and pushed his hand in his boxers. That's when Sophie started to scream. Her voice echoed in her head like an army screaming in unison for this nightmare to stop. *Jay don't do this!*

A thick mist of red-hot anger descended on her, and she snapped. Her fists pummelled his back; she kicked his legs and hysterically screamed in his ear to stop and let go of the girl. He slowly turned around with a look in his eyes so disturbing it froze her to her core. Sophie let go of him and slowly stepped back hugging her arms. His eyes were bloodshot and hungry. The girl wriggled free from his grip and escaped to the exit her white skirt still high up her waist. Her platform sandals skid on the wet floor and sobbing loudly she crashed into the door.

Who is this man? What happened to him? She didn't recognise him, it was as if she witnessed a real life Jekyll and Hyde transformation. His sweaty hair stuck to his forehead and the harsh neon light cast dark shadows under his eyes. He stared at Sophie while he buckled his belt back on, casually, like it was the most normal thing in the world. Cowering under his steely gaze, Sophie slowly retreated to the exit, aware of a dozen suspicious eyes on her and the leaden silence that followed her outburst of screams.

With one last pleading look, *Why?* she turned on her heels and ran off. She fought her way through the crowds, ran up the stairs, dodged the bouncers by the VIP area, ran into a dark hallway, found a heavy door at the end of it and burst through it into the soothing night. The deserted club's terrace opened up in front of her as she leaned against the wall, painfully breathing in the warm sea breeze. She coughed and sputtered. It felt like breathing in hair, long thick strands of hair that coiled inside her throat and made her gag and gasp for air.

Finally, her heartbeat relaxed to a more normal frequency, and she got up and walked over to the edge of the terrace. Apart from the faint tremors from the bass reverberating under her feet, it was eerily quiet and peaceful on the roof of the club. She looked out on the darkness and tried to make sense of her feelings. She had instinctively reacted to protect the girl from the assault, but it was her friend who committed the attack. *What the fuck happened in there?*

A hesitant hand touched her arm, and she froze. 'Sophie?' Jay's shaky voice whispered. Her heart shrunk at the familiar sound of his voice, and the way he pronounced her name with the soft lilt of his Canadian accent made her insides melt. She swallowed back the tears and looked down at her feet. She couldn't face him; she couldn't look him in the eye. Not now. Not after this and she shook his arm off in disgust.

'I'm...sorry'. He sounded rueful. Silence. 'Really sorry...I...I don't know what happened in there.... Sophie?...please'

She bit her lip so hard she tasted the metallic tang of blood in her mouth as anger welled up in her again.

'You don't know what happened?' Sophie suddenly flew around and snapped at him.

'I'll tell you what happened. You and that girl. That girl. You were on her. You kissed her. You were going to... to fuck her, in the men's toilet!' her voice trailed off into a frustrated sob as her finger frantically jabbed into his chest.

'That disgusting toilet smelling of piss. For everyone to see. How could you do this! And what about the girl? You knew she didn't want to. She was trying to escape you!'

In her fury, the words stumbled out chaotically, and her body shook with anger and spite. In that very moment, she hated him and everything about him. His pleading eyes, his bowed head, the low-hanging shoulders, the way he wrung his hands in despair. She hated him with every fibre of her body and she wanted to slap him and hurt him and push him off the edge of the terrace.

'You know what this is called? Attempted...' the word crawled over her lips like a fat maggot 'rape'.

He flinched at the ugly word, and when he looked at her, his eyes were wet with silent tears. His pain instantly ripped her heart to shreds, and she regretted saying it. As much as she willed her tears to disappear, she couldn't help it because despite the hurt he had caused her, he was still hers, and her arms longed to hold and comfort him.

Apparently the girl had approached him on the dance floor and had coaxed him back to her table in the VIP area, they had done a few lines of coke and she had wanted to dance with him. He thought he had misread the signals. Laughing loudly she had been writhing up against him placing his hands on her hips. She had whispered that she wanted him. He had told her he needed the toilet. He had wanted to escape her and go back to the foam-pit to find Sophie. She had followed him into the men's and had started to kiss him. He didn't really want to but he had been so angry at her for being so slutty, for not leaving him alone. And she had insisted. He didn't feel like himself, and the drugs, they had had this after effect on him, they had made him so aggressive he lost control.

He spoke softly as he recounted the events, his hand tightly gripping Sophie's wrist while the dark shadows of the night faded into the brightening day-break. A lonely bird chirped a comforting tune. 'Even the darkest night will end and the sun will rise', she thought as she remembered the Victor Hugo quote from Les Miserables. As they sat on the stone floor with their backs touching the wall, they looked out on the hills fading to pale pinks and rust, like a black and white photograph converting to colour.

'It was terrifying…it just happened. Like something snapped… like the drugs opened a door that had previously been shut. and all the darkness escaped and took control of me. I felt like a an animal. With no control. I know it sounds unbelievable, but I swear it wasn't my intention to force her into doing anything she didn't want to. I wish I could find her and apologise. I never meant to scare her, but I got so angry. It was like a voice kept saying "do it, this is what she wants". Fuck.' he let go of Sophie's wrist and cradled his head. 'Oh god, this is bad.'

'Jay, listen, it's ok. Although I still think this was inexcusable, I understand. Don't worry about it, ok? If we see her on the way out you'll apologise. But listen, this stuff you are saying about the door and the darkness… that's scary. And the voice? Not good. Maybe you should stay away from the drugs?'

She thought of his crazy, evil bloodshot eyes. The confused look on his face when she had challenged him. She suddenly remembered the dog he had killed that time at the hotel pool and the dead rabbit he squashed with a rock the day they first met. A deep sense of uneasiness crept up her spine. And as the first rays of the sun broke through the darkness, somewhere deep down inside her alarm bells began to ring.

CHAPTER 7

Solacium, May 2011 - 7 months after the incident

'Herr Adler! Herr Adler! Phone!'

The phone line crackled and went dead. Sophie waited impatiently, aware her mobile phone was low on battery. She hated the fact that she couldn't talk to him whenever she wanted. She always had to check the times. Telephone slots were daily but had now moved to 5:30 to 7pm only, a frustration added to by the time difference. She was so used to sending emails and instant messages that having limited talk time and no other means of communication except hand-written letters that took over a week to arrive was something she found unusually frustrating.

'But isn't that kind of romantic?' he had joked when she voiced her irritation. In a 'back-to-the-olden-days' kind of way it was indeed romantic, she had conceded. It was also a constant, stark reminder of where he was and what he had done. It made it harder to forget that, even though their conversations were like having a cup of tea with an old friend, he remained a murderer.

'Hello?' he breathed into the receiver with a low voice. Her ears pricked up, and her heart-beat quickened instantly. His voice, its low drawl and slight Canadian accent always stirred something within her. A mix of feelings she couldn't quite explain. Guilt. Hope. Longing.

She shook her head energetically, willing herself to suppress whatever it was she felt.

'Sophie? Where are you?' he continued.

She looked outside the window of the cab into the night. Rivers of raindrops blurred the view but the sights were so familiar, her memory easily placed all the buildings.

'In a cab. I'm on my way to a black-tie awards ceremony.'

She wore a deep sea green, floor-length, Grecian style evening dress, gathered by the shoulders. She tugged at it, worried the luxurious silk would crease on the seat. The bumpy ride made her emerald chandelier earrings clatter against the handset. She could hear him chuckle softly down the line. She imagined him in the formless blue overalls inmates were made to wear and grinned helplessly. Their lives couldn't be more different. They were truly a world apart.

'Tell me what you see', he ordered, his voice laced with melancholy and the memory of freedom.

'We just drove along the Embankment; the Thames is to our left. On the other side of the river, I can see the London Eye and the aquarium. Did you know they have tanks so big they hold sharks? Now we're getting to Westminster. I'm looking straight up at Big Ben. You know I have been living in this city for over eight years now, and I still haven't been inside this place', she reflected. The impressive building swerved to the left as the taxi turned into the square.

'Well, do me a favour, go there next weekend and send me a postcard.'

She promised she would, knowing that he collected her postcards and pinned them on the wall above his bed. With every card she signed off, she hoped she could give him a reminder of the beauty of the world he was no longer an active part of. Sadness crept up in her. She tried to shake the feeling off but it just sat there, at the bottom of her heart, like an anchor.

'How are you?'

'How am I?' he asked as if surprised she would want to know the truthful answer. And indeed she always regretted asking him this question. The typical anglo-Saxon 'how are you?' was now so ingrained in all her conversations that the words would leave her mouth automatically.

'Well, my life seems pretty worthless at the moment' he replied, his voice remaining even and detached. 'Stuck in here I'm nothing more than a burden to society. A mere taxpayer's expense.'

Without a hint of self-pity, he was just stating the facts, and Sophie silently thanked him for that. She wasn't strong enough to hear the full breadth of his desperation. Somehow she felt that despite everything, he had managed to keep a fragment of dignity.

'I don't contribute anything and will probably be left to rot inside these maximum security walls.'

She swallowed and forced a lighthearted response over her lips:

'Well, I certainly feel that I pay enough taxes so don't you worry, I think I've got your end covered.'

He laughed softly. How she loved that laugh, it brought a smile to her face every time. The memory of his smiling handsome face haunted her. His back-from-the-beach haystack hair with sun-kissed skin flecked with golden sand, intense clear green eyes and lips curled into a permanently mocking smile. She felt a hint of regret. He would have looked good in a tuxedo, offering his arm and walking her down the stairs of the great ballroom hall of the Dorchester Hotel on Park Lane.

'Besides don't forget that without you, your wardens wouldn't have a job. So somewhere you do have your place in society.'

'Yeah right, when you put it that way...' he mocked and fell silent.

'What's wrong Jay?'

'Sophie? Why do you call me? No one calls me.Why do you keep calling?' It was an anxious question, and Sophie steeled herself for the answer.

' I...' The line suddenly went dead. Sophie stared at her mobile phone in disbelief. The battery had drained. She cursed loudly and threw it in her designer handbag.

She stepped out of the cab and hurried to the entrance door under the umbrella of the hotel doorman. Ignoring the lightbulb flashes, her thoughts trailed back to Jay. She wanted to hold onto the memory of his smiley beach face. Not think of him as a killer. She wanted to find what turned him. But above all she wanted to know if there was the tiniest chance of him recovering. She needed to know if one day he would be ready to have the conversation she had wanted to have with him before she found out about the incident.

***

Berlin, September 2000 - 10 years before the incident

'So I'll see you there tonight?' Jay had asked, a shade of hopeful expectation in his voice. Or maybe that was just Sophie's wishful thinking. She quickly reassured him she would be there as promised. Now that she had permanently moved away, they hadn't seen much of each other lately but now she was back at her parent's house for the summer break she just had to get in touch.

'Great' he replied and he ran her through the directions to the location one more time. She had a map of the city laid out in front of her on the floor of her bedroom and scanned the streets, following the lines with a biro.

'By the bridge, along the river. The 4th bridge down. In the industrial area, by the disused docks. Ok, got it.'

She marked the spot with an X. As the party was organised illegally, all guests were under strict instructions not to reveal the location, and to get there after sunset. It all added up to additional mystery and excitement. He laughed and hung up. She walked over to the closet in search of something suitable to wear.

'Jay? I'm going to move to London to study' She had told him earlier this year and his curt answer 'Ah yeah London, good choice', and an impenetrable air of aloofness had crushed the last inch of longing she had for him. She did however catch a glimpse of sadness in his eyes when he mumbled, 'You will write to me won't you?'

'Of course I will, but only if you write back', she had promised, wondering how long this promise would last.

Against all expectations, they kept to it, and every other week a thick letter found its way onto the hallway carpet of Sophie's chaotic Streatham flatshare. Her Australian and South African flatmates would tease her endlessly about her mysterious 'pen friend'. But ignoring them she would rush to the privacy of her room to rip open the envelope. Trembling in anticipation she would read the first line. Written in his fluid handwriting, the letters always started with: "My Sophie." She was his.

Increasingly disappointed, she flicked through the contents of her wardrobe, finding nothing remotely cool enough to wear out – she had taken all her best outfits to London when she moved there a few months earlier. She pulled out a bright orange top and held it up to her chin. She smiled sarcastically at herself in the mirror. *You look gorgeous, absolutely fabulous my dear,* she pouted. It looked like all the colour had drained from her face, and a pale girl with grey eyes stared back at her. She sighed and chucked the horrid top on the floor. Orange did not suit her freckled complexion and jarred with her white blonde hair.

She rummaged through her suitcase, flinging tops and trousers around the room with increasing frustration. She kicked the pile of useless clothes despondently, sat down on the worn carpet and regretted not having brought anything funkier to wear. After all she now lived in London, supposedly the coolest city in the world. She knew Jay would have vehemently disagreed with her, and the thought made her smile. He was convinced Berlin had become the heart of the European music and art scene – as he would regularly remind her in his letters. She sometimes hoped that what he really wanted was to convince her to come back.

Frustrated she scratched a spot of dried egg-yolk off her t-shirt and sighed. *This will have to do.* She changed from her sweat pants into her favourite pair of jeans, the ones that hugged her thighs and showed off her pert bottom. She nodded approvingly at herself in the mirror, expertly reapplied her eye makeup and dusted a bit of colour on her cheeks. But even generous amounts of bronzing powder were not going to hide the translucent pallor of her skin.

Tying her hoodie around her waist, she slipped into her skateboard trainers and before leaving the room, quickly rang her best friend Camelia to ask her to come by her house after dinner. Enough time for Sophie to join the family at the table, give out vague answers about her evening's whereabouts and methodically wolf down a bowl of spaghetti. Carbs for the party, a lining for the stomach.

'What's the deal with you and Jay anyway?' Camelia teased her as she sped out of the driveway in reverse. Sophie had to admit to admiring her friend's sporty driving skills, something she could never rival. Especially since moving to London Sophie had avoided driving and mainly relied on public transport to get her from A to B. She gripped the door handle with both hands as the VW Golf swerved onto the motorway at breakneck speed.

'What do you mean Cam?' Sophie answered innocently, trying to hide the blush creeping up her neck.

'Oh, come on. You two have been spending so much time on romantic Ibiza beach holidays together.' She winked 'rolling in the sand at sunset, getting all hot and heavy in the clubs, exchanging kisses in the swimming pool.'

Sophie laughed and shook her head as the blush reached her cheeks.

'It's not like that.'

'Oh yeah, so how is it then huh?' Cam lit a cigarette and exhaled a thick cloud of smoke.

'We're just friends', Sophie coughed, fumbling with the lid of the bottle of some cheap wine she had bought when they stopped at the corner store for Camelia's cigarettes.

'Bullshit, I don't believe you one bit. Have you looked at him lately? The man is hot, all tall and broad shoulders. Moody and cool. And those eyes! Greenest eyes I've ever seen, I'd pay good money for contact lenses that match that colour.'

'Oh, shut up! Why don't you date him then? You seem to like him an awful lot', Sophie hissed defiantly while clamping the bottle between her legs and pulling out the cork with the Swiss army knife Jay had given her for her birthday. *He has one, now I have one too.*

'Would you mind?' She smiled, and Sophie rolled her eyes at her.

'You bitch, you would do that?' The cork plopped, and Sophie took a hasty sip trying not to spill wine all over her t-shirt as Camelia zig-zagged her shabby VW Golf through the evening traffic.

'I'd totally shag him! Unless you tell me there is something going on between you two, then of course he'd be all yours... oh shit, was I supposed to turn left at this junction? Where's your map? God you are the worst co-pilot ever,' she laughed. 'Utterly useless!'.

Sophie reassured her on the directions while she thought about her answer. The honest truth was that she didn't know what was going on between them. Jay had a strange way of showing affection one minute and then the next retreating into his shell and shutting her out so completely that she was left wondering whether she had done something to anger him. She just couldn't figure him out. Then that night at the club in Ibiza happened, and since then they hadn't really been alone together. The scene with the girl in the club's toilet had somehow cast a shadow on the friendship – one that she couldn't dispel.

'Hey Soph, are you going to share that wine or are you going to drink it all by yourself?'

Camelia cut her out of her reverie and snatched the bottle out of her hand. Tilting her head backwards, she took a greedy gulp, one hand shifting gear. Handing back the bottle she gave the middle finger to the Mercedes honking behind them. She drove Sophie nuts with her extreme take on multitasking but Sophie also realised how much she had missed her best friend. Camelia had always been a source of strength when she most needed it.

'Cam? He's home and drunk again. He's screaming at my mum. I'm scared' Sophie would whisper down the phone late at night, her hands trembling.

'Be quiet, don't go downstairs, just lock the bedroom door.' Camelia would instruct her and never ask about the bruises on her back the next day. She also never commented on her weight or her strange eating habits. She was her only real friend.

After a painfully slow start Sophie had managed to befriend her London flatmates and students on her course, but it wasn't the same. Cam was a true and loyal friend, and Sophie missed her and the way they felt mischievous and untouchable when they were together. She looked up to her friend; Cam would never be a pushover, she was fierce. With her tank top, wide Carhartt cargo pants and skateboard trainers, she was a cross between Tank Girl and the lead singer of Guano Apes, all piercings, wild blond hair and go-fuck-yourself attitude. Deep down, Sophie hoped that through spending time with Cam, some of her friend's toughness would rub off on her and she would learn to stand up more for herself.

'It's good to see you Cam. I missed you', Sophie whispered.

'Awww I missed you too chicken. So when are you coming back?' she stared straight ahead, her tone suddenly serious.

'I don't know, when the course finishes I suppose. Jay keeps asking the same question', Sophie answered somewhat sheepishly as she switched on the radio.

'See? I told you he is soooo in love with you. He just wants you back for goo-oo-ood', Cam sung the Take That song mockingly out of tune, swinging her long blond ponytail to the beat of the cheesy ballad.

'Whatever I did, whatever I said I didn't mean i-i-it, I just want you back for gooooooood', Sophie chimed in, giggling and grabbing the bottle off her friend for another swig.

'God that song is shit', Cam guffawed, as she flipped a drum & bass tape into the deck.

With deafening beats blaring from the VW Golf's tiny speakers, they drove around the industrial area for what felt like an eternity. Not admitting to being lost, they tried to seek out the place Sophie had marked with an X on the map sprawled out on her knees. Even if they had wanted to ask someone for directions, they couldn't, as the dark streets were entirely devoid of people. Just as she thought that they must have taken completely the wrong turn earlier, a small sign at the entrance of a closed down factory beamed out at them, bright orange letters saying 'Esoteric Escort'. It was the code name Jay had given her earlier that night. A flashlight in the dark signalled them over, and Cam carefully drove her car through the high metal gates into what looked like a deserted factory courtyard. The sparse yellow light from the street lamp shone down on a lonely parka-clad figure. He jumped up, strode over to the car and peering out from under his military cap he signed Sophie to wind down the window. Cam silenced the radio.

'Hi ladies, you here for the party?' he asked, and they both nodded.

'Drive a bit further down and park the car on the left-hand side. You'll see quite a queue of cars. Just park wherever you find space. Make sure to lock up though. No security cameras here.'

Shortly after, they found a parking space, grabbed their backpacks, ditched the empty wine bottle and stepped out into the warm September night. As they neared to the riverbank, the music grew louder. A heavy drum and bass sound echoed along the brick walls, and they climbed down the dike, clinging to a steep wobbly metal ladder – right into the heart of the party. Hundreds of people had already arrived and spilled over from under the bridge, dancing, smoking by the waterline and ordering drinks from makeshift bars.

The girls walked over to the first bar, a simple fold-out table dangerously bowing under the weight of a children's bathtub, filled to the brim with ice and stocked with beer bottles. Sophie waved at the barman. He nodded and cracked open two bottles of beer against the table with a slam of his wrist. Sophie yelled into his ear whether he knew where Jay was.

'Who?' the guy growled back covering his ear with his hand, his cigarette whipping at the corner of his mouth.

'Jay, he DJ's here tonight. Jay Adler?' She asked, suddenly feeling a bit nervous.

'No. Sorry, no idea kid', he answered curtly and turned away to serve the two guys behind her. Sophie stood there for a moment, at a loss as to what to do next when the barman tapped her on the shoulder.

'Did you mean AddeeJay?'

She wasn't sure but decided to go along with it.

'Yeah AddeeJay, you know where I can find him?'

'Yeah, he's supposed to start his set in about…' he checked his chunky Citizen watch, '…20 minutes. You'll find him by the bar under the bridge with the rest of the organisers.'

Holding Cam's hand tightly, Sophie walked off into the crowd, pushing their way to the front past undulating bodies, ducking under raised beer glasses and breathing in wafts of marijuana smoke, until they reached the raised stage with its turntables and speaker towers. She quickly glanced over to the dark figure hunched over his record-case. As he looked up from under his cap, she realised – somewhat disappointed – that he didn't look anything like Jay.

Sophie's t-shirt vibrated against her chest, and a powerful bass drowned her heartbeat. With her best friend trailing behind her, Sophie edged to the furthest side of the stage, towards the cordoned-off area where a makeshift gazebo made of parachute silk had been provisionally erected. Someone had gone through the trouble of dragging a few old sofas over and had arranged them in a circle around a huge campfire. A group of guys sat roasting sausages on spits, smoking and sipping beer. From where Sophie stood they all looked the same, wearing camouflage coloured army trousers and hooded jumpers. She couldn't see Jay anywhere, and it was making her increasingly anxious. Cam pulled her over to the tall unfriendly-looking guy who manned the entrance of the backstage area.

'Sophie, can you please explain to square head here that we know the DJ and therefore should definitely be allowed in here', Cam's tone was provocative.

As Sophie shyly explained to the hostile bouncer that she had been invited by her friend Jay, her cheeks flushed. *Oh god, I sound like a groupie.* She wished Jay would just show up and let them in. The broad-shouldered man wearing a petrol-green bomber jacket and high laced Doc Martins looked them up and down and laughed sarcastically.

'So you ladies are part of Jay's fan club, huh? I'll have to let you in then!' he pointedly didn't move an inch.

Sophie let out a frustrated 'Fuck you, you fucking Nazi twat' which luckily was drowned out by the music. Someone suddenly waved from over the sofas, and she recognised Frank's familiar pointy face. He hadn't changed much since the last time she had seen him in Ibiza, and he was still wearing his ugly baseball cap and a pair of oversized jeans hanging loosely off his skinny frame. He greeted them with a grunt and yelled:

'Adi, these two are cool, let them in.'

Adi, the bouncer, arrogantly shrugged his shoulders and begrudgingly let the girls pass through. Sophie had to yank Cam's arm, warning her not to repeat the obscene gesture she had made at the Mercedes driver earlier.

'What?' she mouthed. 'He was a total dick.'

Sophie smiled lightly at her hot-headed friend, and they followed Frank to the sofas. They plonked themselves next to a group of heavily-tattooed guys and quietly sipped on their beers, feeling somewhat awkward and wondering how to start a conversation with this too-cool-to-talk-to-girls crew. Frank was seemingly too engrossed talking to his dreadlocked friend to pay the girls any attention. But eventually someone handed them a sausage on a skewer to roast in the flames. When Cam started flirting with the heavily-pierced, spliff-smoking man sitting next to her, Sophie decided to go and search for Jay. By now she was impatient to see him, the alcohol had emboldened her and she just wanted to hold him in her arms, tell him how much she had enjoyed receiving his letters and how much she had missed him.

The rave was starting to kick off now, with a growing crowd gathering in front of the stage. As she walked along the river, leaving the crowd behind and heading towards the abandoned motorway bridge linking the industrial area to Berlin city, Sophie suddenly heard a woman's loud laugh resonate from under the bridge. And as she turned behind a concrete pillar, she saw them. A smiling Jay was lounging on a tattered sofa, his arm curled around an ebony-skinned beauty with a stylish afro and big dark eyes sparkling on her doll face. Having not noticed Sophie, Jay gently lifted the joint from the girl's long elegant fingers and took a deep drag. Slowly savouring the sweet taste of the weed with closed eyes, he sunk back into the depth of the sofa the girl's head nestling comfortably in the crook of his arm. Crushed by a resentful disappointment, Sophie couldn't bring herself to interrupt their intimate moment, and as her heart shrunk to nothingness, she turned away.

'Sophie?' his voice sounded surprised.

She froze but didn't look back and instead stubbornly looked at her feet. She wondered for a second whether she could pretend not hearing him and continue walking.

'Sophie, wait. Hold on!' He brushed the girl on the sofa aside and rushed over. Cam was right, he had changed. He really wasn't the awkward boy with a distant look in his eyes who 'had no friends' anymore. Tall and effortlessly handsome, his unwavering smile was inviting and warm. His hair had grown longer and flopped over his eyebrow. A shadow of a beard framed his strong jaw and Sophie felt a familiar pinch in the pit of her stomach as their eyes met.

Sophie resisted the urge to fall into his open arms and breathe in the scent of his skin, and instead she nervously glanced at the mysterious girl on the sofa. Elegantly draping her long, lean limbs over the couch and shrouded in a cloud of blue smoke, the dark-skinned model sultrily smoked the remains of the spliff. She stared back at Sophie, suspicious of the unexpected disturbance, like a cheetah eyeing its prey. Her black eyes flickered with nascent jealousy. Sophie's awkwardness grew, and Jay dropped his arms to his sides and instead of giving her a hug, put his hands in his pockets.

'Hi', he said with a soft voice.

'Hi.'

She was forcing herself to look at him and ignore the angry stare of the feline woman, but she couldn't help a crimson blush spreading across her face.

'You made it.' He smiled tentatively.

'Yeah.' Her voice sounded like someone had walked on a squeaky dog toy.

'So what do you think? It's a cool location, no? I told you I was going to do this right.'

He looked over to the party, a hint of pride in his voice.

'Yeah.' Sophie was hot and shifted uncomfortably under the glaring gaze of the lonely beauty on the couch. *If looks could kill...*

'What's up Sophie? Aren't you happy to see me?' he asked. The concern in his voice sounded genuine.

'Yeah sure. Errrm… Look I better go…. Seems you're pretty busy anyway, getting ready and stuff so ...err... catch you after your set, ok?'

She turned on her heel and walked back to the campfire, fighting the urge to look back and desperately trying to hide her bitter disappointment. *Fuck this. Fuck him. That bouncer was right. Jay does have a fan club. A pretty good-looking fan club. Fuck.*

She stomped back to the sofas, angry with herself for letting her feelings betray her.

'Did you find him?' Cam rose a quizzical eyebrow upon seeing her friend's thundery expression.

Sophie waved her off and instead reached for the beer Cam handed her. Cam knew better than to quiz her friend further. A real friend knows when not to ask obvious questions. Sophie sat on the edge of the musty-smelling sofa, peeling the label off her beer bottle, something she would usually do when she was nervous. She tried to bury the image of Jay gently folding his arm around the mysterious girl. She broodingly observed the people around her slowly getting drunker, wishing she could get wasted faster. *What am I doing here?*

Empty beer bottles littered the floor, and the heady smell of marijuana hung low in the warm damp air. Sophie stiffened as Jay walked over with the Amazonian beauty in tow. Sophie couldn't look at them and quickly turned to Frank to ask him for a cigarette. Frank looked up and smiled. She knew he was stoned as he only ever smiled when he was high. A few blonde tufts of what looked like a feeble attempt to grow a goatee sprouted on his pointy chin and Sophie itched for a razor to give him a good clean shave. *But not in a sexy way. He is everything but sexy.*

'Hi Sophie. Haven't seen you in a while', he grinned inanely.

'Frank,' she nodded icily. 'Always a pleasure. So what kind of trouble are you causing these days?' She couldn't help but dislike him. She wasn't sure whether it was his oversized baseball cap, the yellow tipped pimple on his nose, the dumb expressionless eyes or that as Jay's best friend he always seemed to know more about him than she did.

'Me?' he feigned innocence that didn't suit him. In the corner of her eye, she could see Jay standing by the stage on the other side of the campfire, silently staring at her. But she resisted acknowledging him and instead jutted out her jaw defiantly. There was no point trying to rival this girl.

'If anything you are the one causing trouble tonight, looking at how Aisha King is staring you down,' he said hinting at the girl standing by Jay's side. *Aisha King, even her name is cool.*

'Is she Jay's, you know...err...well...'

The words stumbled over each other and fell to the floor like dice.

'Girlfriend? Yeah, sort of, I think he fucks her. You can't blame the man for having good taste. She is smoking hot. Halle Berry in Xmen kinda hot', he laughed irritatingly.

She couldn't shake the feeling that Frank was enjoying seeing her squirm with uneasiness at the thought of Jay being intimate with that woman. She struggled to keep a composed look, but all she wanted to do was stab Frank savagely with one of the sausage skewers.

Jay picked up his crate of vinyls and walked on stage leaving a big-eyed Aisha hanging onto to the railing. He shook hands with the departing DJ, pulled the headphones over his ears and laid down his first track.

Sophie held her breath. A tremor ran through the crowd as he expertly faded out the drum and bass track and melted the beats into an otherworldly hum. The dancers slowed down to a halt and looked to the stage, mystified by the powerful change of atmosphere. All eyes were on Jay and Sophie couldn't help but cross her fingers for him while nervously tapping her foot in the dusty floor as the tension increased. And like a lightning strike followed by thunder, the track kicked into gear and rumbled heavy beats onto the expectant crowd. A wave of cheers spontaneously erupted. With arms raised to cloudy skies, the crowd resumed dancing.

His set was beautifully crafted and took everyone into its moody spell. Every track flowed smoothly into the next while each of them told a different story and took the crowd on a different journey. The beats vibrated through each individual on the packed dance floor. As Sophie took another drag from the cigarette Cam had handed her, she had to admit that he was good. He had perfected his skill, and he had the crowd in the palm of his hand. Never looking up at his adoring public, he seemed deeply concentrated and serene with a hint of a smile curling at the corner of his lips. His steady hand glided delicately over the black gleaming vinyl as he spiked the track with short-tempered salves of scratch sounds. The dance floor whooped and cheered in ecstasy.

Cam jumped up from the sofa and with Sophie trailing behind her, shoved her way through the crowd to the front. Letting the music guide them, they danced, they laughed and they whooped in unison and fell into each other's arms. An exhilarated Cam shouted into Sophie's ear: 'Fuck that girl of his. You just go and tell him how you feel. He is in love with you. I know it, and you know it. Just go and tell him. Just do it.'

Sophie wanted to believe her. She wanted to take her advice and talk to him, she just had to wait until he finished his set. The air had become hot and humid, and in the cloudy night sky a thunderstorm was silently brewing at the fringe of the city. Slowly yet inexorably, the dark clouds advanced towards this side of town, one lightning strike at a time.

As they got back to the backstage area, Sophie noticed Frank having a seemingly heated exchange with a group of eastern-European looking men. The middle-aged men sported black leather jackets and thick moustaches and stood out from the crowd of 20-something ravers. There was something about their posture that looked threatening. A nervous knot formed in the pit of her stomach. Frank gesticulated aggressively and suddenly, his face red with anger, he violently shoved the leader of the group, a boxy man with a thick neck, away from the campfire. Shouts erupted, and the man's face twisted into a mask of fury and he suddenly launched himself at Frank with raised fists. Hard blows rained on his shoulders and his back. Too stunned to defend himself, Frank sunk to the ground, covering his head as the angry attackers continued to beat him.

Within seconds, Frank's friend with the dreadlocks jumped over and protectively stood in between a cowering Frank and his attackers. He was immediately joined by the rest of his friends, with whom Sophie had peacefully shared a spliff and a beer just a few hours ago. Kicks and punches followed suit. Bottles were picked up and hurled between the two groups. Sophie's knees turned to jelly, as she stood by, helplessly witnessing the escalating chaos, too petrified to move away from the violent scene that was unfolding right in front of her eyes. A sudden blow to her ribcage struck her to the ground. A bottle crashed next to her head and woke her from her stupor as she frantically tried to scramble to her feet, avoiding boots and trainers trampling her face. The air was full of furious grunts and screams, drowning out the music. *Where is Cam? Where is Jay?*

On all fours, Sophie scampered through the fighting crowd, panic rising fast as she tunnel-visioned her escape route towards the backstage area. She ran to safety behind the pillars of the bridge to the sofa where she had found Jay cuddling his girlfriend earlier that night, and hid behind it, breathing painfully.

Suddenly the world exploded in black and white, lighting the dark silhouettes of the fighting mob in an instant before everything plunged into absolute darkness. Blinded, Sophie held her hands before her eyes. The music had stopped abruptly, and electricity crackled in the eerie silence. The ensuing thunderbolt was so deafening it threw her to the ground. The rain started almost immediately. Heavy raindrops smashed to the ground like detonating grenades, soaking her to the bone within seconds.

Hearing the faint but insistent sound of police sirens, Sophie turned to the river. Through the heavy curtain of rain, the dark shape of a patrol ship approached the shore. Dizzy with fear and adrenaline, Sophie suppressed a coughing fit and breathed loudly into her shaking hands. 200 meters. 100 meters. 50 meters. The sirens blared in her ears and suddenly a powerful beam of light cut through the darkness. A megaphone voice shouted:

'Berliner River Patrol. For your safety, please remain where you are and identify yourself to a police officer. I repeat. This is Berliner river patrol.'

Sophie scrambled to her feet, and as she tried to run back towards the parking lot, she remembered suddenly that she had left her backpack in the backstage area. She turned on her heel and ran back. As she bent down to fish the rucksack from underneath the sofa, two police officers hurried over, pinned her to the muddy ground, and twisted her arms behind her back. And with the click of the handcuffs snapping shut, her screams for help gurgled incomprehensibly into the mud. *Jay help!*

end of part one

Part two - When winter comes

Jay Adler

***

'And when your fears subside
And shadows still remain
I know that you can love me
When there's no one left to blame
So never mind the darkness
We still can find a way
'Cause nothin' lasts forever
Even cold November rain'

November Rain,
Guns N' Roses

***

CHAPTER 8

***

Berlin, September 2000 - 10 years before the incident

Jay Adler looked up at the dark concrete vaults of the bridge; he could hear the music in the distance. A poster sellotaped to the bridge pillar announced an 'Esoteric Escort Rave' with his name at the top of the bill. 'AddeeJay'. He thought the name was ridiculous, but Frank Stahl loved it, and as he was in charge of advertising the night he hadn't made much of Jay's protests.

Nightmares on wax, swirling drone opening, 90 beats per minute, Unkle, 100bpm, Perton Bee, the B-side, flip, crossfader left, triple scratch salves...

Slowly fading into his set he repeated the key tracks in his head. It relaxed him. The order was right, now he needed to loop that drum and bass track out and fade the opening track in. He cracked his knuckles and warmed up his fingers, drumming them against the back of the sofa.

Da rumm da rumm tack tack. Da rumm da rumm tack tack.

The white label, Zen and the white cat, note minute 3:26, the siren, triple scratch salve on that one...

Da rumm da rumm tack tack. Da rumm da rumm tack tack.

He was barely aware of the girl's presence. He looked down as she stretched her long legs over the edge of the sofa, and for a moment he wondered whether he found her attractive. According to Frank, Aisha King was 'sex on legs', and he had insisted more than once that Jay should 'just fuck her' as she was 'gagging for it'. His friend's crudeness had made Jay laugh. But maybe Frank was right, Aisha had been gravitating around him ever since she had joined the motley crew of event organisers.

She nestled her head against his chest and extended a delicate hand with long round shaped fingernails. He looked at the large cocktail ring on her middle finger and then at the spliff she held out for him. He mentally shrugged his shoulders - a bit of weed wasn't going to do any harm, although what he really wished for was a stiff whisky. He drew in the sweet smoke and relaxed further into the sofa.

...the record with the orange sticker, did I actually pack that one? Then bridge over to Phantom x, back to 90 bpm...

The girl felt hot and uncomfortable against his skin, and he suddenly broke out in a cold sweat, his heart raced as he felt a stab of panic in his stomach. Having relentlessly spread the word over the past weeks, Frank had expected over two thousand people tonight. Jay had been more realistic in his opinion and thought the event would be a success if they had a few hundred attending. In any case it was a large crowd to stand in front of for his first big gig. Feeling clammy, he wanted to shake the girl off him as if she was a hot blanket – she stopped him from concentrating his thoughts. He willed himself to remain calm and focused, but his thoughts started to whirl like leaves in the wind. The insistent sweet smell of vanilla emanating from her hair made him feel queasy. Sweat beading his brow, he gently pushed Aisha back into seating position and breathing heavily he sat up to reach for the beer bottle on the floor. *No whisky but it'll have to do.*

Taking a few greedy gulps, he looked up and saw her walk away.

'Sophie?' he heard himself call out. *Was it really her?* He had waited for her to arrive all evening and had almost given up on seeing her tonight, worrying about what or who had changed her mind at the last minute.

Her silver-blond hair was so long it reached far below her ribs and brushed against her bottom. A nice firm round bottom he couldn't help but notice. The panic tormenting his innards vanished as he got to his feet to embrace her. But as she slowly turned towards him, the look on her face stopped him. Her cold eyes stared him up and down and pinned him to the spot. He tried to talk, but her grey gaze shied him. To his embarrassment he only managed to utter meaningless platitudes for which he wanted to kick himself instead of holding her fragile frame in his arms. He noticed the freckles on her pale cheeks. Where was her usual beaming smile? Why didn't she hug him? He needed her to tell him everything was going to be fine. Instead, she made her excuses through razor-thin lips and left.

As she haughtily vanished into the crowd, the gnawing feeling of dread came back spreading through him with its cold tendrils. Aisha coiled her arm around his waist like a tropical snake and whispered seductively: 'Looks like she doesn't think much of you, this Sophie girl. But I know just what you need.' She drew him back to the coffee table and pulled out a slim plastic sachet of the small leather pouch she wore around her neck. She emptied the sachet on the flat surface and using a playing card she expertly chopped the white powder into four fat lines. Jay stared at the ace of spades, and the Motorhead lyrics popped into his head...

...Playing for the high one, dancing with the devil,

Going with the flow, it's all a game to me...

The cocaine flushed through him like a powerful speed-train crushing his fears and insecurities to make way for a new and improved version of himself. He ground his teeth hoping the drug wouldn't numb the tip of his nose, as last time he snorted the stuff he spent most of his evening holding back from scratching an imaginary itch. *Not tonight,* tonight he needed both of his hands concentrating on rocking this party.

Full of a newly-found chemical-induced confidence, Jay calmly picked up his record case and took to the stage. In passing, he shot a filthy look at Frank, who leaned into Sophie on the couch. Jay thought they were sitting suspiciously close. *Dirty bastard. He better not lay a hand on her.*
Later, he thought, pacing himself. First he was going to tear up the dance floor, and he walked over to the stage. The preceding DJ shook his hand. 'Good luck mate, the wheels of steel are all yours', he said and freed the place at the turntables.

Jay ran a finger over the smooth silver surface. Technics SL 1200. The most reliable and durable turntables ever produced.The same model as the ones he had in the basement at home. He gently adjusted the slip mat and pulled out the first record.This was going to be fun. He cracked his knuckles, pulled the headphones over his ears and with a steady index finger he smoothly eased the cartridge onto the groove. He was instantly sucked into a parallel universe where, in this personal video game of his, he had to match unruly beats, align diverging tempos and scratch quirks in the tracks. The outside world had receded to nothing but a fringe of his reality. The celebrating crowd, the whooping and the cheering, it was all far away in another galaxy. He smiled contently. This is where he wanted to be, inside the music. Like waves washing through his body, cleansing and nurturing him, the music lifted him, pure and innocent like a newborn baby. Hours or minutes went by, he couldn't tell the difference; his time was counted in beats per minute and by the starts and endings of his tracks.

Only once, he looked up to see her and her friend dancing in the crowd. *Sophie.* She looked radiant. Her long white hair floated around her delicate face like a mermaid underwater, and her laugh rang in his head. The needle skipped, and he missed a beat. *Concentrate you fool*, the voice in his head urged him.

Suddenly, the turntables shook, as though in the throws of an earthquake and the needles slid off the records. The music stopped with a distorted scratch as the table crashed to the ground under the weight of two men fighting.

'What the fuck!' Jay exclaimed and as he ripped his headphones off, the cacophony of the crowd shocked him into action. He carefully stepped over the writhing bodies, avoiding knocks and kicks and looked over to what seemed to be the heart of the fight. In the middle of the mass of people, he spotted Sophie getting knocked over and disappearing in the midst of the crowd. He jumped off the stage and ran to the spot he'd last seen her. But she was gone.

Frantically looking for her, he ran to the bridge. But a sudden lightning struck so bright the world froze into a black and white photograph. It blinded him for a split second then plunged everything back into total darkness. In the following seconds of eerie silence, he heard a feeble moan coming from behind the bridge pillar. He cautiously walked closer and stopped to find a huddled body at his feet. As he touched her shoulder carefully, she turned her face to him, and he swallowed hard as an ugly gash across her forehead oozed dark blood. A deafening smack of thunder cracked the sky open, and the rain started to fall hard to the dusty ground.

'Aisha, holy shit. What happened?'

He bent down on his knees in the rapidly forming puddle and steadied her gently.

'I don't know... I... think a bottle hit me', she sobbed breathlessly, trying to cover the cut with shaking hands. He quickly took off his jumper and wrapped it around her head. In a makeshift attempt to stop the bleeding he pressed the wound with the cuff. It wasn't going to help much. He gently pushed a stray strand of hair out of the cut and her eyes rolled back.

'Aisha, stay with me', he whispered. Her eyes fluttered open again.

The angry cut was deep, and she was going to need stitches – several by the looks of it. He needed an ambulance. Now. He effortlessly scooped her up. Feeling the warm raindrops streaming down his face into the collar of his t-shirt, he hurried towards the car park. His mind was racing. He needed to find a phone.

What was the number for the emerging services? 911. No that was the number they always showed in American movies. 112. Yes 112. I need a fucking phone.

Holding the helpless girl tightly, he climbed up the creaking metal ladder. Then he heard the police sirens. The piercing noise cut through the thunder and the rain and seemed to come simultaneously from the river and the car park. Panic broke out as people blindly stumbled to escape the police who seemed to have come in force. Out of nowhere, they appeared in full rioting gear, marching in, kettling the crowd and making arrests. People rushed past him, screaming and pushing each other out of the way to run back to their cars.

Cradling Aisha's head between his shoulder and his chest, he ran towards a group of policemen standing by their armoured van. Her eyes were closed; rain and blood streaked down her face as she lay unconscious in his arms. Her faint breath feathered against his chest. Her usually ebony-coloured skin had turned ashen.

The officer in charge immediately ushered Jay over to the ambulance where paramedics took over. She was carefully lowered on a stretcher, removed of her shirt, and someone handed him his jumper back which he distractedly pulled over his drenched t-shirt. While the paramedic cleaned the wound, Jay gently reached out for her limp hand. Her skin was cold against his. Another thunderbolt exploded above their heads, and the ground shook. Jay thought of his mother who had always said that the safest place to be during a thunderstorm was a car. Something about the rubber tires. He shook his head and couldn't remember. He started humming to the Prince song playing in his head.

...Thunder all through the night. Promise to see Jesus in the morning light. Take my hand, it'll be alright. Come on, save your soul tonight ...

Recently he had noticed that when he was stressed, somehow song lyrics would randomly pop into his head and he found it relaxing to sing along, silently, like a mute karaoke to his own personal radio station. He couldn't quite explain it; it was as if he played the soundtrack to his life in his head. The doors slammed shut, and they drove off, sirens blaring and blue lights flashing.

'Your name? Hello?' the man next to him nudged him with his clipboard. Put on the spot he told him his real name and regretted it instantly. This was going to have consequences. The police would find out the names of the organisers of the illegal event, Mark, Frank, Josef, Alex, Karl and me... and looking over to Aisha. *Aisha.* Her eyes were still closed; she had lost quite a lot of blood. The paramedic said something about a possible transfusion and asked whether Jay knew her blood type. He didn't. *I only just met her,* he thought sadly. The paramedic shrugged his shoulders and scribbled something on his clipboard before loosely applying a gauze dressing to Aisha's forehead. She moaned softly and gripped Jay's hand tighter.

Only now he took notice of the two other guys in the back of the ambulance, one tilting his head backwards holding a bloody compress to his nose and his neighbour with a vacant look in his eyes had his arm in a sling. One cursory glance reassured him that he didn't know either of them. He thought of his friends and hoped they were alright. He tried not to think of the crate of records he had left behind in the rain. It pained him too much to think of losing them. Records he had patiently collected over the past years, hours he had spent sifting through rows and rows of vinyls at his favourite store, headphones tightly screwed on, listening intently to every beat and chorus. A world away from school with its grades and finger-wagging teachers insisting he could do better. Ever since that night at the club in Ibiza he had it in his head to become a DJ. *And now?* His heart sunk.

Nice one, good job, first gig and all descends into chaos. Fucking loser.

Confused, he raised an eyebrow at the two guys to his left. *What?*

But they didn't seem to pay him any attention, too busy with their injuries. He could have sworn the whispering voice came from their end. He tried to steer his thoughts away from tonight's deception and suddenly he saw her face in his mind's eye. *Sophie.*

Her long silver blond hair framing her pale face, the look of contempt in her clear grey eyes. She had seen right through him as if she had known what a loser he really was. His stomach lurched, and he caught his breath. He had left her behind. He helplessly clenched his fists as the ambulance sped through the stormy night.

CHAPTER 9

Solacium, June 2011 - 8 months after the incident

The alarm buzzer rang the same insistent ring like every other morning. It pierced through his sleep and chased away the foggy remnants of his dream. Jay slowly drifted back to consciousness, his mouth dry, the taste metallic. He wanted to shake out the drowsiness like a wet dog. The meds still coursing through his veins; he tried to sort his thoughts like normal people would sort their laundry, whites on this pile, colours on that one. It wasn't easy, most of the time he would forget where he was and would look around the room in disbelief, wondering what the hell he was doing here. Looking over at the two other beds in the small room, the occupants stirring, a feeling of nausea took hold of him. He wasn't alone.

The walls were bare, and the morning dusk seeped through the dirty window panes. No curtains, just metal bars instead. With the realisation he was still at Solacium, the sense of bottomless despair was soul-destroying. *Another day. In here.* Still dizzy from the drugs he tugged at his t-shirt. It was soaking wet. *Again.*

A loud fart echoed in the room. His roommate Karl, a hot-headed 25-year-old schizophrenic in remission, giggled without apologising. In response his other roommate Tarek, a quiet older man who had apparently stabbed his wife in the eyes with a screwdriver, coughed up his lungs and spat into the bin. Jay shuddered in disgust. His fellow inmates knew no manners and no boundaries. He thought of them as a disgrace to humankind. Jay itched to tell them off; his fist balled, idly he thought about how it would feel to punch them in the face. It wasn't just the farting, the coughing and the spitting, it was the snoring that got to him most.

They both snored so loudly, he found himself wishing he would go deaf. He fantasised about shoving pencils in his ears. He grew tired of their constant jibes as they bullied him relentlessly about the distinguished way he spoke, calling him Posh Boy. Ever since his father had visited, leaving an expensive bathrobe and a bottle of exquisite perfume as parting gifts, he had become the butt of many jokes.

He had complained to his wardens, but all he succeeded in doing was igniting a row that cost him his daily 5pm walk in the park.

One lunch-time, his roommate Karl waved a letter in his face that he had stolen from Jay's locker. Mimicking a child's voice, he started reading out loud the private thoughts Jay had written down for Sophie, for everyone to hear. Jay had reacted simply and efficiently. One blow to the head sent his roommate straight to the floor, howling in pain as he cradled his broken jaw. Flushed with red-hot anger, Jay kicked him repeatedly in the abdomen until the man groaned in agony. Within seconds, inmates gathered around the two fighters, chanting and taunting, and the violence spread like wildfire. Mayhem broke out in the cafeteria, and many used the ensuing chaos as payback time for the various disagreements they harboured with each other. The guards quickly waded in, and hiding behind plexiglass shields they forced their way through the fray, wielding their batons at anyone who moved. Jay and Karl had been found guilty starting the unrest and were each charged with a week of solitary confinement.

It had been a long week with nothing to do but stare at the walls, count the ridges in the tiles, walk the four square meters of the cold cell and watch the daylight intensify and fade on the cold concrete flooring. The nights were the worst, and Jay suffered claustrophobia-induced panic attacks so severe he thought he was going to self-combust. Heinz, the sadistic warden who got a kick out of exerting his power on the inmates, wanted his stay to be longer, unconvinced Jay had learnt his lesson. To Jay's immense relief, Solacium's psychiatrist Doctor Steinbach had recognised the distress the solitary cell caused him and ordered for an early release. Once back in his room, Jay didn't raise his voice again and when the taunting resumed he swallowed his pride and ignored them. It was like being back at school. He hoped that eventually the bullies would grow bored, and he would become invisible.

**

Berlin, October 2001 - 9 years before the incident

He woke up to the rhythmic sound of raindrops incessantly drumming against the window pane. His head throbbed painfully from the excesses of the night before. His right lower abdominal ached. He could feel the bandage stretch across his skin. With his eyes still firmly shut, he clumsily fumbled for the bottle of painkillers he knew he had stowed away in the drawer of his night table. He rose slowly. Peering through heavy eyelids he picked up the water bottle by the bed and swallowed a handful of the tablets. The water tasted stale and he suppressed the urge to vomit. He inched back under the covers and buried his head into the soft cushions, willing the headache to subside. Unable to go back to sleep, his thoughts whirled in time with the drumming raindrops, throwing up random flashbacks from the previous night.

At Frank's. Impromptu jam session. Hits from the bong. A giant bowl of pasta. The bar. And another bar. A joint in the alleyway. A trip to the tattoo studio….Queue to the club. Tequila shots to numb the pain of his freshly inked skin. Strobe lights flashing. Dancing people. Coke in the toilets. Dancing. Walk home. Rucksack stuffed with spray cans. Underground train station. Photo of the finished piece. In bed. Sex...

The memory of her lean body hardened him. Slowly he slid one hand in his boxers, the other reaching for her warm, smooth back. She stirred in her sleep as he gently traced his fingers along her spine to the two dimples in the small of her back. Her hair spilled across the pillow, and carefully he ran his finger lightly over the dark scar on her forehead, a zig-zagged line at the base of her hairline.

'Jay' she moaned still asleep, rolling towards him, her full lips slightly parted. Feeling increasingly horny, he tore through the sheets, ran his eager fingers over her chest and cupped her small firm breast. He gently rolled a hard nipple between his fingers as she sighed and nonchalantly lifted her hand to her breast. He held his breath and slowly his hand slid down her tight stomach, feeling every muscle breathe under her silken skin. As if he had switched her on, her onyx eyes suddenly opened wide as he reached between her thighs. With a groan, she wrapped her lithe self around him, supple like a panther and bit his neck hungrily.

Blood rushed to his head, and he felt dizzy with lust. He wanted her, his cat woman. *Now.* The Fleetwood Mac song hummed in his head.

Got a black magic woman, Got me so blind I can't see, That she is a black magic woman, She's trying to make a devil out of me…

Effortlessly he rolled her onto her back and holding her wrists tightly, he pinned her to the mattress. She writhed to escape his iron grip, her legs kicking his back, but to no avail as he was all strong, lean muscles. She gasped as he entered her and with every thrust bringing him closer to climaxing, she moaned louder, turning him all the more on. As he reached an all consuming orgasm, a red hot flash of pain exploded in his head.

He rolled off her panting body, holding his head, groaning in agony.

'What's wrong? Jay? Are you ok?' she murmured, her voice thick with worry. Black dots impaired his vision, and his speech was slurred when he finally uttered: 'Fucking hangover.'

He woke up hours later to the smell of fresh coffee. Still feeling bruised and his eyelids heavy, he pulled his trousers on, wondering what had happened to him earlier. The unexplained flash of pain had burst through his brains as if all synapses dissolved at once into one mushy matter. Lights out. Intense pleasure immediately followed by extreme pain. Not that he didn't see the attraction of sadomasochistic practices – but this was not what he had in mind.

The sleeping had helped, but time was still a floating concept and he didn't know for how long he had been out. *Wasn't I supposed to be somewhere today?* He tried to recall what it was he had forgotten but to no avail.

All the headache tablets had done was numb him. Sitting in the nape of his neck, the low throbbing pain was still lingering like a dormant threat. The nagging thought of forgetting something buzzed around his head like a persistent mosquito. When his feet touched the cold wood of the floor he shivered. His girlfriend's laugh echoed in the corridor. *My girlfriend*, he smiled, still finding it incredible she had chosen to stay with him. And now he had her name tattooed below his belly button. She was his forever now. That was probably not my best idea, he shook his head. *How high was I?*

The kitchen's bright lights made him squint, and the overpowering smell of bacon and eggs made his stomach churn. Wearing an apron, Aisha was busy frying eggs sunny side up.

'Help yourself', she mouthed, sliding the eggs off the pan onto two slices of toast, and with the telephone on loudspeaker she continued chatting away to her friend Val. Aisha clearly didn't approve of something he had done the night before. Her velvety voice drowned out as he looked down at his plate wondering whether he could stomach eating at all. If he did, he worried he would mark her white walls with a permanent vomit stain. He chuckled at the thought. She was a real neat freak. He would risk being permanently banned from her flat if he did. Probably not a good idea. He liked her flat. Although small, it was clean and bright, in a nice trendy area of Berlin, Kreuzberg. He stabbed the egg yolk with his fork, and it bled over the toast in technicolour yellow. Aisha plonked a bowl of strawberries next to his plate, blew him a quick kiss and returned to her animated conversation.

Hey, psst!

What? His eyes widening in surprise, he looked over at Aisha.

She had her back turned to him and stood by the sink, wearing nothing but thick woollen socks and his grey sweater. Her smooth dark legs were infinitely long and disappeared under the XXL jumper. He idly wondered whether she was wearing any knickers and just the thought of the possibility that she wasn't, aroused him again.

Hey, psst, over here!

The whisper came from the table and confused, he looked at the bowl of strawberries. Slowly he lifted a finger and touched the seedy fruit.

oh!

He prodded it again.

Stop it!

'What the fuck?' He exclaimed, delicately picking up the fruit and placing it on the plate in front of him. He stared at it for a while, waiting for it to say something else, or maybe it would open its eyes and wink at him? *Of course, it wouldn't, it's a fucking fruit,* and just as he thought it, the insistent whisper resonated in his head again.

Loser!

'What the fuck?' he whispered again, perplexed. *I'm being insulted by a strawberry?* He wasn't sure if he should burst out laughing or whether this was beyond funny.

'Aisha, did you just hear that?' He asked somewhat bemused. Still chatting to her friend, she didn't look up and undisturbed, lifted a wait-a-second index finger.

You forgot about Sunday; the strawberry said reproachfully.

Shit, suddenly it dawned on him. *It is Sunday.* The headache reared its ugly head again and angled its way up his neck with long winding tendrils. The long awaited Sunday and of all Sundays, it had to be the one he had a monstrous hangover and felt like shit.

Ha ha. Told you, you fuckwit.

He could have sworn he heard the strawberry giggle. That goddamn thing was messing with his head. Stay calm and rational, he willed himself. *This doesn't make any sense.* And then the memory suddenly clicked into place: Frank handing him a plastic bag full of dried mushrooms, smiling ahead of a good trip. Even eaten as pizza topping, they had tasted like soggy cardboard but nevertheless their effect had been potent. The rest of the night was spent in fits of giggles, seeing flashes of coloured inspiration, people morphing into cartoon characters and holding pointless discussions. While they worked on an elaborate graffiti piece in a deserted U-Bahn station, Jay remembered arguing with Frank about whether Smurfs had genitalia or whether they were just asexual under those tiny white pants. What was the point in existing if you didn't have a dick? Jay had wondered while emptying his spray can on the wall.

This is bullshit, I only hear you because I got so wasted last night, ok? He thought.

No, I'm here. To stay. You need me; it continued.

The headache had spread to his forehead like slow rising poison and sat in the curve of his skull, a dark, menacing mass ready to burst into another flash of debilitating pain. Jay wanted that damn fruit to shut up already. Exasperated he lifted his arm and with one hard blow he splatted it flat to the wood of the table. He could swear he heard it squeal in terror and then silence. Blood red juice ran down the palm of his hand, along his arm, into the cuff of his shirt. He incredulously looked on as Aisha, suddenly standing next to him, fluidly leaned over and with a wry smile, licked the inside of his wrist with quick laps of her pink tongue. Like a domesticated panther. All elastic, gleaming and subtle power. He wanted to grab her by her elegant neck, feel his way under the oversized sweatshirt up to her breasts, and...

'Hey, Jay! Stop staring at your plate. Come on. We need to get ready; we're running late... you said your mother is quite particular about time-keeping?' Aisha interrupted his thoughts with a tone that bore no patience.

It was that Sunday. He looked out of the window and noticed it hadn't stopped raining. Dark clouds of doom descended from the sky, hanging low and forecasting no improvement for the afternoon ahead. The flood was coming, and he wished for an ark to rescue him. With a heavy heart, he threw on his parka and dragged himself to his car, an old draughty Jeep his mother had branded 'a dreadful eyesore'. She regularly urged him to scrap it and buy a 'decent' car. But there was something so comforting in its trusty defiance that almost made it look human. Jay lovingly patted the leaky hood and ignored the rust patches that had formed at the sides of the door.

They drove in silence for a while, through the curtain of heavy rain, concentrating on the slow traffic, lulled by the incessant drumming of raindrops and the persistent damp smell lingering inside the car.

'Are you nervous?' She looked over to him, her eyes narrowed to black slits. She expected him to be. He had dragged this day out for months and finally, after much nagging and her eventual threat of turning up uninvited, he caved in and complied to her demands. She was to be finally made his official girlfriend by meeting his mother and stepfather, and he was dreading it.

'Not really, I know you will do just fine. They will love you', he lied through clenched jaws and continued concentrating on the road, avoiding her probing stare.

She nodded slowly and thankfully didn't ask any further questions. They drove through the crawling traffic into the posh neighbourhood where his mother had moved when she remarried.

The car turned left, and he flicked the remote control towards the huge wooden gate. It slowly creaked open to give way to a gravel path. The tires crunched forward, painfully slow as if to drag out their arrival. The house that appeared behind the barren oak trees was of impressive size, a ten-bedroom Victorian townhouse with a tennis court and a swimming pool. Jay was acutely aware of Aisha's widening eyes. He cringed inwardly. The reaction was almost always the same. As soon as people found out how his parents lived, they would start treating him differently. It wasn't an in-your-face change, but small sly comments crept up in conversations that widened the chasm between them. His friends would drop a humorous "you pick up the tab, your parents are minted", to a more paining, dripping in envy "What have you got to moan about, ask mommy she'll fix it". He always felt he should be happy – didn't he have everything going for him? Wasn't he destined to succeed in life? And yet, he sighed with the freedom-starved heart of a prisoner, it wasn't his to choose.

'What, this is where your parents live? Are you joking, this is a fucking castle! I didn't even know villas of this size existed in this neighbourhood!' she gushed excitedly.

'My mother and her husband', he corrected her moodily. It annoyed him when she called them his parents. He was his stepdad. And it wasn't a castle, but he let it pass.

He parked the mud-caked Jeep in the garage, at odds between his stepdad's gleaming Jaguar and his mother's brand new Mercedes. They hurried up the steps to the main entrance, sheltering from the lashing rain under their hoods. As the doorbell echoed between the limestone walls, an excited squeal resounded behind the thick teak door. It swung open, and a giggling whirlwind of blond curls jumped up and folded its legs around Jay's waist.

'Jaaaaaaay, I waited all day yesterday and all day today and finally you are here!' Skinny arms clamped around his neck, her clear laugh and large grin made his heart sing.

'Pearl. It's so good to see you. I didn't think you were going to be here. I thought you and your brother were at Ma and Pa's?' He ruffled her beach-blonde hair and noticed she had grown since the last time he saw her. She hooked her little hand into his and smiled at him adoringly. He had missed coming over to see her and her brother. Ever since he had got over the shock of coming back from a summer holiday with his dad, to find that his mother and his stepdad had adopted two children, Milana and Maxime, they had become his family.

A car had picked him up from the airport and on arrival, Karl the butler had walked him over to what had been his games room. Jay found out that, in his absence, it had been transformed into a nursery. He had been greeted hurriedly and waved over to the crib where the babies slept. He had leaned over and looking at their rosy cheeks, butter-soft skin and blond downy hair he knew everything was going to change. He was ten years old.

The door opened more widely, and his mother stared at him with cold eyes and a thin smile. Her dark-brown hair was tied severely into a knot at the base of her neck, and the dangling emerald earrings were the same colour as her eyes. The fine lines accentuating her features bore no secret that Elisabeth von Schoenefeldt had once been an exceptionally beautiful woman. Frail as a bird, she leaned in and gave him a barely noticeable squeeze, lightly as not to crease her silk blouse. In a fleeting moment, he had wanted to press her fragile frame lovingly to his chest but he didn't. She wasn't that type of person; she didn't do hugs. At least not with him.

His brother Maxime appeared in the doorway, and peering through his thick blonde fringe he eyed up Aisha suspiciously. She gave him a little smile which he ignored.

'Who is that?' he asked rudely pointing at her. Jay's mother batted his hand down with a severe look.

'Don't be impolite Maxime,' she hissed and turned to Aisha. For a split second, her stern composure faltered, but she caught herself. Overly formally, and with an icy smile she greeted Aisha.

They were let into the house, and Aisha marvelled at the marble floorings, the tastefully decorated interiors with classic and contemporary art splashed across the walls, and white designer furniture. While the twins went to wash their hands as ordered, they sat down in the drawing-room and Karl the butler brought out a tray of champagne glasses. Jay downed his in one gulp as his stepfather entered the room. His mother had always had this innate sixth-sense for picking out the right suitors for her ambitious lifestyle. A material man for 'the right kind of marriage', with a smooth manner and a thick wallet.

Caspar was tall and tanned with a permanent just-came-back-from-Mallorca glow that he chose to show off with a crisp white shirt. 'He always wears bloody perfect white shirts', thought Jay. And he always itched to give the twins a pot of Nutella and instruct them to give their adoptive dad a hug. For his early 50s, Caspar was a handsome man, and Jay knew he had quite a following – he was that kind of man, a talented surgeon with a sharky smile. He mastered getting the attention of women perfectly and played his female fans like fiddles. He gave Jay a quick and strong handshake, his grey eyes narrowed on Aisha all the while. His head arrogantly cocked to the side, he took her in, from head to toe, not making the slightest effort to hide that he was checking her out.

'Oh hello. You must be Aisha. It's a pleasure to finally meet you. Jay has talked about you in the most positive terms but he had never mentioned just how exquisite you look in the flesh.' Aisha giggled nervously at the overly pompous greeting. Jay hated his stepfather's leering gaze and even more so his glib tone. Busy picking fluff off the cushions on the sofa, his mother didn't seem to notice, or if she did, she didn't seem to care much.

'Jay, can I get you to help me with the wine for a second. The kitchen please', she ordered him icily.

Once in the kitchen and out of earshot, she jabbed a bony jewel-clad finger in his chest and hissed at him.

'Why did you not tell me that … you know... she is...' Not wanting to say the word she gave him a telling look.

'What? A girl?' Jay looked down at her with contempt.

'Very funny. No, I mean, well... this isn't easy son. You are bringing this on yourself. I am your mother and I need to look out for your best interest, and you know our family's reputation is paramount. She is black? Your girlfriend had to be black? Did you do this on purpose to annoy us? Are you acting out like a teenager?' she hissed dripping venom.

'I don't see your point mother, you just sound... racist.'

She recoiled at the ugly word, and he swore he saw a hint of a blush colouring her pale cheeks. No, she didn't like to be called a racist; she had just wanted him to date someone more of his standing. Not a yoga instructor whose only ambition was to get into event management. No, she wanted him to date a double-barrelled lady of ... preferably a white Aryan who would make him lots of blond and blue-eyed babies to perpetuate the white supremacy. He bit his tongue. He knew he was getting angry.

'You don't even know her. Don't be so judgmental.' He grabbed the bottle of wine and left her standing, alone and dwarfed by her oversized chrome designer kitchen. Such a waste of space, they hardly ever dined in.

The rest of the afternoon was painful. The conversations were stilted and full of passive aggressive hooks for arguments. His mother had as usual lectured him on his future. When was he going to sort out his life? She still smarted from last year's encounter with the police, and Jay's community service sentence for illegal event organisation had been the gossip of the tennis club. Rolling her eyes dramatically at his stepdad, she launched into belittling his current day job. Working as an inventory clerk in his father's factory wasn't what they had in mind. They urged him to study business administration to be, one day, groomed to take over the multi-million publishing empire his father had in turn inherited from his parents. He was the rightful heir. He was the only son. He had the responsibility to carry on the legacy of the family. When was he going to realise that more was expected of him?

Jay didn't look up from his plate but could sense Aisha shifting uncomfortably in her chair. At least they had moved on from grilling his poor girlfriend with questions. They had wanted to know where in Somalia she had come from and what her parents did for a living. Her dad was a handyman and her mother had raised four kids and worked as a nurse in the district hospital, she replied, politely unaware of the meaningful looks Jay's mother shot her husband as if to say "see I told you so'. Why had she moved to Germany? To escape the civil war that had torn apart the country. And then they had launched into a heated debate on whether political refugees syphoned off the governmental benefits from a lackadaisical states benefits system. Aisha fell quiet.

'And how is your lovely friend. What was her name? Sophie?' Just when Jay thought it couldn't get any worse, Caspar raised an eyebrow and threw a curveball into the conversation.

'Oh yes the one you spent so much time with before she left to go studying abroad. Was it law or business she chose? Where is she now, are you two still in touch? She is delightful', His mother interjected with calculating eyes and a paper-thin smile.

He confirmed quietly that indeed Sophie had left Germany to go study at a renowned London business school. He kept silent about his letters to her, since the night of the party by the river, her answers had been rare. Lately they had only been a quick note scribbled on the back of a postcard.

She had been working very hard for her final exams and was hoping to get an internship in a bank. He didn't want to admit it but he missed her long funny letters in which she described her daily struggle to keep sane, grappling with untidy housemates and the interminable mishaps of her day-to-day life, trying to adapt to London's stiff upper lip. By now he had given up on the idea of visiting her.

The twins seemed oblivious to the adult conversation if not a little bored by it all and discreetly played with their food. Caspar shot his adoptive 12 year old daughter a warning look, and Milana dropped the fork with a loud clatter, her lower lip quivering. The headache awoke and clawed its way to Jay's forehead, pulsating darkly. Jay noticed Caspar had put a domineering hand on her thigh. *That bastard, he really shouldn't touch her like that.* It was that child's voice again, whispering urgently in his ear. It wasn't a bloody strawberry; it was a child's voice. In his head.

Save her. Now. The creepy voice hissed.

Jay got up and all the while looking his stepfather squarely in the eye, forced a cheerful tone and said: 'Pearl, come with me, we are going to get some ice-cream'. Caspar withdrew his hand from her leg and Milana leaped up to rush into the kitchen with him.

The drive back to his flat was long and silent. It was still raining, and it had suddenly got very dark. Jay's headache was now so severe that Aisha had to drive while he stared out of the window waiting for the tablets to kick in that his mother had pushed into his palm. When Aisha complained about the loaded atmosphere he resisted the urge to say 'I told you so'.

'Your mother, she is quite tough isn't she', Aisha had continued. He had nodded. But the problem wasn't his mother, Aisha got that wrong, the problem was his stepfather.

CHAPTER 10

Solacium, July 2011 - 9 months after the incident

His head resting on his hand, Jay surveyed the canteen with a bored stare. It was a lunch time feeding frenzy at the looney bin. Even after having spent six months at the asylum, he still found the sight surreal. All these crazies wearing blue jumpsuits and stuffing their faces like it was their last supper. A great collection of mental illnesses in human form on display in all its fucked up glory. *Don't you fit in here marvellously.*

'Hey…hey… man …Are you going to eat this?' a fat finger prodded the fishcake on his plate. Jay sighed and answered:

'No George. Not anymore, now you've stuck your finger in it, you can have it'

George made a high-pitched giggle and greedily scooped the cake onto his plate.A thread of drool slid down his double chin as he opened his mouth wide open to swallow the cake whole.

Jay sighed again, *Bloody George*, every meal time he would seek Jay out in the canteen and sit next to him staring at him with big puppy brown eyes until he would raise his index finger, pretend to pick up a stray breadcrumb and then slowly inch towards Jay's plate. If Jay looked over to him, his finger would freeze and then tap onto the plastic table cloth like the equivalent of someone whistling with guilt only to resume its stealth operation to sink its nail into whatever food morsel would be closest to the edge of the plate. It would have been comical if it hadn't been so tragic.

The man's stomach folded over his trousers like the top of a muffin and his forearms were triple the size of Jay's. How could he be mad at him, the poor man was a simpleton. He was completely nuts but he was a good guy at heart. Jay wondered whether George was bulimic or whether it was the pills he was given that made him so hungry. Although slightly grossed out by the man's food fingering habits, he figured it didn't really matter. He had to watch his weight anyway and eating half of his daily ration was probably a good thing. As he side eyed George frothing over his desert, he made a note to ask for clearance to the gym at his next psychiatric evaluation.

Who are you kidding, you fat slug. The gym…hahaha what do you think this is? A spa? the familiar voice giggled *Forget about it, just let yourself go, who do you need to get slim for anyway? No one is visiting you in here*

'Shut up!'

George turned to him, mouth still chewing and eyes wide with consternation.
'Sofffrry, wroat ditch I doph?' pieces of the apple tart sprayed out of his mouth towards him.

'Nothing George, that wasn't meant for you, I'm sorry'

'Ish Dan schtill there? or ish it schthe white lady? I think I like her more.'

'George, it's nothing ok. Here have my apple tart' he sounded much more abrupt than he wanted to, but sometimes he wished he hadn't opened up to George about Dan and the white lady.

Anyway, the apple tart tasted more like chemicals than actual apples, probably manufactured somewhere in a factory of the East block of Russia.

Full of poison. Of course. It's part of the Russian's plan to ensure world domination. Poison the food of the West Europeans, make them all weak with cancer and then. Boom. In they march. Russian soldiers everywhere

Jay pushed his tray away from him and got up. He knew he needed to report the voice, the psychiatrist Doctor Steinbach insisted asking him the question at every session. Jay knew that this time he really needed to report that the drug dosage had slipped and allowed the voices to come back, like a bunch of party goers rebuffed at the entrance but entering the club through the backstage door instead. They weren't always there, and not all at once but sometimes, on bad days, the paranoid thoughts returned and spiralled in endless loops around his head, inside his skull, like a game of roulette when the ball rolls around the barrel, faster and faster, without ever settling on red and uneven.

'Bye George, enjoy the cake.'

He politely nodded at the warden on duty, exited the canteen and walked over to the 'Pill Box' as the inmates nicknamed it - where the Queen of Pills, Mrs Rot handed out the little paper cups with the daily dosage of chemicals to keep the loonies sedated.

'Good afternoon Mrs Rot. I hope you are well. Would you be so kind to give me my prescription? Adler West Wing G7, inmate ID 31102010.'

'Adler, yes yes yes. The Canadian. Here you are.' she mumbled.

The Canadian - they had nicknamed him that after he had pointed out that his accent wasn't American and his mother was originally from Toronto. Since then the moniker stuck. Jay didn't mind, he was just glad that since the fight in the canteen, no one dared to call him Posh Boy anymore and there now was a flicker of respect in the inmates eyes every time he'd look at them.

'Adler what time is it?' she looked at him over her reading glasses.

Jay frowned, opened his mouth to say something and then instead looked at the clock behind Mrs Rot.

'14:05 Mrs Rot'

'And what time are you due to pick up your pills?'

'By 14:00?' he ventured a smile he hoped to be disarming but probably came across as an awkward grin.

'Oh look at that, you are not as dumb as you look pretty boy. Yes indeed. You are late. This will have to go on your record' she shook her head and drew a cross next to his name on the registrar. 'I would be more careful next time Adler. You get minus points for that, and you wouldn't want to be downgraded, now would you?'

'No Mrs Rot, I will be more careful next time.'

'I'm sure you will.' she smiled a smile that didn't reach her eyes.

Panic rose up in him. *No I can't be downgraded, they'll revoke my visitors access.* He pushed his hand in his pocket and the paper of Sophie's letter rustled between his fingers. 'I'll be in Berlin in a few months time, for Christmas and I thought I could come to visit if that's ok with you'. His heart beat fluttered irregularly at the thought of Sophie coming to visit him in Solacium.

***

Amsterdam, November 2002 - 8 years before the incident

'My Sophie,

We haven't spoken in a while, and I miss your letters. Sophie, I think I'm in trouble. Nobody can know about this, I trust you, you're my friend. I think there's someone in my head. He calls himself Dan. He's unpredictable and comes and goes whenever it pleases him. He likes to creep up on me at the most inappropriate moments and then he starts to whisper and once he starts, I can't shut him up. He's torturing me.

In the beginning, I thought it was the drugs, and I tried to stop taking them for a while. Sophie, I'm not a druggy. I can see you shaking your head in disbelief, haven't you always teased me for being scared and weak. I know I walked out on that Alien movie we watched together when we were kids but that thing erupting out of that guy's stomach, I couldn't watch that. However desperately I tried to impress you, the movie just made me sick with fear. You just laughed that sunny laugh of yours. I miss your laugh; it makes the world a better place.

I don't know why I seem to find it so hard to say no. Everyone around me seems to have a good time, and I just want to fill that void inside of me. I'm a hollow shell. I know I promised you I would quit, but I just need something to numb this pain. Coke, mushrooms and weed. Too much of it. I'm glad in a way that you live so far away, I don't think I could face the disappointed look in your eyes. I know it's all messing with my head, and I need to get a grip.

At first I thought I had it all under control but now, I don't know. The drugs seem to open doors that I can't close again and coming in from the dark side, he slips in. Dan seems to visit me every time I'm anxious about something. I now know more or less when he is planning on talking to me. The headaches seem to be a telltale warning sign.

Sometimes the pain gets so intense I have to lock myself in my bedroom and draw the curtains. I close my eyes and try not to panic and then I hear him, his voice echoes in my head. It's crazy. Some days he's in a good mood, and he cracks a few jokes but more often than not he's angry, and he sees everything. When people stare at me in the street, he hears them whisper about me. Music seems to be the only way to block him out; the headphones provide a sound barrier protecting me from his constant comments. Sophie, this is driving me crazy. I'm scared.

I don't understand what Dan wants and why he doesn't go away. It's not like I haven't tried to make him leave, but he just giggles. It's creepy. Sophie, this is slightly nuts, right? Fuck, sometimes I just don't know if I'm making this shit up and writing this down makes me realise how crazy this sounds. Don't tell anyone, I don't think people would understand.'

Jay looked at the last words he had penned down and frowned. *What the fuck am I doing?* The elegantly-slanted words laughed at him, mocking his pathetic attempt at a cry for help. He crumpled the pages in anger and hurled the paper ball at the bin. It bounced off the rim and rolled back towards him as if to taunt him to rethink his action. But he didn't pick it up. He couldn't tell Sophie he was hearing voices as he feared that she was never going to talk to him again or worse, talk to his family and they would get him locked up. He pointedly ignored the crumpled letter and instead looked out of the window into the sombre evening sky. The flat felt empty without Aisha. It had been the most devastating argument they had ever had and after what had been said, he wasn't sure if they would survive as a couple. He wondered what would happen next.

He rested his head against the cool glass of the window; snowflakes whirled in the hazy streetlamp light behind the steam of his breath, and he wished he had never agreed to that gig. From the start, it had failure written all over it but he had ignored the warning feeling that had wrenched his gut. When the organiser called him to confirm his DJ slot at the BMX Games in Amsterdam, he had said yes. Amsterdam sounded like an adventure he had to take. Jay had insisted his friends to be added onto the payroll and the organiser had begrudgingly agreed after Jay promised to split the wages three ways. After factoring petrol costs in, he wasn't going to make a penny out of this gig but he didn't care. He couldn't break the code of honour that bound him to his friends; you always included your mates.

And so on Friday evening, after he finished his shift at his dad's company and had picked up Frank and Matthias in Kreuzberg, they had trekked off in his old jeep. It was a small miracle that the car made it all the way from Berlin, across Northern Germany to Amsterdam, braving the adverse weather conditions. 700 km in ice, rain and sleet.

The roads had been kept reasonably clear, and the sturdy tires of the all-terrain off-roader had kept them on a steady course. Mid-morning the next day, they had checked in, exhausted, at a cheap hostel in the city-centre nearby its Central Station. They collapsed face down on their rattling bunk beds, ignoring the other occupants of the dingy room. A group of Norwegians were getting ready for a day of sightseeing or as Jay presumed, it was more likely that they would spend the day hanging out in a coffee shop sampling the hundreds of weed varieties on the menu. Something Jay and his friends walked out to do too, once they woke up from their coma-like nap, wiping off cold roaches stuck to their damp foreheads and scratching bug bites in their necks.

A few bags of super skunk later, the boys ordered pint after pint of beer and finally, feeling lightheaded, they made their way to the BMX venue, on the fringe of the city centre. Jay wondered how they managed to avoid collisions with trams, cars, and the ubiquitous bikes emerging out of clouds of low fog, all the while following Frank's vague efforts at giving him directions, the city's map sprawled awkwardly across his lap, a joint dangling in the corner of his mouth.

They eventually found the place and walked, record crates in arm, into an old gymnasium that had been converted into a BMX street ground including stunt modules, ramps in various sizes and an accident-inducing half pipe. Just looking at it, Jay's joints ached in remembrance of his own attempt to master the tough sport.

He hadn't given up even after he had broken his shoulder in ten places from an unluckily timed backflip, and he would shrug off the numb pain caused by the metal pins screwed into his humerus bone. He had just started making a name for himself on the scene. He hadn't even minded the thick scar across his collar bone where the bone had pierced the skin. But a sprained wrist and a broken thumb later, he had preferred to keep his dexterity for drawing and making music, and had hung up his bike for good. Looking at the fresh talent bunny-hopping their way up the competition, flaunting their bike's shiny frames and colourful grips, Jay couldn't help but feel a stab of regret. He missed the blood, sweat and masochistic pain of pushing his body to the limit, something even the toughest gym session could not restore.

Instead, he kept his head down and concentrated on his set. A flawlessly executed warm up session, preparing the crowd for the post-competition party later that night. He always preferred taking his own turntables to a gig. The atmosphere was good despite the cold weather and the bikers competed with Olympian effort.

Later that night, as he took a break from his set, Frank walked up to him, and said: 'Jay, a few of us are going to do some late night sightseeing' Frank winked at him knowingly. Jay nodded with caution, and glanced over to the girls Frank was trying to convince to join them. They looked excited at being invited and giggled, their eyes sparkling flirtatiously.

Since his early teens, shrouded in a heavy cloak of sadness, he bore a sense of aloofness that his classmates often mistook for a detached arrogance. He never realised that his quiet demeanour, geeky passion for music, alternative sports and striking good looks attracted girls like moths to a flame. His father mocked him for being a hipster, he wasn't quite sure what that meant, but coming from his dad, it sounded like an insult.

The sultry Brazilian girl standing next to Frank was quite attractive, with long shiny hair she liked to flick and graceful limbs in masculine cargo pants. Her hand wandered up Jay's arm as she gazed expectantly at him. For a second, he felt tempted but then he shook his head. Even if things weren't going that smoothly with Aisha, he wasn't the type to gratuitously chat up girls. His face fell as he recalled their argument before he left Berlin. He didn't understand what was happening to them.

In their first two years together they had been so happy, he loved her and wanted to spend more time with her and naturally they had been discussing moving in together. It had made sense at the time. And then once they did, inexplicably, slowly and inexorably he had sensed a distance growing between them, a moody silence, dripping with resentment and peppered with arguments. Aisha was so damn beautiful, and whilst he once adored every inch of her, he grew tired of standing up to the greedy stares of the men in her path, and the wolf whistles in her wake.

She claimed he exaggerated and insisted that no one flirted with her, but he knew, he had seen it. The near imperceptible flicker of lust in the eye of the attractive barista when they picked up their coffees. She would pretend to ignore the longing gaze from the shopkeeper at the video store. Even his friends made no effort to hide their seedy admiration for her fitness instructor figure. He caught himself looking for signs of her infidelity. The fake coy looks she shot her clients at the gym, while parading her pert derriere in tight lycra. He hated her for making him feel so powerless and rejected. Despite often being told that he was an exceptionally good-looking man – tall, dark and chiseled – and that she felt she was lucky she had found him, looking in the mirror he had only ever seen the shadow of the man he was expected to be.

He had started criticising Aisha for wearing skirts that showed off her long lean legs and asked her to dress more casually, her jeans to be loser to hide her shapely curves, her t-shirts to minimise her chest and cardigans to cover her smooth arms. Even if she had agreed to comply with his unreasonable demands, which she hadn't since she had vehemently refused to even consider dressing to his whim, only a full body burka would have shielded her away from prying looks. In the end, it had been a ridiculous fight. Knowing he was being unreasonable, he had caved in, made a grovelling apology and hadn't breached the topic again since. It hadn't bettered their relationship.

She resented him for going out too much; 'You only live at night!' she had yelled slamming the door to her room in his face. Well, he had to, as a DJ wasn't that part of the job spec?

'You don't care about anything else!' she had screamed and she had meant the music. Well, surely he had to be good at what he did, so didn't he need to practice his set?

'You're not making enough money', she argued and he disagreed, he made enough.

'Your mother is right. You should really start thinking about your career', she meant taking over his dad's business. He had shook his head. Aisha didn't get it.

He had offered her the chance to come with him to Amsterdam to patch things up. He had envisioned them on romantic walks along the frozen canals, high with love and dope, boots crunching the fresh snow, breath steaming into cups of hot chocolate, kissing snowflakes off her eyelashes. But she had dispelled his sugarcoated fantasy with one acerbic "I hate your friends". That's where he drew the line. They were slightly unsavoury sometimes, he conceded to that, with their ever-increasing drug consumption and their philandering ways, but they were still his friends. His crew. His posse. They had his back. They would always extend an arm and a spliff to welcome him back from yet another depressing standoff with his mother and stepfather about his future. Jay didn't grant Aisha a response and turned on his heel, silently seething with anger. Flinging his duffle bag over his shoulder, he stomped off to work, leaving her standing in the doorway looking lost and tired.

Now he was here in Amsterdam, with his friends, it seemed easy to go along with the flow. Feeling the excitement of an explorer, he agreed to join the merry band when they suggested a late night excursion into the red-light district. After recharging their batteries in one of the various coffee shops lining the canal, the air thick with green smoke, rubbing shoulders with international backpackers and dubious-looking locals, they ventured out into the cold night. They ambled deeper into the dark narrow side-alleys, away from the hectic canal side and away from the ticket touts who spent their night luring groups of British stag dos to seedy shows The streets narrowed to the width of their shoulders, and they grazed the wet brick walls with their parkas. A soft red glow bled over the snow and illuminated their faces. And then he saw them. The narrow red windows. The writhing ladies waving at the punters with brash makeup and barely-there underwear. The boys lined up and started picking their favourites.

'Look at the tits on this one' The remark drew some wolf whistles.

'Plastic, all plastic' sniggers.

'Plastic is good!' shoulders shrugging.

'This one looks like she would know what to do with that tiny prick of yours.'

'Man, I couldn't she looks too much like your mum.'

'Fuck off at least she's not like your mother. Your mum's like a mosquito; you'd have to slap her to get her to stop sucking.'

The cat-calls fused as they goaded each other to put their inhibitions aside and knock on the window of their choice.

'Right, who is going in first?'

'I certainly wouldn't want to go in after you.'

They laughed collectively at their jokes laden with guilt, horniness and excitement. Jay withdrew further into the hood of his parka. Hiding deep behind the thick fur trim, he didn't want to be there. He was cold and tired. The adrenaline of his set had left him, and if he was honest, he longed for a warm bed, a joint and... Aisha's warm curves. He hadn't spoken to her since he had left Berlin. Thinking of her made him edgy. If only he remembered where the youth hostel was. He looked around. Every cobblestone street looked the same to him. Then he remembered the damp stink of the bedsheets and the bug bites he could still feel stinging the back of his neck, and thought that perhaps he wasn't looking forward to finding his way back there. His head ached.

That bitch. All she ever does is prance around town showing her ass off. She's just a gold digger. As the Heir of Adler Enterprises, she's got her bets on you.

Shut up, he thought. He didn't want Dan to talk like that about Aisha. He nervously fiddled with the cord of his headphones. He wanted to pull them over his ears and sink into the music, away from Dan's evil whispers.

'Jay, Hey! What's up? Which one are you going to go for? The ugly fat one that looks like Matthias' mother, or this one? ' Frank taunted him pointing at a raven-haired eastern European beauty with large breasts in nothing but a neon thong and suspenders and a pair of 12cm dominatrix heels. Jay looked at Frank's shiny red face; he was enjoying every second of this. Jay was going to pass, but Frank wasn't having any of it. He was fed up with Jay's somber mood over the past six months and insisted he had earned himself a bit of fun. His idea of fun. Jay shook his head, clearly they weren't on the same page.

'Make up your mind dude, I'm going for the platinum blonde one over here' he waved over to the last window at the end of the alley that hadn't drawn its curtain yet.

One after the other, each of the boys went in. Under the cheers and whistles, offering a salute, like gladiators going into the arena they tapped on the window and disappeared behind the heavy red curtains.

Nervously shuffling his cold feet in the snow, Jay took a gulp from the whisky bottle Matthias had handed him. It wasn't warming him up. His hands were freezing in his gloves. He tried to ignore the insistent whispering in his head and the sense of dread that hugged him tightly.

Come on you coward. Do you really think Aisha gives a shit, given half the chance she would fuck your best friend for money. And not hesitate a second. You know it.

The remaining guys gathered around him like a hungry pack of wolves, pushing and shoving each other, and started chanting:

'Jay, Jay, Jaaaaay. Are you gay, gay, gaaaaay.'

'Come on you fucking pussy.' They were all in this together. No one in the group was going to default and make them question their behaviour.

The raven-haired prostitute's smile had started to freeze on her painted face and made way for an exasperated grimace. This wasn't a joke to her, rather it was her livelihood, and he was holding up her business. She probably had rent and bills to pay, maybe an ill mother to support, or a child to send to university. He shrugged his shoulders. Walking in was half the problem.

He tapped on the window and with a stern face, she let him into the warmth. The door closed to the cheers of his mates that faded into a faint murmur, once she drew the thick curtain, shutting them off from the outside world. He looked around a white walled room, only big enough to fit in a small sink, a bar stool and a single bed. *No sleepovers allowed here then I guess*, Dan joked. Jay didn't know what to say. How does one behave in such a situation? Was he to shake her hand and ask her name?

'Hello', he muttered. She nodded without looking at him.

The place smelled strangely of disinfectant and cheap vanilla perfume. The prostitute switched a little portable CD player on and the small room filled with gipsy-style music. He listened to the first cords and suddenly laughed out loud. She looked up from oiling her large surgically enhanced breasts; her big kohl-circled eyes alight with surprise. 'Hey, I know this', Jay said. 'This is the soundtrack from the Yugoslavian movie 'Black cat, white cat'. She broke into an incredulous, genuine smile. She had beautiful straight white teeth.

'Not many people know this music' She drawled in a heavy-accented English. He nodded; he wanted to tell her how much he had enjoyed that eccentric gangster movie. How after much research he had finally found the record in one of the music shops in downtown Berlin. He wanted to tell her how he had weaved the music into his set. But he didn't. Her nipples stared at him. Her eyes meant business. She motioned him to sit on the bed. Obediently he sat down, not knowing where to look, the palms of his hands sticking to the plastic sheet covering the mattress. A nice touch. The plastic. He wondered how many clients had already sat their naked sweaty asses on this mattress. He was glad for the plastic cover.

She threw back her waist long gleaming black hair and stretched her back, pushing her breasts closer to his face. He swallowed hard. His pants stretched over his groin.

'You are good-looking man. Dark hair, green eyes, big hands. Like man from my country. Where you from?' She twisted her long lean legs outwards and slowly squatted down to his level and looked him straight in the eye with piercing blue eyes.

'Germany. Berlin', he whispered hotly, clutching at straws. Maybe they could just talk about their respective countries, discuss the atrocities of the second world war, terrorism, genocide, anything was going to be more pleasant than what followed.

'Good. Good. So what do you want? You get 20 minutes for Suck and Fuck. 50 euros. Cash. Any extras, boob touching, anal, toys. Cost extra. OK?'

Her guttural voice rasped over each vowel like she smoked two packs a day and washed it down with whisky. She probably did. But it didn't show, beneath the thick layer of trowel applied make up she looked young. He guessed her to be a couple of years older than him but not much more. Her voice turned him on more than her inflated chest. He weighed up his options. Apologising and leaving would piss her off and then he would also have to face endless jibes from his friends. He could offer to pay her the full fee and agree on drinking a cup of coffee until time ran out but then he wondered, never mind the awkwardness, if that would hurt her feelings.

He could tell her he was gay. He looked down at the bulk in his pants, and it was there for her to see that clearly he wasn't. She smiled as she undid his belt. In one fluid movement, she expertly zipped it off and whipped it on the floor with a loud crack that made him flinch. His mind fogged up. Dan was giggling victoriously in the back of his head wrapped in a dark blanket of headache, ready to strike him with a bolt of pain.

Through a hazy veil he saw her long fingers weave through the buttons of his flies, and within seconds she had fished a condom from a side pocket on her garter, ripped the cover with her teeth and rolled it over his cock with her mouth.

He gasped at the warm wetness, his mind made a feeble attempt to stop her, his hands wandering to her head, he fisted her hair to pull her away from him but when she cupped his balls, he surrendered to her rhythmic mouth movements. Her tongue ran up and down with professional enthusiasm, and he sunk back into the plastic cushions with a low moan. Her hands working the shaft of his cock, he felt waves of pleasure coursing through his body foreboding an intense climax. Suddenly it stopped. He opened his eyes to the red-lit room and found her at his feet taking his shoes and pants off. Getting up, she slowly slid her neon thong down her thighs. Time for the second part of the deal.

Something snapped in him, and he got up, grabbed her roughly by the neck, kissed her hungrily on the mouth ignoring her widening eyes as he shamelessly broke the no kissing rule. His voice thick with lust, he whispered in her ear:

'Please just continue what you started.'

He forcefully pulled her down to her knees, and as he held her firmly by her long black hair, he pulled her back to his groin. She obliged with more abandon the second time round, and he fell deeper and deeper into a bottomless well of lust. Soon every rational inhibited thought receded, fading into the background with one only animalistic thought remaining front of mind: fucking this girl's grotesque painted face. Hard. Selfishly. Guiltily. Vengefully. Helplessly. His orgasm was short and powerful.

As he slowly released his hand from her hair, stray strands hung lifelessly off his fingers. He pulled up his pants. Her eyes had watered, and mascara traced two black rivers down her cheeks.

Her red lipstick had stained where he had kissed her. She looked beautifully disheveled. Her fierceness had vanished, and she looked younger and vulnerable. She stood a little unsteady on her high heels and Jay carefully wrapped his arm around her shoulder. Her mouth opened and with a slightly confused look in her eyes, she seemed to lean in for another kiss. He wanted to wipe the tears from her face with a delicate finger but she recoiled and within seconds recomposed her face to the stern expression she had cultivated for so long.

'You happy?' she enquired with a bored voice, only her sparkling blue eyes betraying her attraction for him.

Happy? Not remotely, he thought but he nodded politely as ten tons of guilt crashed on his shoulders, in slow motion...Aisha.

'Kissing is not allowed, you know', the prostitute continued. 'I never do. For money'

'I'm sorry', and he was. His eyes shone as he looked at her earnestly. 'I don't know the rules. You were just... so good'. he blushed. 'I kind of lost... mmm... control'

She smiled lightly, flattered by the compliment and fished out the bundle of money from his trouser pocket. She swiftly counted the notes and locked them into a safe box.

'For you I make exception. You have something, raw, wild. But you are kind.' She tiptoed over and hung her slender white arms around his neck and gently kissed him on the lips.

'And fragile', she giggled. 'Yet so tall, so big', she glanced at his crotch and winked. 'So big'.

'Sorry' he offered.

'What for? Don't be, this is my job, handsome, my job', she winked again. Jay grabbed his parka as she turned to the sink to splash her face and sanitise her hands. A shiver crept up his spine as he opened the door, and the icy air pulled him back out into the freezing night.

The next day, they drove back to Berlin. It had stopped snowing, but Jay decided to remain cautious, fearing that the rain would turn to ice and transform the motorway into a lethal ice rink. His trusty Jeep hadn't given up on them, and the strong profile of the tires slushed through the snow. The boys were in a jovial mood and weed smoke steamed up the windows. Their banter was rife with salacious references to their encounter with the red light district girls the night before.

'Dude, that blonde chick was hot. A real centrefold, a fucking playboy bunny. Even the old Hugh Hefner would have married her. Those tits, man. They felt as hot as they looked.'

Frank had been particularly vocal about his sexual prowess and having been the last of them to resurface from behind the drawn curtains, he claimed the prostitute had begged him on her knees to stay longer and give him some more of the 'Frank loving'. The rest of them had laughed, and his comments sparked a laddish competition amongst them, each one trying to outdo the other in virility, endurance and 'special' requests.

Jay remained silent and concentrated on the traffic. He noted absent-mindedly that it had slowed dramatically since they crossed the border into Germany, and trucks and lorries had now claimed the road. Jay and his friends had been driving for what started feeling like an eternity. Snow covered the asphalt, the blue light of the motorway lamps faded and alighted endlessly, a monotonous pattern only disturbed by the red rear lamps of the trucks in front.

The headlights pierced through the fog, and Jay yawned, stretched his arms over the wheel and rubbed his stinging eyes, thinking that soon he would get Matthias to take over the next driving shift.

'You know what amazes me the most, is that that shit is legal and only in Amsterdam would you get prostitutes to pay taxes on their revenue. I mean, get this: the government makes money out of them wanking punters off. It's perverted.'

'Well, at least they're not scrawny heroin addicts. The girls are clean and, you got to admit, smoking hot.'

They agreed. Jay stayed silent. He didn't want to talk to them about his experience. He was fed up, consumed by guilt and just wanted the trip to end. He wanted to be home, and sleep for two days solid to make up for the lack of it over the past few days. The sweet smell of marijuana inside the car made his head spin.

Suddenly his vision blurred. He shook his head and rubbed his eyes again. As he reopened them, a white figure appeared in the middle of the road. A girl in an ankle-length white dress with long blonde hair shone eerily in the beam of his headlights. She slowly lifted her arms in front of her chest in a warning gesture. His reflexes instantly kicked into action. As he slammed on the brakes and yanked the steering wheel to one side, the Jeep swerved sharply to the right, narrowly avoiding colliding into her and skidded towards the hard shoulder. The car crashed into a roadside barrier and swivelled around 360 degrees. Jaws clenched and arm muscles tensed, Jay fought to regain control of his vehicle. A gasp of horror rippled through the car as all its occupants scrambled to grip onto something. To their right the 12-ton lorry they had been trying to overtake earlier swerved off its course in what seemed like slow motion. It crashed onto its side in the middle of the road. Missing the Jeep by centimetres. As the car spun around, Jay spotted the inflammable sign on the rear of the truck, flashing up in the headlights.

'Shit', he hissed, realising the imminent danger and slammed his foot on the accelerator to regain momentum. The jeep howled in protest and jumped forward. A loud crash echoed in their ears and the car shook. Looking in the rear mirror, Jay saw the truck behind them crashing into the one lying across the highway like a beached whale. A flicker lit up and suddenly the truck was ablaze in a loud roar. The Jeep sped off ahead, and the lake of fire shrunk in its rear window as they escaped the inferno.

For a while, they were too shocked to speak. Frank stubbed out his spliff and hugged his legs under his chin. 'Fuck, fuck, fuck'.

'Jesus guys, what the fuck just happened?' 'Did you see that ...explosion?' 'Fuck man.'

Jay stared straight ahead, his knuckles white from gripping the steering wheel tightly. They stopped at the first petrol station, a few hundred meters ahead and sat down for an instant cup of coffee. Although there was much head-shaking and incredulous swearing as they grappled to understand what had happened, it was clear to them that Jay's quick reaction had saved them.

The conversation hotted up, and they began to speculate wildly.

'I saw it had a Spanish license plate.'

'The driver probably fell asleep after speeding halfway through Europe to meet his employer's deadline.'

'He probably only fell asleep for a split second before he shot awake realising he was losing control.'

'He panicked as he saw the barrier he was about to crash into and braked, turned and skidded on the icy road.'

'Why did it blow up? From the warning sticker at the back, it probably contained flammable liquids, you know, explosives?'

Until Jay quietly said 'Guys, we need to call the police, and we better do it quick. God knows what happened to the driver and the other trucks that piled into him.'

Over the past hours, he had kept so quiet that they looked at him somewhat surprised to hear his voice. He didn't look up from his coffee, but his remark sparked a new debate. Most were in favour of not calling the police. They were high, and the car boot was filled with king size peanut jars. And upon closer inspection, as would the duly diligent German highway police undoubtedly do with a car full of red-eyed young men back from Amsterdam, they would quickly discover that when unscrewed and spooned into, the jars of peanut butter would be half full of creamy peanut butter, the rest being weed. They couldn't take that risk.

Jay excused himself and walked towards the bathroom. When he came back, they paid for their coffees and exited to the car park, ready to face the final leg of their journey back home. As they walked out, police sirens howled and several ambulances and fire trucks sped by in a haze of flashing lights. Jay looked at them and nodded knowingly. He was going to remain the anonymous tipper.

After he had dropped off the boys and after swearing solemnly, hands raised and all, that "whatever happens in Amsterdam, stays in Amsterdam", he drove back to the small flat he shared with Aisha.

The thought of her cold dark eyes both filled him equally with dread and excitement. He missed her, or rather the girl he met three years ago. She had been funny, relaxed and above all in love with him. Now, she hated him spending time with his friends. They were a bad influence; she said. To his immense shame, he now knew that she was right. This whole trip proved it. He smoked and drank and ended up getting his cock sucked by a prostitute. This wasn't right, at all. He needed to get a grip on his life before something else did. That included Dan, he needed to get rid of him, he was poisoning his judgement. *Muzzle him. Stop the drugs. Spend less time with my mates. Get a real job.* A real career that brought in more money than the shifts he pulled at his father's company. A proper day job instead of pulling all-nighters night after night, DJing and partying. Yes, he smiled to himself; this was going to be the dawn of a new beginning, a new style of life. The decision made him lighthearted, and he hummed along to the music in his head.

Little darling, I feel that ice is slowly melting
Little darling, it seems like years since it's been clear
Here comes the sun
Here comes the sun and I say
It's all right

He thought back to the girl in white on the road. She had stood there to warn him. Like a guardian angel. The thought of having one comforted him. Everything was going to be alright.

He parked the Jeep and walked to his flat, fumbling for the keys with stiff fingers. He was weary and longing for a shower. He hoped she would open the door with a smile on her face. It was still snowing and in the yellow streetlamp light, the row of parked cars shone eerily.

Suddenly he dropped his keys and stopped to look for them in the foot deep snow. He swore under his breath at the coldness on his bare hands, while he sifted through the snow. He looked at the car next to him and paused, keys dangling in hand. He knew that car. A silver Jaguar. A 1988 XJ. 'Unmistakably broad-shouldered and sleek cut, just like me' his stepfather would brag at dinner parties. Jay brushed the snow aside and there it was, the defacing scratch on the paint job from the time, when as a ten year old he had sneakily borrowed the keys, taken the prized car for a spin in the driveway and had tried to reverse the then brand new car into the garage. His stepfather had beaten him senseless and since had never been allowed anywhere near it again.

He wondered why his stepfather's car was parked in his street, it wasn't a dangerous area but it was a far cry from his stepfather's posh neighbourhood in the southwest of Berlin, when the front door suddenly swung open and a dark, tall shadow stepped out. He wore a felt hat and a long black cape. Jay instinctively backtracked to the wall and melted into the darkness. The man with the hat scurried past him, clutching an old-fashioned black leather doctor's bag in his arms. He walked to the car, paused to open the door and turned around to look up to the flats above. The permanent tan, the vainly plucked eyebrows, the square jaw and the light blonde hair with the nazi parting. *Caspar, what are you doing here?* Jay followed his gaze and looked up to the window on the first floor. The curtain swept aside, and a slim silhouette seemed to wave goodbye. Jay's eyes widened as he recognised her face and he cursed under his breath.

Caspar raised his hand to answer, turned on his heel, brushed the snow off the windshield and drove off.

The front door opened and as Aisha greeted him with a surprised look and an 'Oh I thought you were coming home tomorrow?', Jay couldn't get Dan to shut up whispering in his ear.

How come there was so much snow on Caspar's car?

***

Jay walked away from the window, sat down at his desk and wrote a few lines in his fluid handwriting.

'Dear Sophie, I hope you're well. Here are some photos I took of my latest graffiti. I hope you're coming to Berlin for Christmas.
Yours, Jay'

He stuffed the envelope, added the photos, and sealed it. Then he started crying.

CHAPTER 11

Solacium, August 2011 - 10 months after the incident

The radio blared in the background while the inmates sat at their workbenches. Despite the vacant look in their eyes, they tried, under the watchful look of the wardens, to concentrate on the task at hand. The air was stuffy with boredom, and a contagious yawn jumped from inmate to inmate. Jay had become quite skilled at tuning out the drag that were the asylum's communal activities and gratefully retreated into his bubble to entertain his own thoughts and hang on to flashes of his memories. They were his escape route, his treasures. The glowing thoughts of his memories were kept safe in a treasure chest which he was reluctant to open too often out of fear that the memories would fade too quickly, like polaroids in the sun.

Suddenly the song on the radio bore through his fogged up mind. Red Hot Chilli Peppers' Under the Bridge played and the soft guitar notes took him right back to the time he had roamed the city, homeless and free.

...Sometimes I feel Like I don't have a partner
Sometimes I feel Like my only friend
Is the city I live in
The city of Angels
Lonely as I am

Together we cry…

Rain drops obscured the view through the bars of the workroom windows, green hills blurred into the damp horizon. Occasionally an ominous black crow squawked into the summer rain. The repetitive sound of paper being cut, scissors clanking on tables and paint brushes spreading glue over cardboard and linen was hypnotic. Jay bit his lip in concentration as he meticulously folded the pages, flattened the pack and clipped them together. He picked up the thick bookbinding needle and pulled the red waxed thread through. Slowly he stitched the pages together, careful to keep a perfect alignment before he moved onto to fixing the hardcover. There was something soothing about this task; page after page, thread after thread, a book came to life in his hands. And it was always with a sense of completion that he would drop the finished, freshly bound book into the wicker basket on the wardens' desk.

Conscious of the skill required to master the artisanal art of bookbinding, Jay was keen to progress. He looked forward to perfecting his trade to graduate to the next stage which involved bound leather covers. He knew the books were destined to sit on dusty shelves in the city's library but he found it a comforting thought to know that perhaps a young student would find the answers to his philosophy thesis in the works of Nietzsche, Hegel, Kant and Schopenhauer that he had bound.

…I drive on her streets
'Cause she's my companion
I walk through her hills
'Cause she knows who I am
She sees my good deeds
and She kisses me windy
and I never worry
Now that is a lie…

He sighed at the paper-cut on his thumb and sucked on it pensively, the metallic taste of the blood filling his mouth.

Heinz, the sadistic warden with a nervous eye twitch, stared at him, wondering whether or not Jay's pause signalled rebellious behaviour.

Jay smiled apologetically and hurried to resume his task. He had learned fairly quickly that at Solacium, the warden was king and any form of rebellion against the rules was reprimanded severely. He had suffered the consequences many times after his initial protests, a week at a time in solitary confinement, food restriction and revocation of library access, so he had resigned himself to remain meek and docile.

Over time, his pacifistic tactic had come to fruition and he had finally reached security stage two. Under strict surveillance of an armed guard, he now had permission to exit the premises, to go food shopping at the village grocers. It had given him immense pleasure to set foot outside of the psychiatric hospital. He had been so excited that he had barely slept the night before. The ensuing disappointment of the awkwardness, when he spoke to the suspicious shop-keeper, had only slightly dampened his enthusiasm. He was happy to be outside and to have reclaimed a form of independence, albeit infinitely small. He had spent the little money he had painstakingly earned from his bookbinding job on basil, watery tomatoes and supermarket brand pasta. The meal he had cooked that night in the communal kitchen tasted like a delicious triumph. One step closer to freedom. One very small step.

***

Berlin, December 2003 - 7 years before the incident

Jay looked up from his coffee to see her come through the door. Her cheeks flushed from the icy winds; she wore a black parka with a hood so large it framed her face in snow-covered fur. She struggled through the thick curtain of the entrance, kicking it off her shopping bags with a snow-covered boot. She turned around somewhat flustered, and anxiously looked for him in the crowd. As he stood up and waved, she broke into a large grin. With a look of sheer relief on her face she waved back.

'Hi Jay! I'm so sorry I'm late, it's heaving with people out there, it took me ages to get here. Gosh I'm glad you're still here, I thought you'd gone already!' She bubbled, her grey eyes shining with excitement as she hesitated what to do next. Instead of hugging him, she plonked the bags on the floor, shook the snow off the big winter coat before flinging it on the chair Jay had pulled out for her. 'It's been a while', she exhaled.

'What would you like to drink?' he offered, smiling at the little blonde whirlwind.

'Hold on just a second, I haven't seen you in bloody ages, let me look at you' She stepped closer and looked him up and down, tugging at his arm. He looked skinnier than she remembered him, when they last met four years ago. The combination of a grey roughly spun wool cardigan, navy low-slung jeans and sturdy Red Wing boots gave him a rugged outdoorsy look that suited his tall frame. He had grown into a man, she joked with a wink.

'Don't embarrass me', he laughed.

'No, I mean it. Look at you, all trendy and handsome. So your dad told my dad that you are on your way to becoming famous? This music thing is really kicking off? Apparently you are DJing in clubs? I'd better ask you for your autograph now, before international stardom hits!'

'Yeah', he looked slightly uneasy, not sure whether she was mocking him. 'So are you just going to stare at me or can I get a hug?'

She laughed, a little surprised by the slight undertone of urgency in his voice, and threw her arms around his neck for a big bear hug. Jay held her closely and breathed in her perfume.

It was good to feel her slight body pressed against his, and the void in his soul suddenly didn't feel as deep anymore. Only now that she was here, a frail bird in his arms, did he realise just how much he had missed her.

They sat down; he waved the waitress over and, looking at Sophie he ordered her a cappuccino and another black filter coffee for himself. His childhood friend smiled as he remembered how she liked her coffee. The coffees came, guests joined at neighbouring tables, drank and left but the pair barely noticed, trapped inside a time bubble, they had eyes only for each other. Studying each other's faces, they looked for signs of ageing. He recognised the familiar crease above her eyelids that slightly slanted her eyes, so she looked like she permanently smiled. Her white blonde hair was cut shorter than the last time he had seen her. She looked happy. The coffees went cold, untouched, so they ordered another round.

'Was it really that long ago? Was the last time we saw each other at that Esoteric Escort party by the river?' , she flicked her straightened hair over her shoulder.

All too conscious that his hand on the table was only inches away from hers, he remembered the fateful night of the illegal rave party that had so unluckily descended into chaos. *If I stretch my fingers I could touch her.*

'Yep, it is that long ago. Man, that night didn't end too well', he said as he thought back to the anxious hours he had spent pacing the sterile corridors of A&E, desperate to know whether Sophie was safe while the surgeon stitched Aisha's forehead back together.

'Mmm yeah, you got into trouble, right?'

He had written to her that the police had confiscated all the equipment. He nodded at the painful memory.

'Did you ever get your record case back?' she continued.

'No.'

He winced at the thought of the rare bootleg recordings which now probably rotted as confiscated evidence in the archives of the police station. He somehow doubted Herr Hauptkommissar was keen on big beat and probably preferred Wagner to be played in his living room on Sunday afternoons.

'But I did some great community service, 12 months of cleaning public spaces. I picked a lot of chewing gum from a lot of park benches, and a certain church in Charlottenburg was particularly clean for a while', he smiled sarcastically.

'I bet your dad went apeshit.'

Jay's eyes darkened at the mention of his father. He had mentioned in one of the more recent letters to Sophie that things weren't that great with his family.

'Huh, yeah… we aren't on the best of terms.'

He was relieved when Sophie didn't dig any deeper, and when he asked about her life in London, she changed the subject to her recent promotion. After months of late nights at work, she had been promoted from her intern position to analyst on the trading desk at a big American investment bank. She was finally starting to make some decent money. Jay was equally appalled and intrigued by the macho world of greed she had joined. It was apparent from the confused look on his face that he couldn't quite understand what had motivated her to choose this career path.

'Out of all the possibilities you had, you voluntarily chose to go into finance? But why?' Lost for words, she thought about it for a bit, licked the foam off her spoon. Eventually she leaned forward and said earnestly:

'I'm not sure to be honest.' She laughed at the absurdity of her remark. 'It's a combination of different reasons I guess. I liked the challenge; it's a guy's world and I was keen to make a mark. I like the idea of understanding complex financial formulae, watch the world's economy unfold in rows on spreadsheets, predict trends and talk to interesting decision-makers. Plus I always had this geeky thing for mathematics. It's clean, logical and emotionless. Like a reassuring anchor in a chaotic universe.'

'Mmm yes, I get it, sounds so very interesting…' He mocked her gently while pretending to yawn.

'How do you parents feel about this? I bet they're proud', he said quietly, thinking of the frequent arguments he had with his parents and how time and time again they made no secret of how they deplored his poor career choices.

Her parents hadn't been that fussed, she replied. They were glad she found a job after getting her master's diploma, that she was happy and had earned financial independence.

'Although they both think this is just a phase, some sort of a rebellion. Kids always tend to do quite the opposite of what their parents expect them to become. And as both my parents are arty types and very creative, I had to find the diametrical opposite of their life ideology. I'm not sure I'm making much sense', she shook her head laughing. 'Ok, how about this: I somehow got the job, and it earns me quite a bit of money. Guess I was fed up growing up wearing hand-me-downs, being bullied and belittled. So I chose a job that encourages greed, bullying and belittling, and at least now I can afford better clothes.' She laughed some more and concluded 'I guess I just have something to prove.'

'You have nothing to prove. You're a forest nymph with an arrow and bow. With a steely core. I still don't entirely get why you want to work with a bunch of greedy wankers, but I'm proud of you. I guess it doesn't really matter where you work. What matters is that you are making something of yourself. You action your ideas and move forward. If only I had a smidgen of your steely determination, we could easily rule the world.'

'You mean us getting married, inherit your dad's publishing empire and control the news?' she smiled as she remembered their midnight teenage pledge, when they were sitting on the roof of their house on Ibiza, planning their future together.

'If it means saving you from withering away on your trading floor, why not?' he joked. She looked so small, Jay couldn't help but wonder if she ate enough. In one of her letters she had hinted at an eating disorder. He ordered them a plate of tapas. While she picked at the pickled olives, he wondered about her comment. *Us getting married.*

'Enough about me and my capitalistic career choices. So tell me, how have you been?' she asked. He knew she wanted to know whether he had a girlfriend.

Suddenly pensive, he looked out of the window into the dark streets of the capital, his brow knitted. Wrapped up passers-by rushed home from the stresses of last-minute present shopping. Bowing down to brace the icy winds turning snowflakes into tiny shards of ice, they were eager to return to the comfort of their warm living rooms and finish decorating their Christmas trees and pack their presents. He hadn't celebrated Christmas with his family last year. And he wasn't going to this year either. Instead he was going to get a volunteering job at the soup kitchen again. He was going to, just as he did the previous year, pack and post his gifts to his step brother and sister, and leave it at that. The thought of spending Christmas Eve alone sent a wave of anxiety through him, and he lit up a cigarette to distract himself from the lonely vision he conjured of himself.

'Well...'

Standing in the hallway of Aisha's apartment, the melting snow dripping off his boots onto the black linoleum, Jay looked at her beautiful face in the doorframe, unsure how to react. He just witnessed his stepfather leaving her flat, and he thought it was odd, because she always insisted that she didn't like the way Caspar leered at her. Jay thought of confronting her.

Ask her straight out, the voice whispered in his head. She looked at him with big blank eyes; the door was ajar, and the sickening sweet smell of incense floated into the cold, bleak corridor.

She shivered and pulled her cardigan over her lace vest top. He noticed the expensive looking french knickers and didn't remember having seen them on her ever before. A wave of rage overwhelmed him as he pushed her aside and walked into the flat.

'What the fuck is going on, it smells like a brothel in here!' he shouted, flinging his bag on the couch.

Hahahaha that's a fitting comparison considering where you have just come back from, Dan giggled.

The curtains were drawn, and candles bathed the place in an eerie light. He switched on the light and snuffed out the candles, one by one.

'What is the matter with you? I thought you were in Amsterdam with Frank until tomorrow! You come back unannounced and then you walk in here and shout at me? What the fuck is going on with *you*?' she yelled back.

He looked around the place for further evidence of her late night bootie call. A bottle of wine on the living room table, two empty glasses. He switched the jazz music that played softly in the background off and grabbed her by the arm and forced her next to him on the sofa.

'So, my darling, how was your evening tonight?'

His sudden change of tone was disconcerting, and Aisha looked at him suspiciously but knowing better, decided to go along with it, carefully. Catlike, she tucked her legs on the sofa while her eyes nervously flitted between her boyfriend and the wine glasses on the table.

'I'm fine thank you. A bit tired and was about to go to bed', she mumbled defensively, straightening a fold on her cardigan.

'What did you do?' he motioned over to the bottle of wine on the table. 'Did you have someone over?'

She squirmed slightly.

'It's not what you think it is. I can explain', she looked at him pleadingly, wringing her hands anxiously.

'Please, I'm all ears', he growled, feeling the anger well up in him like slow rising poison.

'I had someone over I needed to talk to', her voice quivered, and her eyes shone with fear. 'Jay this is difficult to say...'

You better come out with it, you bitch; I know exactly what you are about to say. More lies.

'... I...I...', her eyes welled up and a single tear rolled down her cheek.

I fucked your stepfather.

She breathed in and braced herself.

'I am pregnant.'

Jay sunk back into the sofa as if struck by lightning. The images in his head collided. The memory of the prostitute in Amsterdam, and the *deja vu* of his stepfather leaving his flat, merged with a vision of a tiny dark-skinned newborn. The thoughts in his head whirled together and then unravelled, loose ends snaking for answers. It didn't make any sense. He felt hot and nauseous.

'Jay, say something. Anything.' Aisha begged.

His throat was dry.

'Are you sure?' he whispered with a low croaky voice. *I am pregnant*. The words resonated in his head like church bells. In the three years they had spent together they had never discussed the baby issue. Moving in together yes, but they never talked about the next steps. Marriage. Children. And now...a baby. The perfect mix of their genes.

She nodded slowly while her eyes scanned him anxiously, desperately hoping for a reaction or some indication of his thoughts.

'But we were careful', he continued at last.

'Not careful enough', she whispered.

He was torn between feeling elated and a sudden sense of dread. Having a child required responsibility, a decent job, money. A home. They would need a real home. Not this hipster flat in the middle of one of the busiest areas in Berlin. They could move to the suburbs, have a garden with a swing. As he pictured a living room with toys and baby equipment piling up to the ceiling, he wondered whether it would be a boy of a girl.

'When did you find out?'

'A couple of days ago, but I have felt it for a while.'

He continued to fantasise about a cute dark skinned toddler with green eyes. His legacy. His chest filled up with joy and then suddenly he was all too aware of the two glasses and the wine bottle on the coffee table.

'Who was here tonight?' he demanded an answer staring at the glasses he noticed one was still half full.

She sobbed quietly, 'Caspar.'

Jay nodded in disgust.

'Why was he here?'

'Please don't shout, I called him. Don't look at me like this Jay. I didn't know what to do. You and me had a fight; you were gone and didn't call me. I didn't know where you were, and I needed to talk to a doctor.'

'But you could have called your regular GP, why him? You know I don't trust him.'

Sunday lunches at home had been increasingly nightmarish since Caspar had started to make no effort to hide his obsession with Aisha. It had started with a few compliments on her appearance and then Jay caught him leeringly glancing across the table, his hand always seemed to be on her arm unnecessarily or on her waist. His sly derogatory remarks on how such a clever and gorgeous girl like her could date a failure like his son were supposed to be said in jest but stung deeply. Jay had started to loathe him quietly, not only because he was shamelessly flirting with his girlfriend, but also because he couldn't stand that he was referring to him as his 'son'. What right did this man have over him? The visits to his parents had since then been kept to a minimum. And on the rare occasions that his sweet sister could convince him to come, he grew increasingly aware of the uncomfortable atmosphere whenever Caspar was around her. Jay felt increasingly protective of his sister Milana having to share the house with her adoptive father. *Yeah he totally is a cheat and … a paedo* hissed Dan.

'I couldn't see my regular GP. I... I ...needed to talk to your stepdad about...', she hesitated and wiped the tears of her cheeks.

'Is it mine?' He couldn't look at her. She hesitated just a moment too long.

'Of course it is yours', her voice was shaking.

Look how she hesitated? That's because she's lying. It's not yours. He wished Dan would just shut up and stop planting these allegations in his head.

'How do I know you're not lying?'

'Please believe me. You're doing it again', she pleaded, more tears pooling at the corner of her eyes. He looked irritated and breathless as he got up and started pacing around the room.

'Please stop being so paranoid. This insane jealousy needs to stop, Jay. I can't take this anymore.'

Frozen and statuesque, her cheeks wet with tears, she looked down at her feet and whispered with a voice so quiet it was as if she didn't want to hear the words she was saying.

'I don't want to keep it' she sobbed.

She wants to abort the child, because its Caspar's. He wants no traces of his affair. He's paying her to get rid of it.

'Jay, you make no sense. Listen to yourself, I beg you. Please stop. What do you think of me?' Only then, he realised Dan had managed to speak the words through his mouth.

Once he recovered his own voice, Jay tried to reason with her, and he gave her all the possibilities if they kept the baby. He was going to give up the night gigs, get a well-paid day job. He was going to quit smoking weed and stop seeing his destructive friends. He told her about the near accident on the motorway back in Amsterdam and that an angel had saved him. He said it was a sign, a good omen. She didn't believe him; she had heard it before. He was always full of good intentions, but the lure of the illicit life always took the upper hand. He didn't tell her about the prostitute. And she didn't tell him she knew about all those nights he awoke next to her, eyes wide in terror begging Dan to leave. She didn't mention that every time he had one of his depressive episodes, she had the feeling that something was irreparably wrong. Although he always tried to hide it, she knew that sometimes he would become so paranoid someone was out to get him that Jay would refuse to leave the flat for days on end. But she chose not to tell him.

She had to promise him not to ask his stepdad for advice again, and instead see her regular GP and in return he hadn't mentioned his suspicions to her again. Although deep down, he knew. When she went ahead with the abortion, he came with her to the clinic. He held her hand and with every second the procedure came closer to completion, he felt bits of his soul evaporating into the disinfectant-heavy air, freeing up space for a growing pool of hatred aimed at the man he considered the source of their pain. Caspar.

Numbness had settled into them as a coping mechanism. They buried themselves in their everyday boring routine while he desperately tried to be there for her as she mourned the unborn baby they had killed, but she was cold and distant. He kept his promise and gave up smoking. He seldomly drank more than a couple of beers. And on his resident DJ nights in the underground club he went home straight after the end of his set rather than hanging out in the VIP lounge as he used to do. His mind was clear and strong. Dan had been good and had rarely manifested himself. He applied for a masters at the Berliner Kunstakademie, one of the most renowned arts and music schools in Germany and when he received the acceptance letter, he had never felt so proud. He took classic art courses and digital design. He had started playing the drums again and every now and then played at jam sessions at Club Baudelaire, a dimly lit jazz club buried in the backstreets of Kreuzberg.

It seemed to all be coming together for him, but Aisha refused to see it. The relationship had changed for good, and even if they both tried to hold on to golden memories of their once so perfect relationship, the cracks started to show. Then one day he woke up, and she was gone. She had packed her bags during the night and stuck a lonely note to the refrigerator: 'I'm sorry'. Falling off the wagon had never been so easy.

***

Jay breathed in slowly. The air was cold and smelled of grass and humid soil. He extended a hesitant hand and felt a soft carpet of moist leaves under his fingers. His body ached in unusual places. He opened his eyes an inch to a blurry daylight. The world presented itself to him in soft focus, and as the mist lifted slowly, he looked straight into two small black shiny pupils.

'Hello!' it said cheerfully and hopped closer. Jay's eyes widened in surprise. Careful not make any brisk movements, he sat up. A bunny. A soft fluffy white bunny. It sat on its tail only a short metre away from him, twitching its nose curiously.

'Hello!' it said again in the same playful tone and sniffed the air. Jay felt his mouth drop open in wonder. Another rabbit peeped from behind a daffodil and sniffed the air. And another one hopped over from behind a rock and looked at him with its head cocked to one side

'Hello!' it echoed in the same voice. Within moments he was surrounded by a whole army of small white rabbits, all fluffy with twitchy noses and bushy tails, looking at him, their cute little heads to one side, seemingly expecting an answer.

'Hello!' 'Hello!' 'hello!' a wave of hello's echoed from one edge of the clearing to the other. 'Huh?' Jay croaked, his vocal cords refusing to function properly. His throat was dry, and his head swam. The rabbits squeaked in unison at his unwelcoming greeting and hopped a few inches backwards into the bushes from where they had emerged. He frowned and stared at the bushes for a few moments, expecting them to reappear. But nothing moved. He scratched the stubble of his three-day beard and looked down at his feet. He was fully dressed, wearing the same clothes he had stepped out in the night before. He removed a few leaves that clung to his elbow and wondered what the fuck he was doing here in the middle of what seemed to be a deserted park. *Full of rabbits. Talking rabbits as well. What the hell was that about?*

He had no recollection of how he got here in the first place. As he slowly got back to his feet, a sudden surge of dizziness forced him to seek balance against a thick oak tree. Nausea brutally took hold of him and as he lurched forward he emptied the contents of his stomach against the tree trunk.

Wandering out of the park, he realised it was the Berliner Tiergarten he had chosen to wake up in. As he walked out into the sleepy Sunday morning city, he wondered, somewhat perplexed, at how he got here in the first place. Still feeling out of sorts, he vaguely remembered starting the evening by drowning his sorrows in a glass of wine, or had it been a bottle? He shook his head, knowing he had probably overstepped the mark again. He had been at home, on his own, shutting himself off from the rest of the world, unable to pick up the phone to his friends.

What was he going to tell them anyway? That he sometimes felt like he couldn't breathe? That he could spend hours lying on his back unable to lift a finger, that he desperately wanted to cry but no tears ever came? His so-called friends were only interested in seeing the confident and funny Jay, not the train wreck he had become since Aisha had left him to return to live with her parents. The doorbell had rang and rang, and when he refused to open the door, Frank had climbed up the drain pipe and knocked on the window. Startled, Jay's heart jumped in his throat, and he was ready to push the intruder back out the window when he identified the hooded stranger in his window as his best friend. Frank, persuasive as ever, had dragged him to a house party, where more alcohol was consumed, a bit of weed had made the rounds. And some of the guests suspiciously kept disappearing into the toilets from which they emerged rubbing their noses excitedly and grinning somewhat manically. Jay had kept to himself most of the evening and only took a quick drag from one of the passing joints, while he found it more and more difficult to converse with his increasingly high friends.

He remembered walking home later that night, it had been a long way from Prenzlauer Berg to his flat in Kreuzberg, and he tried to hitch a ride on the night bus. Maybe he fell asleep on the bus, he wondered. It hadn't been the first time this happened to him, and in recent months, around the same time Aisha had moved out, he had started waking up in the most improbable places. Once he woke up in a paper recycling bin, wrapped in newspaper to keep warm. The following week it had been a gusty wind that had woken him on the top of an 18-storey building. Lying close enough to the edge that when he lifted his head the city unfolded below in panoramic view. A couple of times he had woken up under an upturned boat by the river shore, smelling of turpentine, his clothes smeared with boat paint. Every incident had the same narrative; he had no recollection of how he got there. His memory was a black hole. For a while, he tried to figure out what triggered the blackouts, whether it was the drugs or the drinking. *Probably both, you idiot*

Suddenly a memory hit him with such unexpected force that he stopped dead in his tracks. Cars honked in the distance and swerved past him in slow motion while he backtracked to the pavement, shaking.

Frank. The memory clicked into place. Frank was arguing with this guy, Michael, an unpleasant heavyset part-time dealer with a permanent acne outbreak on his chin. Someone owed someone else money; Jay wasn't sure what caused the outburst but guessed it was about a deal that had gone wrong. It didn't help that Frank had been reasonably drunk, possibly high on cocaine and was itching for a fight. They had taken it outside, and a few fists flew. Frank and his friends had quickly overthrown the dealer and pinned him to the floor. Someone had pulled out duct tape, and they proceeded to tape the poor sod to the nearest tree in the garden. Laughing and taunting him they had rifled through his pockets and relieved him of his abundant drug stash, not before selecting a few strips of LSD which they forced into the dealer's mouth, duct-taping it shut. A lesson, should his brain survive the meltdown the powerful hallucinogenic drug would most certainly induce, he would never forget.

A deep feeling of anxiety spreading, Jay had seen the whole scene unfold before his eyes. And although he felt no pity for the unsavoury character when he got taped to the tree, he did object to subjecting him to chemical torture. He had yelled to stop Frank from sending the guy on a one-way trip to hell, and ripped the duct tape off the poor idiot's mouth to retrieve the lethal dosages.

But when he finally succeeded to shake off Frank and remove the strips, the drug had already entered the damned dealer's bloodstream, his eyes had rolled back in his head. And he had started grinning uncontrollably.

Jay sat down on the pavement as the sun rose, and he remembered the actions of the night before in vivid colours. He shook his head in horror. How had Frank allowed this to happen? What had possessed him?

That had possibly been one of the cruelest forms of torture to inflict onto another human being. The incapacity to differentiate between reality, and drug-induced hallucinations like giant hairy spiders crawling under one's skin, and an uncontrollable heartbeat threatening to burst through ones thinning chest. Elation fighting despair and the sheer terror of not ever coming back. *The poor guy, I know what that feels like.* For all his small-time crookedness, the dealer hadn't deserved a punishment that destructive. The only thing Jay had been able to do was to call an ambulance and ruin the party.

Still trying to piece the events of the previous night together, Jay reckoned he must have left at around the time the ambulance arrived and had wandered off in the night on his own before blacking out. By the time he got up from the pavement and bought himself a cup of coffee, he had made up his mind. He could not go on like this. He didn't want to be associated with people like Frank, who was clearly going off the rails and was likely to lead him astray as well if he stuck around. Last night had been the wake up call he needed. No more hanging out with that psychopath Frank, he vowed. Secondly he needed to tackle the blackouts. Waking up in increasingly strange places conversing with rabbits wasn't a sign of good mental health. He worried about his alcohol addiction. And there and then, as the spring sun spilled over the pavement into the coffee house, he decided to check himself into rehab.

***

'Oh' Sophie looked him straight in the eye and wasn't sure what to say. Avoiding her piercing stare, he looked over to the bar discreetly waving at the waitress for the bill. It had stopped snowing, and the streets were emptying.

'So when did you come out of rehab?' she whispered.

He shifted in his seat. 'Two days ago'.

'Oh.' Silence. She hadn't expected this. 'What about your parents?'

'My dad was shocked but welcomed the decision when I told him about the blackouts, the drugs and the drinking.'

'And what about...' She hesitated for a second.

Jay angrily tossed his spoon into the empty coffee mug 'That asshole? I haven't spoken to him since.'

She had meant Aisha, for whom for some reason she still harboured uncontrollable feelings of jealousy, for she had been the perfect one that had charmed her way into her Jay's heart, Aisha, the poisonous temptress.

'Caspar?'

Jay nodded silently 'I wish he would just die and give me back my family', he whispered. The suppressed undertone of hatred in his voice sent shivers down Sophie's spine.

The waitress came with the bill. After paying, they slipped into their furry parkas and headed out into the snow.

CHAPTER 12

Solacium, September 2011 - 11 months after the incident

'Are you feeling any better?' Sophie asked cautiously, as she paced around her bedroom, the handset glued to her ear, aware her question might upset her friend.

'What do you mean? Like generally? Yeah, I feel more in control of my thoughts now... well, most of the time at least.'

She knew he wasn't telling her the truth; she could hear it in his voice. She didn't like it when he pretended things were okay when in fact they weren't.

'Jay, you know what I mean, the morning sickness?'

A few months ago, he had told her that he would wake up every single morning with nausea so severe he would throw up the medication he had just swallowed. The nausea would carry on through breakfast and only much later in the day would he feel well enough to able to hold down a slice of toast and glass of milk. Sophie had been alarmed at the news and together they had evaluated the possibilities.

Was it the new drug dosage? Was he allergic to something he had eaten? Was he sick? The most disturbing theory was one she kept to herself and she had only asked one question.

'Is Dan back?'

Jay had firmly denied it, but she couldn't shake off the scary thought. Trapped in a psychiatric hospital, the grimmest of places. Incarcerated for probably the rest of your life with a horde of schizophrenics and psychopaths and other deranged individuals. Guarded by a group of sadistic wardens and incompetent psychiatrists. And you so desperately seek an escape, what other option is there? How would you kill yourself without any ropes, or knives or glass shards? Would it be possible to just not eat anymore? Throw up anything you swallowed? She shuddered at the thought.

'Well, the nausea is still there. But you know, on the bright side, I've lost a lot of that excess weight, so when you come for a visit at Christmas, I'll be a lot trimmer.'

'Jay? Have you spoken to your psychiatrist about this?'

'Yeah, sort of but you know she just seems to nod and then scribbles something on her notepad. I don't think she cares much, although she did ask me the same question about Dan.'

'She would. What do you think causes it?'

'I don't know. I wake up and before I even open my eyes, I can sense them next to me. The others. I can smell them. I can hear them. And they repulse me. Another day in their company. Another day where I get thirty minutes in the morning to walk around the courtyard and another thirty minutes in the evening. At least I'm no longer wearing those hand and foot cuffs so I can actually walk and not shuffle along like cattle in chains. Sophie, every day in here is so desperately dull and grey. I have no means to escape or find some solitude. Even in my head. I'm constantly observed and someone with a notepad is always writing those observations down. If you don't participate in group activities, you get a warning. After three warnings they withdraw your library access. You know what the group activities are? Debating on your fantasy football team. I fucking hate football. I would rather stay in bed all day than mix with these idiots and their imaginary football tournaments.'

Despite the tragedy of the situation, she couldn't help but giggle. They had both hated football as teenagers and had often mocked Frank for being a proud Hertha BSC fan. Spurned on by her laughter, he continued to rant about the life as an inmate at Solacium. He told her about his roommate who hid food under his mattress, forgot about it and then wondered what caused the pungent smell of rot that regularly flooded their shared room.

Jay's other roommate slept with one eye open – 'for real Sophie, I don't know how he does it!' – for fear that Jay would pounce on him in his sleep and slit his throat.

'With what? My fingernails? I should be more afraid of him, apparently he drove a screwdriver through his wife's eyeball. Then there is this other nutter George, I nicknamed him Meatball, who always insists on sitting next to me at lunchtime and systematically pokes at my food. Every fucking meal. To test if it's warmer than his. If only he didn't scratch his balls all the time.' They snorted in unison until suddenly their laughter died out and the familiar subdued feeling seeped back into their conversation as if suddenly something pulled them back into the darkness.

'Jay, promise me you'll get help for the morning sickness. I'll call you back soon. Stay strong', she whispered and hung up.

***

Berlin, January 2004 - 6 years before the incident

The silent city was asleep under a thick blanket of new year's snow. The dimly lit streets were eerily empty. A cold wind blew snow whirls over his boots as he crunched through the snow-covered streets towards home. His breath steamed in the icy night as he buckled under the burden on his shoulders. A thin layer of ice had crusted over the snow, and he walked slowly, careful not to slip. As he stopped by his front door and fumbled for his keys, the hooded bulk on his back shifted and moaned.

He looked over his shoulder. The girl half opened her eyes; her makeup had run, and the dark circles under her eyes looked like bruises. She wiped the corner of her mouth with a gloved hand and hiccupped loudly. He smiled forgivingly. She'd had too much to drink. He didn't blame her; it had been a great party. He hadn't expected so many people would turn up. It had only been his second gig at the club, but by word of mouth the place had soon been heaving with people. The owner, Patrick Steinberger, one of Berlin's up-and-coming party promoters had patted him on the back and yelled with a whisky-infused voice; 'You got pulling power man, I like that. Look at all these beautiful young ladies. They are all here for you. Make the most of it', he winked.

Jay carefully shifted the girl off his shoulders, lowered her to the ground and steadied her back against the entrance door to his flat. He looked at her and his heart melted. Her white blonde hair spilled out from under her beanie hat, and she looked disheveled and vulnerable. Jay felt a familiar pang of desire rushing through him, a disconcerting mix of protective instinct and lust.

She is so beautiful. As if she heard his thought, Sophie smiled a dreamy smile and slowly slid to the snow-covered ground, her arms and legs floppy like a rag doll. He gently scooped her up and opened the door with a leg kick and carried her into his flat, straight into his bedroom, and eased her onto the bed.

Patrick Steinberger had been right; the women had all looked glamorous in their slutty high heels and tight, sequinned dresses barely covering their assets. But he hated how they shimmied up to the DJ booth and fawned over him, batting their grotesque fake eyelashes. *I wish they wouldn't try so hard.* He ignored them and had instead asked Sophie to join him behind the decks for an impromptu set. She had met him at the club earlier that day, and he had been keen to show her a few tricks on the decks. To his surprise she had been rather good at matching beats. Headphones screwed on, she had mocked his signature impassible face, although he was quite sure he never pouted like her duck face suggested. She danced around the DJ booth, giggling, and lifted her hands dramatically to the ceiling to motivate an empty dance floor. It had the rest of the club staff in stitches as they prepared for the big new year's eve party. He faked great offence and had dared her to play the two songs as he had taught her, only this time with an audience. Later that night, after a few beers, she had given in and joined him behind the decks. Her bravado was only a front, and she cut a contrasting figure standing next to him in tiny velvet black shorts and knee high boots, half his size, her hands shaking.

Sophie tried to curl up as he removed her snow-covered boots and steadied her legs. He went to pick a clean shirt from his wardrobe to find her sitting up looking at him with a vague stare. He noticed her eyes were red-rimmed and she looked terribly pale. *She still looks stunning.* She wasn't wearing a bra under her t-shirt, and when she slipped the oversized shirt over her slender frame, Jay quickly had to look away. She didn't bother doing the buttons, mumbled a slurred 'thank you' and slumped back into the cushions while Jay sat on the edge of the bed, removing his shoes and trying to control his growing erection.

Her white-blonde fringe hanging low in her eyes, she had bit her lower lip in concentration, her right hand clamped over the headphones while her left hand hovered over the vinyl in anticipation. He had laughed when she missed a beat, and the needle skipped off the record. The music stopped abruptly, and she had stared at the crowd, her eyes wide with growing panic but he had been quick to rectify the mistake for which she thanked him for with a grateful smile.

Stripped to his boxers, Jay curled up next to her on the bed, his body tired but his mind awake. He looked at her, fast asleep, breathing softly, her head next to his. He hadn't drawn the curtains, and the faint glow of the street-light softly lit her face. She looked peaceful and innocent. With every breath, her long lashes quivered under the dense layer of mascara. The red lipstick had smudged a bit where he had kissed her, and the memory of the kiss hardened him some more. He bit his lip and worried, as he slowly felt one his headaches brewing. He wondered, irritated, whether it was sexual arousal that triggered the blinding headaches. He reached out for the pills on his bedside table.

After he'd finished his set, they hit the bar. Relieved she had survived public humiliation, she had challenged him to tequila shots, even though she stood no chance of winning. Midnight came and went, and they stumbled into the new year with a drunken kiss. A kiss that made him long for more. Her soft lips felt incredible against his. He loved the taste of her tongue and her body pressed against his.

They had danced and laughed. High on life and alcohol they had felt eternal, young, careless and endlessly happy to be in each other's company. Too drunk to drive and too high to bother trying to find a cab, they had staggered off into the night, arm in arm, their loud laughs echoing in the night. Her high-heeled boots hadn't been the best choice for a walk home in the snow. And when she complained she couldn't feel her feet anymore, he lifted her up and carried her the rest of the way.

Now she was snoring softly next to him, and when he bent over her to delicately push a stray strand of hair behind her ear, he noticed the shirt had shifted slightly, exposing a small pert breast. He swallowed hard and the temptation to extend his hand to touch her overwhelmed him. He closed his eyes and reached out slowly.

Rapist!

He flinched, his hand immediately retracting and scanned the room cautiously, wondering where the voice came from. He narrowed his eyes. A menacing shadow hovered above his desk.

Go ahead. Touch her. She won't mind; she is passed out.

Jay shivered. Lately, Dan had become more than a creepy voice in his head; he could now see him. A dark silhouette with long spindly fingers, blending into the shadows, barely visible but every time more explicitly ordering instructions that Jay found, absurdly, increasingly difficult to resist.

During an episode, he now felt more and more like the puppet and Dan the master. Unable to resist, his fingers slowly caressed her breast.

You like that, don't you? You dirty horny lowlife.

He did, and he hated himself for it. Her skin was soft, and her nipple hardened under his touch and all he wanted to do was to take it into his mouth. Suddenly Sophie stirred in her sleep, and he retracted his hand, slid off the bed and walked into the kitchen. Wiping the sweat of his brow and catching his breath, he poured himself a glass of cold water. This wasn't right.

When he had leaned in for another new year's kiss, Sophie had gently put a finger on his lips and with a sad smile had told him that she had a boyfriend who she loved and that she and him could only ever be friends. Of course, didn't she always have a boyfriend? *The lucky bastard.* He had dismissed her plea with all the aloofness he could muster, all the while fighting to repress the overwhelming feelings of anger, jealousy and loss bubbling up in him. He turned to the bar and downed another tequila.

'Where is he tonight?'

Away on business, she had said with a hint of defiance in her voice. His loss, Jay had thought, and he had whirled her away from the bar and back onto the dance floor.

Get the knife, Dan ordered.

Jay looked at the kitchen knife gleaming on the sideboard. Its blade shimmered dangerously in the moonlit kitchen, and Jay extended his hand to grab it. When he slid a finger along the paper-thin edge, the blade effortlessly cut into his flesh.

Feel how it cuts through your skin like butter. It feels good doesn't it? Like ...deliverance. Dan's shadow lingered on the kitchen wall.

Jay picked up the knife. It was heavy and powerful in his hands.

I know a way she could be yours forever, the evil voice resonated in his head as if Satan spoke to him directly from the hellfire pit.

Slowly Jay lifted the blade to his face. In its reflection, his eyes shone dark and emotionless. Dan's dark shadow spread across the wall, long bony fingers clawing along the curtains and crawling up the ceiling. His sinister giggle echoed in Jay's thoughts.

***

Sophie rolled over, extending her arms to her sides, and her fingers slid through the soft cool silk sheets of an unfamiliar bed. Suddenly she opened her eyes in shock. *Oh god*, she thought, and through a hazy tequila fog, she struggled to remember where she was and how she got there. The left side of the bed was empty. She peeked under the blankets, and noticed she was wearing someone else's shirt. Panic rose inside of her and her mind raced. *Where am I?* In the soft winter sunlight shining through the windows, the bedroom looked tidy and inviting. She gingerly threw back the expensive cashmere blankets and slid into a pair of plush black bath slippers waiting for her by the side of the bed.

The carpets were thick, and the pattern oozed exotic craftsmanship. The dark wooden bookshelves overflowed with hardbacks and upon closer inspection it turned out the owner of the room had a penchant for travel guides, design, photography tutorials and French classics like Baudelaire's Les Fleurs du Mal, and Le Horlas by Guy de Maupassant. The shelves covered half of the wall, and as she walked past rows and rows of books, she noticed that each one of them had bookmarks. It wasn't the usual cardboard bookmark, they all were pages of newspapers painstakingly folded to fit the individual sizes of each book.

Her index finger trailed on the covers until she stopped and folded back one of the bookmarks on Immanuel Kant's 'Critique of pure reason'. The date on the top of the newspaper read 23 January 1999. She wondered if the owner of these books had indeed read all of the books and that the bookmarks were there to remind him of passages he had liked. Or if indeed he had just inserted them randomly to pretend to be well read. Next to Kant she found a small silver frame with a black and white photo of a young woman, in her twenties, with long hair and a flower pinned above her ear. She looked ferociously beautiful with big intense eyes. The next frame hid behind an Anthropology tome, as she turned it around she looked into a young handsome face. She noticed the same intense eyes. His were green. She recognised this boy, in a classic white polo shirt and beige shorts, standing next to an expensive looking car, a Jaguar as she identified the iconic panther on the grid. It was Jay. He must have been about ten years old and judging by his intense frown into the camera, he seemed deeply unhappy to have his picture taken. In the background, she noticed two small babies peering out of an old-fashioned pram.

She carefully put the frame back, out of sight behind the book and sighed in relief. She had woken up in Jay's flat, not some random stranger's home. In her drunken state, she couldn't remember most of what happened after that wretched painfully embarrassing moment when she had tried to impress Jay and stepped into the DJ booth. What a failure she had felt when she messed up. Luckily there had been plenty of tequila shots to numb the shame, but after about her seventh shot she couldn't remember much about how she got back to his flat.

She wandered over to his desk, ignoring her rumbling stomach. A simple white surface, upheld by metal trestles, the desk was a chaotic mess of pots of pens and pencils. A dark palette of acrylic paint tubes and brushes of all shapes and sizes nestled between sheets of thick paper and canvas, some blank, some covered in black and white kohl sketches. She picked up the one on top. It showed a young girl with long flowing hair, sleeping in a curled up position on a large bed, wearing nothing but a loose shirt and exposing a small breast. A dark shadow descending from the ceiling seemed to pray menacingly on her with long spindly fingers, ready to pounce. The sharp strokes of the pencil had captured the scene's raw horror, and a strange sensation of *deja vu* made her shudder as she carefully put it back onto the stack of drawings.

Next to the desk stood an easel with a half-finished painting of a black cat. The painter's style was quite abstract, and the canvas had been splattered with layers of blood red paint from which the cat emerged, clawing its way out the bloody mess with glistening fur and white narrowed eyes. She stared at it for a while, wondering why her friend seemed so obsessed with such darkness in his work. No doubt he's talented, she thought, but she wasn't sure whether she liked it. Noticing a further twenty or so canvasses neatly stacked on the wooden floor, she carefully flicked through them. There was unquestionably a reoccurring theme to his work; they seemed all to have been painted in great haste and violence, the colour heavy and bleeding into the linen in broad angry strokes. But at the same time they exuded a great vulnerability, the lone figures in them seemed both lost and overwhelmed by a stormy force beyond their control.

More than once she noticed the subjects in the paintings appeared desperate to escape their predicament, forced out of their position to flee from an encroaching dark matter, threatening to engulf them. Looking at the nightmarish scenes depicted she felt fascinated, if not slightly uneasy. Suddenly her eye was caught by a canvas right at the back of the stack. Backed up against the wall and half hidden by the thick curtains, it was larger than the other paintings and showed a grotesque grown man devouring a child. The white bulging eyes of the man shone with madness. His mouth gaping and bloody, he feasted on the torn limb of the lifeless infant. It reminded her of the Goya painting she had once admired in the Museo del Prado in Madrid. At the time she had thought the Spanish painter was a visionary, symbolising the Spanish fatherland sacrificing its children to a useless war. Now looking at Jay's interpretation of it, she somehow knew this wasn't related to history of any kind apart from his own.

Pensive and intimidated, she pushed the painting back against the wall and folded her arms. His gothic style didn't quite fit the genteel demeanour of the man she had known for over ten years. 'Maybe this is his dark phase', she mumbled. Shocked at the sound of her own voice, she quickly turned to the door, suddenly aware that Jay had to be somewhere in the flat. She didn't want to get caught snooping through his belongings.

She stepped to the door and peered into the hall. It was dead quiet. Rays of pale winter sun streamed softly through the windows and dust sparkled in the air. Wearing the fluffy slippers, she quietly tiptoed into the kitchen and held her breath. The place was a spotless chrome and white space, a huge American double fridge stood next to a professional steam oven. The sink was an old fashion white ceramic trough with a matching water pump instead of the usual tap. She stepped forward onto a gorgeous blue-and-white, Moroccan inspired mosaic-tiled floor. The kitchen looked a flawlessly tasteful mix of classic fixtures and modern equipment. She had known her friend was a passionate cook, but she hadn't appreciated to what extent. She who couldn't cook to save her life and once managed to burn a boiled egg, marvelled at the neatly-stowed Mason jars on the shelves. Rows and rows of small glass jars, all marked with labels written in tidy handwriting, displayed dried sage, shiitake mushrooms, vanilla pods, saffron threads, black peppercorns, sea salt flakes and more. On the kitchen island, next to the inbuilt electric waste disposal, she found a post-it note that read 'Off to get croissants. You'll need coffee… Machine is charged, just press the button. Back shortly, J.'

While the coffee machine whizzed her a foamy cappuccino, she looked up at the high ceilings and the Victorian crystal chandelier and wondered at the mismatched opulence. This flat reminded her of the ones photographed for designer magazines. She couldn't help but wonder how Jay could afford a place like this. She had heard from friends and family that his fame as a DJ had skyrocketed over the past year. He had started to invest in music production and was now working for an independent electronic music label. Last night he had mentioned something about a record he was about to release, but to her disappointment her hungover brain struggled to remember the details. She remembered him mentioning the possibility of him guest-hosting a show at a club in Ibiza for the coming summer, and that he had seemed very excited at the prospect.

She sat down at the window and looked out onto the snow-covered garden. She thought about Martin, her boyfriend, and hot anger welled up in her. She was mad at herself. For she had told him not to worry, not to be jealous, Jay was just a friend who had invited her to his gig at one of Berlin's trendiest clubs. What was she supposed to do on New Year's eve without her boyfriend? Stay at home moping and wait for his Happy New Year text message before going to bed with a hot cocoa? Of course she had jumped at the chance to spend the night treated like a VIP, who wouldn't have?

It wasn't until she saw Jay waiting outside her parents' house, leaning against his battered old Jeep, smiling, hands burrowed in the pockets of his coat, that she remembered her feelings for him. Something about this man would always make her heart yearn. It was his way of switching from close to distant, making her feel totally comfortable in his presence one minute and the next be a million miles away. The resulting confusion left her permanently wanting to please him, to look her best and be her funniest. He had a way of looking at her with such intensity that his green eyes seemed to look right into her soul, laying her bare and defenceless. It made her want to kiss him in wild abandon. Or as her friend Camelia had bluntly put it: he was hot. Smoking hot. Camelia would put a hand to her forehead in a dramatic pose and sigh, not understanding how on earth it was possible that the friendship had never extended to something a bit more gossip-worthy.

And indeed after a few drinks she had found it increasingly difficult to resist touching him. She had forced herself to hint at him not to flirt with her, but really she had an almost irrepressible urge to rip his clothes off and run her hands over his muscular body. She chuckled at the thought of her drunken horny self, *how embarrassing was I?* Blushing as she suddenly remembered that on their trek home to his flat, she had succumbed to a violent bout of nausea and sought out the nearest bush in which to relieve herself. Jay's soft laugh rang in her ear. She remembered him holding her hair back and rubbing her shoulders as she shuddered and coughed into the snow. Looking down at the spiky ends of her hair, she was suddenly very aware that she probably looked a fright and smelt like a brewery and, maybe worse – dried vomit.

'Urrgh', she exhaled, mortified, as she slipped into the bathroom, slid out of the borrowed shirt and stepped into the black marble shower. The warm water washed all the alcoholic sins off her, and her headache disappeared in a soap bubble down the drain. Once she had finished scrubbing her hair thoroughly, she picked up a black bathrobe and walked out into the hall, just as the front door opened and Jay walked in, clutching a bag of croissants in his arm.

'Ah, you are up. Great. How are you feeling?' he greeted her and smiled broadly while shaking the fresh snow from his boots.

'Huh, yeah I'm good I guess. I ...err... used your shower, hope that's ok?'

She looked down at the oversized bathrobe she had borrowed, conscious she was very naked underneath it.

'Course, glad you did, think some of that... err... from the accident... on the way home...you know', he pointed at her hair, a mocking smile widening across his handsome face.

'Yep. Squeaky clean now', she nodded. 'By the way thanks for... looking after me last night?' She shifted shyly from one foot to the other as he peeled himself out of his coat. He wore a navy blue coarse wool jumper and when he pulled up the sleeves she noticed bandages on both his arms.

'Jay, what... are these? What happened to your arms?' she pointed at his right arm where blood had flowered on the white linen.

'Err, nothing.' He hesitated, looking trapped and embarrassed.

She looked at him quizzically. He certainly didn't have these on last night.

'Ok tiger, I wasn't going to make a big deal of it, but you fought ferociously for your side of the bed. Next time, keep your claws retracted, ok?' he laughed. Sophie knew he was lying but she decided to ignore it.

'Ha ha. Really? I mean I was pretty drunk last night.' When she realised they had shared the same bed, and she couldn't remember anything because she had passed out, she suddenly regretted drinking so much.

'You were missy. Scary drunk. You should be ashamed of yourself', he laughed, ushering her into the kitchen, keen to drop the subject.

'Soooo, time for breakfast. I see you managed to work the coffee machine, good girl... I was a bit worried you wouldn't find the 'on' button.' He chuckled. A keen gastronome himself, he had always made fun of her inability to cook. Blushing with embarrassment, she stuck her tongue out at him.

They sat down at the kitchen island. Sitting side-by-side, looking out into the garden, they tucked into a copious breakfast. A group of squawking magpies had gathered and were picking the snow in search of something edible. Sophie idly looked at the large oil painting on the kitchen wall when she suddenly noticed the wall to the right of the picture was riddled with lacerations and holes. In some places, the plaster had crumbled, and the paint had flaked. *How come I didn't notice this earlier?* It looked like someone had violently hacked the wall with a sharp object. Her arm accidentally brushed against his and made him flinch; he winced in pain.

'What really happened to you Jay? Stop bullshitting me.' She pointed at his muscular forearms, her eyebrows raised inquisitively.

His mouth pressed into a hard line; he remained silent. His face had turned serious, a shade of pain clouding his handsome features. Sophie got off her stool and, curiosity getting the better of her, walked over to inspect the defaced wall. Dark brown streaks crisscrossed the plaster. She leaned over to scratch them with her fingernail. It looked like dried blood. Jay's cough made her jump, and her foot jerked into a sharp object. When she bent down and searched the heap of dust, she found she had walked into a blade. It turned out to be half the blade of a kitchen knife. She recovered the other half and lifted it up. Both halves fitted together exactly. She looked up at Jay.

'Jay?'

No answer.

'Did you do this? You stabbed the wall? What was on this wall?' Despite her best effort to appear calm and collected, her voice sounded shrill. His eyes glazed over, and Jay looked like he had gone into a meditative state. When he finally spoke, his voice sounded robotic and emotionless.

'Do not touch this. It's evil. Put it back on the floor. This knife is dangerous ok?'

'What?'

'Sophie PUT THE GODDAMN KNIFE ON THE FUCKING FLOOR!! NOW!'

Sophie's eyes widened in shock. Her lower lip quivered. She had never heard her friend shout at her before. As a matter of fact, she had never heard her friend raise his voice at all. She immediately dropped the two halves of the knife to the floor and backed away from the wall.

They stared at each other for a few seconds, unblinking, and as he opened his mouth to speak 'Sophie, I am ...' the doorbell rang. He looked away, an expression of relief flashed up on his face. With an insistent 'don't go near that knife' he rushed to open the door.

Sophie looked around the kitchen a bit at loss for what to do next, her head filled with questions.

What was he about to say? When did he do this? Last night? How come I didn't hear him? Was I that drunk?

As she looked out into the hallway, she caught a glimpse of Jay awkwardly hugging a fur-clad silhouette. As the woman turned around, Sophie looked into a pair of cold green eyes and recognised the woman from the photo in Jay's bedroom. Jay's mother Elizabeth. Sophie remembered meeting Elizabeth before, at her 18th birthday party. The same night she had eavesdropped on a conversation when Elizabeth had complained about Jay not having any friends. Elizabeth's face tightened into a sour smile as she released her son from her embrace, removed her fur hat and extended a delicate gloved hand.

'Oh hello, Sophie isn't it?'

Her tone was glacial, and the elegant older woman looked Sophie up and down like a serpent preying on a tiny field mouse. A skinny pale girl with wet, unbrushed hair, no makeup, wearing a bathrobe so big it could have slid off her bony shoulders with every movement. Sophie swallowed, well aware she wasn't making the best impression. She nervously pushed a strand of hair behind her ear and shook Elizabeth's hand with an awkward:

'Hello, yes, I'm Sophie. Jay's ...err... friend. Happy New Year...' She tried her most affable smile. Elizabeth nodded; her grip was steely and didn't linger a second longer than necessary.

'Son, be a darling and fix me a cup of coffee. Latte of course. Semi-skimmed milk please', she ordered in a low authoritarian voice. While Jay obediently went to execute her wish, the two women walked into the living room. Jay's mother striding on the thick carpet in high heeled fur boots and Sophie shuffling behind her in borrowed oversized slippers, trying not to lose one on the way.

'And... son?' Her voice was cold, her Canadian accent clipped. Jay poked his head out of the kitchen door. 'Yes mother?'

'While you are at it make one for your...' she eyed Sophie up with barely detectable disdain '...friend.'

Her mocking tone wasn't trying to hide the incredulity in her voice. Not daring to mention that she already had a cup of coffee, thank you very much, Sophie blushed. *Clearly, she thinks she walked in on us. Thank god Jay is dressed.* The thought of him not wearing any clothes made her smile. She quickly dispelled the image of his abs she had conjured up in her mind.

Sophie sat down at the furthest end of the designer sofa and perched on the edge of it, comforted by the fact she could easily make a break for it if the questioning turned ugly. Careful not to show more than was decent, she continually smoothed the folds of the oversized bathrobe over her thighs. Jay's mother folded her legs neatly on top of each other and proceeded to pluck a few invisible hairs from the cushions, pretending she was the only person in the room. The silence was unbearable. They could hear the coffee machine whirring away in the kitchen. Jay whistled softly, unaware of the uncomfortable tension that hung over the two women. Wishing herself far away, Sophie felt like telling the snobbish woman that it wasn't what it looked like; that that Jay and her were just friends and that she had a boyfriend. But she didn't as even in her head it already sounded too much like a lame excuse, if not an even worse version of what Elizabeth thought she had uncovered.

Instead, Sophie picked up the TV program on the coffee table and leafed through it, faking indifference, all the while glancing furtively at the tight-lipped woman with diamond chandelier earrings. Sophie knew Elizabeth was the type of woman who wore real diamonds. Draped in cream-coloured cashmere, Jay's mother was tall and bony. She exuded the kind of aloofness and steely self-assurance of women born into decades of well-bred families. A woman for whom life was either lived in luxury and fame, or not worth living at all. A woman who lived by her motto to scheme, divide and conquer.

'It's grotesque, isn't it?' Her sharp voice cut through the silence like a scalpel. Sophie looked up, surprised, wondering whether Elizabeth had meant her in her oversized bathrobe. *I do look grotesque.*

'These paintings.' She pointed at the large painting that hung above the fireplace. It was one of Jay's, Sophie recognised the unmistakable style. A lone silhouette sitting on the edge of a cliff, legs dangling in the air, looking down at the black sea and waves lapping up poised to engulf him. Dark, depressing, tortured. Definitely one of Jay's.

'This one and the others in his room.' She waved dismissively in the direction of the bedroom. 'I don't know where he gets his inspiration from. I for one am certainly not encouraging this. It's not like he is any good at it really, he just seems to waste all that paint.' Sophie looked at her in surprise.

'Don't look at me like that', Elizabeth spat back. 'I know my way around fine art and these are just the immature works of an attention-seeker trying to pass for a tortured artist.'

Her words were dripping with contempt and Sophie was too shocked to utter a word.

'Thank you mother. As usual your comments are just delightful.' Speaking with deadly calm, Jay put the silver tray on the coffee table and handed her a cup. The look of steely resignation on his face gave away that this wasn't the first time he had heard the outspoken opinion of his mother.

'Oh son, when will you abandon this fruitless hobby of yours and concentrate on a real career, your father and I are very concerned about your future. Don't you think you have rebelled enough now. Isn't it time to get serious?'

'Is that why you are here mother? I wondered what this visit was for.'

'Well, can't I wish my son a Happy New Year?' she retorted with a fake innocent look across her face, but she wasn't finished. '... and I thought while I'm at it, and your new year's resolutions are still fresh, I am here to drop off these MBA brochures.' She reached into her camel-coloured Hermes Birkin bag and retrieved a pouch she carefully placed on the coffee table.

'These are all business schools with excellent reputations. Caspar suggests you check out the one in Mannheim, he has some valuable contacts on the board, which we will definitely need since your recent study choices won't be deemed fitting enough. Art school, what were you thinking! Hanging around those bunch of socialist good-for-nothings, smoking drugs and wasting time. You were never going to learn how to run your father's business there. Thank god Caspar is well connected.'

She flashed a quick shadow of a triumphant smile.

'Thank you mother. I'll give these careful consideration.'

The underlying tone of his voice was one of pure contempt. So far he had managed to hide his bandages under the sleeves of his jumper, but it was time Elizabeth left the house before she started to snoop around. So he started walking her back to the entrance, handed her the fur coat and hat and with a curt 'Always a pleasure mother', he sent her on her way.

Then he turned around and smiled at a somewhat baffled Sophie. 'So how about you get dressed now, and we go for a walk in the park? I don't know about you but I'm certainly in need of some fresh air right now'.

CHAPTER 13

Solacium, October 2011 - 1 year after the incident

It was still dark in the room... and hot, extremely hot. They still hadn't repaired the boiler, and as Jay lay on top of the covers, he could feel beads of sweat forming in the nape of his neck. Damn this place, he thought. Every morning he woke up to the sound of heavy snoring that he loathed even more than having to share a tiny bathroom. The mismatched vibrations resonated in the bedroom; the air was stale and as usual Jay tried to concentrate his mind on visualising his safe place. The golden beach, the warm breeze, the jagged rocks, the open ocean in front of him.

The grunting next to him dragged him back into the room, and he ran a shaky hand through his hair. *Will this never stop? I need to breathe. I need to get out of here.* In the dark heat of the room, he felt the numbness creep up his legs. *In a few moments, the alarm will buzz, and they will unlock the doors. They will come with their white coats, clipboards and medication dispensers and ask their usual questions about my sleep patterns and with stern faces they will scribble their notes.*

The panic slowly swelled in the pit of his stomach, and the nausea took hold. He sat up and downed the glass of water on his nightstand. With trembling hands, he reached for his headphones. Led Zeppelin's 'Since I've been loving you' streamed into his heart and his mind wandered off, beyond the walls of his prison, far away from the frozen hills and the barren land, to his safe place. He walked down the beach, warm sand beneath his feet, his head light and his heart filled with music. Her smiling face shone in front of him; her long floating hair shimmered in the rising sun, and she extended a hand.

'Come on', Sophie laughed. He loved the sound of her laugh; it carried the promise of fun and freedom. He smiled back and let her lead him to the sea. The waves lapped at his bare feet and the beautiful turquoise sea unfolded in front of him like a picture-perfect postcard while he slowly followed her for a sunrise swim.

I did what I could, 'cause I love you, baby, how I love you, darling, how I love you, baby, how I love you, girl, little girl

They had been partying all night, after a few drinks at Pacha they hitched a ride on the boat to El Divino on the opposite side of the harbour. They enjoyed a few vodka lemons at the bar and followed up with a few tequila shots to get dance-floor ready. With their relaxed attitude, lacking a Rolex on their wrist, Jay and Sophie didn't fit the posh jet-set crowd, all oil shipping heirs and billionaire daughters, but they couldn't care less. They laughed and joked and after a joint on the balcony, they floated on to the after party in Space. The club opened in the early hours of the next day and was a haven for substance abusers and hedonistic partygoers unable to find peace.

But baby, since I've been loving you, I'm about to lose my worried mind

Finally on their way home, they walked, barefoot, on a dusty road back to their parents' villas. Holding hands, their hearts full of the golden glow of youth. They sat on the rocks overlooking the sea, the salty breeze frosting their beach hair, and talked about their deepest secrets, their souls touching. As Sophie fell asleep nestled against Jay's chest, her soft breath on his warm skin, he held her tightly, flooded with love for the slender girl who stole his heart. Lulled by the soft sound of waves and the incessant cricket chirp, he rested his head on the sand and stared at the starry night sky. As the sky turned pink in the east, he fell into a dreamless sleep.

It kinda makes my life a drag, a drag, drag, Ah, yeah, it makes a drag. Baby, since I've been loving you, I'm about to lose, lose my worried mind

The harsh buzz of the alarm cut through the last notes of the song, and he opened his eyes to the doctors entering the bedroom. *Another day at Solacium.*

***

Berlin, February 2005 - 5 years before the incident

Tired and weary, Jay flicked through the channels, looking for the Space Night program. He liked that program, it showed the planet shot from some lonely satellite slowly circling the earth, filming the continents, drifting along its circumference, recording the planet's oceans and mountains. By the time the satellite reached the furthest corners of Australia, the background ambient music usually lulled him to sleep. He had just rolled a joint and took a few calming drags. The sweet smelling marijuana smoke filled his lungs, soothing his anxieties. He had found himself smoking more regularly again after the period of self-imposed abstinence following the messy break up with Aisha. It had been nearly two years since he had last seen her. Although not always successfully, he managed to avoid thinking about her most of the time.

During his stay in rehab, doctors and psychologists had repeatedly warned him about smoking weed. They had told him that his mental state was fragile and smoking was only going to exacerbate the symptoms of depression. During the many assessments, Jay had been subjected to endless tests and psychological evaluations and when the question came up "Are you hearing voices?" he hadn't told them about the recurring visions of the talking rabbits, his guardian angel the girl in white, or Dan. Puppet master Dan. Jay knew for sure that telling the doctors that Dan would constantly whisper in his head, *he continually comments on every one of my thoughts*, would be a telltale sign that he was going crazy. *And crazy people aren't just given a few pills in rehab. No, crazy people are sent off to a mental institution and locked up with other crazies.* Based on scenes in 'One Flew Over the Cuckoos Nest', Jay could only imagine such a place being completely off the social grid, a soulless prison for sick and dysfunctional individuals. *A place where dreams come to die.* He had no desire whatsoever to be sent to such a place, and henceforth decided to keep quiet about the voice in his head.

Jay only told the doctors about feeling low and the headaches he was regularly plagued with. As well as being prescribed bags of potent painkillers and anti-depressants, he was sent to a cognitive rehabilitation program where he attended a marathon of self-finding classes hosted by a string of renowned psychologists and experts. Jay didn't think much of the so-called specialists he saw.

They always seemed to take a keen interest in the circumstances of his parent's divorce and his adoptive twin siblings.

'How did it make you feel Mr Adler when your parents divorced?' they enquired and he felt like screaming *Guilty! Fucking guilty!* But he kept his mouth shut.

'How did you feel when your mother and stepfather adopted your twin siblings?'

I don't know, I fucking freaked out! But he remained impassible.

Although he didn't feel the sessions were helping him much, he still liked the fact someone was prepared to listen to him, but as a precaution he always kept the conversation quite courteous. The psychologist, a soft-spoken woman in her late forties, would shake her silver hair and scribble furiously into her notebook.

On the surface and in the eyes of most of his friends, Jay remained the quiet pleasant guy who was only just short of being a musical genius, at least when he played the drums. The type of guy people constantly solicited for social events. Having created a name for himself in the music scene over the past few years, he was offered regular nights in Berlin's most renowned underground clubs. He had DJed at semi-legal raves in abandoned warehouses. He was flown out to Ibiza to perform at its biggest clubs. His name crept up the headliner list until it reached the top of the bill. AddeeJay. His name up in lights. The opportunities kept flowing in and he was flown to Paris, Amsterdam, London and New York to play to adoring crowds.

One day, lying in bed with a debilitating headache, recovering from jetlag combined with a raging hangover, the phone had rung. The man introduced himself as Martin Williams and offered him a collaboration on his next album. The record company paid an attractive advance and Jay had happily accepted. It had meant many late nights, sleep was at a constant shortage and caffeine, whisky and coke were the little helpers that got him through most days.

Tonight he had come back from one of the more intense studio sessions. He had been frustrated at his partner for not showing up, leaving him dealing with a highly strung singer who was lending her vocals to one of the tracks on the next album. He didn't get along with the short-tempered diva. Every time she dissolved into a tantrum he had to show restraint, stopping himself from slapping her. Instead, he swallowed his anger as he so often did, smiled good-naturedly and got on with the job.

When he finally finished off the last reviews of the song, he had switched off the lights and locked the doors to the recording studio, drove his battered old Jeep through the empty streets of West Berlin back to his flat to collapse on the couch. Exhausted, he had wolfed down the remains of the previous night's Chinese takeaway and rolled himself a spliff, his end-of-day reward. He was convinced the weed helped him keep control over his thoughts. The weed kept Dan at bay. The weed drowned out the permanent white noise he seemed to have developed in his left ear.

The satellite had reached Africa and the continent unfolded in vivid colours on the screen. So many countries he had yet to discover, so little time. *My life's too short to explore it all*, he thought not without a hint of melancholy. He wondered who else watched this program, then he guessed most people were asleep at this time of night and the only probable audience were either insomniacs or party people on a come down. There wasn't much else on at that time anyway, now was there? His curiosity piqued he grabbed the remote control and lazily flicked through the channels.

The shopping channels blared aggressive sales pitches at him, endlessly flogging items he didn't know existed or ever thought there was a demand for. He didn't linger for fear of being brainwashed into buying an overpriced but utterly useless snuggle blanket with sleeves, or a battery-operated potato peeler. If it weren't so tragic, he would have laughed at the absurdity of this consumer-led society. Useless junk stuffed down unsuspecting gullible throats. Yet somehow he felt tempted to watch the show and test his willpower to see how long it would take to go from 'I couldn't care less for your set of fluff removers' to 'Oh I could do with this, now where is my phone'. The lady presenter flaunted her breasts and paraded her ass on stage while suggestively purring into the camera. The evil producers really knew how to grab the attention of their dimwitted audience. 'A fantastic offer, only 19.99. The clock is ticking, only 10 left in stock, pick up your phone now and dial...' he quickly switched to the next channel.

'...0190 333 666! I'm up all night for you, call me...' a cheap-looking blonde bimbo whispered huskily into the camera while strutting across the screen in red suspenders. A good idea it was not, unsuspecting punters would be charged at premium rate, to listen to a recorded bored housewife who probably did the ironing while suggestively moaning into the headset. No, not really what got him excited. He took another drag on the joint. The smoke he exhaled momentarily blurred the screen to reveal, once lifting, a leather-clad dominatrix brandishing a whip and screaming 'Call' whip crack 'Me' whip crack 'Now!' Now that was mildly exciting Jay reckoned, before smiling at the absurdity of it all.

For a second, he was tempted to call Sophie to see what she was up to. He hadn't seen her in a while since she moved back to London to start her new job. He had been disappointed to see her leave again so soon. She had been back in Berlin for a few months. She said she was only here, staying at her parent's house, to lick her wounds and figure out her next steps after being made redundant from her high-flying banker job. All that time, her boyfriend Martin had remained in London and came to visit her every other weekend; something Jay had found irritating at best. If he was honest with himself, he wanted to enjoy Sophie's company without her boyfriend. They had been going out every other day and he felt safe and comforted around her. He loved her sense of humour, her fascination with his art and her ever-positive outlook on life in general. He missed her when she wasn't around. Even if their relationship was platonic, he felt alive and hopeful when she was by his side. When the job offer came, he had only half-heartedly tried to convince her to stay, knowing very well there was nothing much he could offer her here. She loved this man who waited for her in London. From the photos she had excitedly shown Jay, he had reluctantly had to admit that he looked not only handsome, but kind, and he had wished them a quiet 'all the best'.

'I will miss you too Jay' she had said with big sad eyes. 'We had an incredible few months. Thank you for taking me to all these cool events and parties… but this is not the end of it. You know we'll stay in touch. We've been friends for too long now, we can't let each other go that easily. We have phones and emails and you said you might be coming over to DJ. So I expect an invite soon to some swanky party in London, ok?'

He had nodded silently and had let her go, her white-blonde hair bobbing, disappearing with a little wave past the security gate to catch her flight.

He checked his watch. 4:30am. He didn't think Sophie would appreciate a late-night call on a Tuesday night. He snapped his mobile shut and switched the channel away from the sexy night calls.

'A trained gynecologist and a trailblazer in aesthetic surgical procedures, he was the first plastic surgeon to introduce Botox in Germany and he is a pioneer in double D breast enhancements… Ladies and Gentlemen, please welcome to the stage one of the most renowned surgeons in our country…. Doctor Caspar von Schoenefeldt!'

Jay nearly choked on his saliva. In between two fits of coughs and through watering eyes, he saw him. The man he had grown to hate walked on stage with a smile as bright and arrogant as that of a US politician. He strode across the stage soaking up the applause of the audience, shook the hand of the presenter with great confidence and sat on the couch ready to answer interview questions from the talk-show host.

Jay usually liked the late night program and its affable host. Harald Schmidt was a well-known Swabian actor with bags of charm and a naughty twinkle in his eye, his show had been around for years and his guests were always illustrious public figures. Until today. What on earth was the man thinking when he booked his stepfather as a guest? Admittedly, Caspar had been successful with his new clinic and his reality TV show with the predictable before-and-after format had given him plenty of media exposure. But surely there were more deserving people out there whom Harald Schmidt could have chosen to interview? Jay hoped the talk show host was going to give his arrogant stepfather a good grilling.

'You're looking good Herr Schoenefeldt!'

'Now thank you Herr Schmidt, but please do call me Caspar.'

He flashed a genuine-looking smile at the audience who whooped at his wink. What an actor and a skilled manipulator, Jay thought, with distaste and, even if he wouldn't admit it, a hint of envy. Caspar hadn't been on stage for more than five seconds and he already he had everyone eating out of his hand.

'You must get this all the time, these compliments about your looks', Harald adjusted his trademark glasses, a wicked smile curling his lip.

'All the time indeed, but let me tell you Harald, it's a good thing I look like this. I mean, my face is kind of my business card, no one trusts an ugly plastic surgeon, do they?' he laughed, smoothing his coiffed hair. Jay nervously dragged on the joint dangling from the corner of his mouth only to discover that he had let it burn out. Not taking his eyes off the TV screen he reached out for a lighter.

'I've got to ask this though, as a plastic surgeon, are you ever tempted to do some work on yourself? I mean some of your patients describe you as a god, but even you must have the odd 'ugly day'? Have you had any procedures done? A little facelift perhaps?' Harald Smith loved asking his guests uncomfortable questions. Jay grinned.

'Of course Harald, of course, as part of the final exam of their training, all my assistant surgeons get to operate on me.' Cue laughs from the audience and a mock horrified look on the talk show host's face.

'Surely not! Now, you are the man who first brought Botox to Germany. As you know, ladies and gentlemen, Botulinum toxin A, more commonly known as 'Botox', has flooded the beauty market and rapidly became one of the most affordable and popular anti-ageing drugs in the world. And this man ran the authorization trials for the health authorities to commercialise the drug in Germany. Am I right Caspar?'

'Yes indeed.'

As Caspar launched into a professional yet witty description of the trials and tribulations of cutting through the red-tape of German bureaucracy to make the drug available to plastic surgeons, Jay couldn't help but feel anger rise in him. Jay had never been able to warm to the man he felt had ruined every chance of him ever bringing his parents back together. It had been bad enough that Jay, without consciously wanting to hurt his parents, had told his dad that, on that fateful morning, he had walked in on his mother in the arms of the tennis coach. It turned out the tennis coach was, in fact, the snobby Caspar von Schoenefeldt. Jay shook his head while he pulled out another Rizzla. He looked down at his fingers. The skin at the tips had a yellow tinge. He probably smoked too much. But he shrugged his shoulders, at least he managed to curb his drinking. He couldn't give up all his vices at once. He picked at the bud he carefully extracted from his weed box while thinking back to that awkward moment he had found out his mother was having an affair.

Seeing the horrified look on his mom's face he knew he shouldn't have been there. His gym class had been cancelled that morning and he had decided to meet his mother an hour earlier at the tennis club where he knew she had classes on a

Friday morning. The club was only a few streets away from his school and he walked to meet her there every time she was late to pick him up. She often was, and he usually found her at the club bar drinking Bloody Marys, holding court to a gaggle of adoring men. She laughed upon seeing her young son, and with a flick of her long mane, she knowingly winked at the men's surprised faces. Despite being a mother, Elizabeth, or Liz as she had them call her, still looked extremely attractive, and she knew how to take advantage of that.

That day she hadn't been at her usual haunt at the bar, and the barman had pointed him in the direction of the tennis courts. He skipped past a group of giggling older women in white tennis skirts, excited to show his mother the Halloween costume he had made in his arts and crafts class. He pushed open the door to an equipment room and in the corner he saw a woman, in her late thirties, canoodling up to the man whose lap she was sitting on. 'Mom?' he had blurted out, praying for the woman to look up and reveal herself a complete stranger. But his prayers went unanswered. The woman turned around. It was indeed his mother.

Elizabeth quickly pushed the man's hand away from under her shirt and pulled down the white tennis skirt, which had ridden high above her thighs, exposing her tanned skin. She coughed and spluttered and jumped to her feet.

'Meet my...err...friend Caspar', she mumbled, scraping back her hair into a hasty bun. Caspar stood up. With a winning smile he extended a hand for Jay to shake. Jay didn't move and suspiciously eyed up this man who just seconds ago had touched his mother where only his father had the right to touch her. His 10-year-old mind was sure of that.

The world he had created, a world in which his parents lived together in perfect harmony, shattered around him with such force that he stood rooted to the spot, breathless. His idealistic version of being a family had the naivety of a cereal advert where Mum, Dad and Son laughed at the breakfast table with big toothy smiles. The shards of his broken illusions stabbed him deeply. Something shifted. His world was out of kilter. Forever. Silent, he turned on his heel and ran from the horrible scene. He ran and ran, tears streaming down his face until he arrived home. He locked himself in his bedroom and wouldn't come out, until eventually, he opened the door to his father's worried face. His father had confronted him, he had insisted on knowing the reason for his son's tantrum. Looking over his father's shoulder, he could see his mother anxiously biting her fingernail, and Jay had shook his head. He couldn't tell on his mother and so he carried the heavy burden of the secret for months to come.

But one day, running away from a heated argument with his mother, he had vengefully left a hot sobbing voicemail on his father's work phone. As he hung up the receiver, a pang of regret hit him instantly, but too late. As he frantically punched in the numbers again, he realised he didn't know how to erase the message. All he could do was wait for his father to come home and then what? Armageddon? He had paced in his bedroom like one of these hyenas he had seen at the zoo. Back and forth, back and forth. Head bowed, jumping at every noise down the stairs, waiting for the inevitable knock on his bedroom door. But nothing happened for a while. The arguments had ceased and made way for a stony silence, which in fact he had learned to fear more than his parents' constant rowing. Every comment at the dinner table "Pass me the salt please" was a laden time bomb, skidding between the wine glasses and plates, ready to self-destruct in an all-flattening explosion. But nothing happened.

And one day his parents had called him into his father's study. As instructed, he sat down as they both towered above him. His mother studiously avoided looking him in the eye, her voice monotonous and controlled. She wasn't wearing her wedding ring. They tried to sell him the idea of two homes, two bedrooms, twice the amount of toys. But it sounded rehearsed.

Ignoring the words that came out of their mouths, all he heard in their voices was a tone of accusation. If only he had kept his mouth shut. It was all his fault. He had betrayed his mother and grassed on her. He had driven his father away. Turned out that tennis guy was a surgeon. A plastic surgeon whose obsession was to turn normal, healthy-looking women into caricatures of themselves. Identikit blond bimbos with permanently frozen smiles on tight faces. He had driven his mother away from his father into the arms of a man hell bent on plastifying the world, one woman at a time.

'Thank you, Doctor Schoenefeldt, and for the benefit of our viewers, a recap of the stellar career progression of the surgeon who changed the way we think about beauty.'

A series of photos filled the screen and the off voice commented: 'Graduation at the illustrious Royal School of Surgeons in Ireland; a post-graduate intern at Stanford University school of medicine in California; the opening of Praxis Schoenefeldt in Berlin; introducing Botox for the first time in Germany; winning the Mannheim award for first facial reconstructive surgery'. A photo showed him shaking the Chancellor's hand. Another flashed up showing Caspar standing in the middle of a group of stunning young women at the TV launch premiere of his TV show 'Before and After'.

'But amidst fame and fortune, he is also a family man. Married to the socialite Lady Elizabeth von Schoenefeldt and father of twins.' Jay looked at the last photo filling the screen and wasn't surprised to see that he had been cut out of the picture. He had kind of expected it. Since he had accused him of cheating with Aisha, Jay's already strained relationship with Caspar had completely broken down. They avoided each other whenever possible and he rarely made an appearance at their home for fear of confrontation, not wanting to upset his mother and siblings. The few family dinners he hadn't been able to make excuses for were spent in sheer agony. Remaining courteous had become a real torture when all he wanted to do was to break his fist into his stepdad's surgically perfected face.

At every opportunity Caspar tried to convince Jay he never had an affair with Aisha. Discreetly, out of earshot from his wife of course. This time round, Jay hadn't said anything to his mother, resolutely shouldering the heavy burden of guilt. His poor unsuspecting mother, who worried every day about her fading looks, a cliched fear beautiful people have in common. She must have known something, at least subconsciously. She was married to a successful and, at least to certain standards, handsome man. He only got better with age, and she, well, she wilted. Slowly but inexorably. He was surrounded every day by young and beautiful women with toned bodies and silken skin. While she complained about stretch marks - the ones she had gained while carrying Jay into the world - mapping her once flawless stomach like silvery trenches from a past battle.

Jay had noticed his mother's face change over the years. Comparing photos in his mind's eye, she now sported tight, somewhat frozen features. Her eyebrows seemed a little higher these days, and her lips a bit fuller. Her cheekbones were just that little bit more shapely, and he could have sworn that his mother's neckline had inflated, which looked a bit odd on her tiny frame. Suddenly he wondered whether all these procedures had been carried out by her husband. Well, of course, he thought. *Private consulting at home. How convenient.* He remembered photos of his mother in her mid-twenties, happy and au natural.

Now she seemed to dip in and out of depression. She was addicted to her anti-depressants and obsessed with her appearance. But wasn't her husband to blame? Didn't he drive her to feel inadequate? And by being his wife, wasn't she supposed to be the flip side of his business card? Surely as a plastic surgeon he couldn't have an ageing woman by his side? Jay gasped at the sudden realisation that by keeping the affair of her husband secret he had pushed her further into the vicious cycle of self-hatred and co-dependance. And this 'can't do no wrong' man of hers seemed quite willing to experiment procedures on his wife, feeding her anxiety and lack of confidence. A nagging feeling of guilt tugged at Jay. But he couldn't tell his mother about Aisha. He couldn't make that mistake again.

As Caspar droned on about how he much loved his gorgeous wife, even though he was perpetually surrounded by beautiful young women on his hit show, Jay finished rolling his next joint. He licked the inside of the cigarette paper to seal the cone, tapped the finished spliff on the back of his hand to compress the tobacco and lit it. By now the potent weed had helped him wind down from a long day at the studio and he felt light-headed. The anger he had felt upon seeing Caspar on the show was pushed to the back of his mind. He let the soothing waves of the weed wash through him. His regular trips to Amsterdam were not only a good opportunity to stock up on fresh pot, but he also had devised a foolproof plan to get his monthly rations sent over to him. He had befriended Joost, the owner of a smokey coffee shop on Prinsengracht by the canal, and had Joost regularly post him a package. When the boxes arrived, they always contained a jar of Dutch peanut butter.

His friend took great care to remove the seal, scoop out the right amount of peanut butter to accommodate the airtight plastic sachet of marijuana, before painstakingly resealing the pot. Now, every first week of the month, Jay went to pick up a package at the postbox he had taken care to open at a post office across town. It always came with a postcard, mainly pictures of cute kittens in front of the city's sights. And flipping it around it would always read some sentimental nonsense such as 'How much I miss you, darling grandson of mine! Hopefully, you will come to visit me soon. Kisses, Yolande'.

The talk-show host engaged his famous guest in a series of questions about the dangers associated with the normalisation of plastic surgery. Caspar's TV program showed many young women with a wish to surgically enhance their features, sometimes to caricatural proportions. Didn't plastic surgeons have a social duty of care to prevent the young from life-changing and in many cases irreversible surgeries? Harald asked, and what about the risks?

Jay scoffed at his stepfather's feeble attempt to justify his crass TV show by shifting the blame to society in general: MTV for showing only video clips with semi-naked, perfect women, and human nature for seeking perfection and immortality. 'I'm just actioning the changes', Caspar said shrugging his shoulders innocently. Bored of seeing him weaseling his way out of every challenging question, Jay felt his eyelids flicker. Jeez, this weed is quite strong, he thought. His limbs felt leaden all of a sudden. He felt himself slowly drifting off.

'Well yes Harald, there is someone else you don't know about, and no, the rumours aren't true.' Jay forced his eyes open. His head hurt. What had he missed?

Caspar looked directly into the camera with sly eyes. Magnified this close up, his groomed eyebrows looked like a pair of blonde caterpillars. Jay shrunk into the sofa cushions. There was something about his stepfather's eyes that scared him. Something cold and steely. Something mad and obsessed. And then his voice resonated from the TV into the living room like an all powerful satanic messiah's calling.

'Dear audience, you should know that I have a stepson.'

Jay cowered as Caspar's voice boomed, looking right at him from the TV screen across the living room. 'He's the one wrongly accusing me of having had an affair with his girlfriend. I vehemently dispute these accusations. He is a paranoid young man. I have nothing but patience and compassion for him and have tried on many occasions to help him back on the right path. I offered to cover his tuition fees to return to school, to get a proper job, to succeed in something. But the poor fool won't listen, he's not entirely right in his head. Wastes his life in nightclubs. Smokes too much marijuana. Jay you are such a lost cause, come back to us, let us help you.'

Caspar's glowering eyes bore into his mind like the headlights of a speeding truck. Jay was pinned to the spot. *Is this actually happening?* Was Caspar really attacking him on national TV? In front of millions, with no chance for him to retaliate? The asshole was making him sound like he was a total basket case. Panic rose inside him as he scrambled over the sofa to fish the remote control off the floor. With trembling hands he switched off the TV. But the voice still echoed in his head and Caspar's evil eyes swam before him like wildfire. His chest tightened.

He couldn't breathe. The panic attack sat heavy on his lungs. He coughed and retched, desperately trying to free his airways, but like muscle cramp, the more he attempted to inhale the more his windpipe tightened. His head swam and he slipped out of consciousness. Goddamn weed, he thought, as his knees buckled and he fell to the floor. His head hit the rug and as he lay there, flat on the floor. 'Fuck', he thought, 'I'm going to die now'. *And I haven't even told her that I love her.*

Then he saw her, the lithe girl in the white flowing dress, the one he had seen on the motorway back from Amsterdam, the one who saved his life. She stood in the doorway, her long white hair flowing down her sides. Her face was serene and pale. An angel, his saviour, his escort over the threshold. She whispered a silent prayer and crouched down next to him. As her hand hovered above his head, he felt calm. His muscles relaxed. He breathed in and the cold air was sweet and life-giving. Every cell rejoiced at the oxygen supply as he opened his eyes. She was gone.

CHAPTER 14

Solacium, November 2011 - 1 year after the incident

Jay was lying on his bed, staring at the ceiling as he so often did, passing time for hours on end and locked in his thoughts. The rough spun wool blanket scratched against the skin of his calves. He thought about Sophie's latest postcard. He ran his finger along the edges of the card. The blue ink bled into the yellowed cardboard and Jay noticed her handwriting was somehow different, the letters flat and elongated as if pulled apart by sadness. If it weren't for the antipsychotic drugs he was taking, his paranoid brain would have thought someone else had written it, but it was unmistakably her signature at the bottom. The way she curled a heart at the end of her name. He chuckled softly into his beard, it was a habit she hadn't changed since she was a teenager. A corny little heart at the end of her name. He loved it.

Reading her description of the deteriorating health of her father, his heart ached at the thought of her pain, and he had never wished more to be close to her to wrap a protective arm around her shoulders. But somewhere he knew that the imminent death of her father was in some way a deliverance. Pensive, he flipped the postcard around and stared at the beach on the front of it. Cala Conta. That was the beach, his safe haven. He smiled at the memory of those halcyon days. They were a thousand miles apart, and yet she picked the one beach that in his mind he walked every morning before he got up. His smile widened as he ignored the second alarm buzz; he was going to be late.

The staff at Solacium were quite strict with time and the inmates only had a 30-minute window to get out of bed, answer the series of questions about how they slept for the psychiatric log before showering, slipping on their ugly blue overalls and then congregating in the refectory for a tasteless porridge breakfast. Ever since he started suffering from inexplicable morning sickness, Jay found the morning routine extremely challenging. His new psychiatrist Doctor Klein, a stern-looking woman with no-nonsense eyes, had subjected him to various degrading tests, but none of the results had been conclusive.

Finally, with a deep sigh, Jay pushed himself off the bed, swallowed his medication and chased the pills down with the drops he'd been prescribed for nausea. Stripping his t-shirt off, he shuffled to the tiny bathroom he shared with his roommates. As usual the T-shirt was soaking wet. He never remembered the nightmares but deep down he knew he heard the screams again, the howling screams of agony. The eyes, the terror in them... A wave of nausea coursed through him like an electric current, and he gripped the sink, heaving. He coughed and retched, but he willed himself to keep the medication down.

The reflection in the mirror stared back at him with expressionless eyes, his gaze as vacant and dull as he felt. Only upon closer inspection a spark of humanity was still flickering in the dark green gateways to his soul – or so he hoped. A full beard hid his sallow features, and his skin had the waxen colour of a man who only got 30 minutes of sunlight per day. He had gained a lot of weight, an unfortunate side effect of the drugs, and he now weighed over 150kg. For an athletically built man who had spent his youth used to an effortlessly toned and muscular body, the sight of man boobs filled him with a self-loathing so intense, he wished he could take a knife to his chest to cut off the excess fat.

He ran a long fingernail along the industrial shower tab, scratching at the lime scale that dulled the once shiny metal. The water was a welcome barrier against the nausea, and he savoured the moment the cold water ran down his broad shoulders. He rubbed his arms with a bar of cheap soap, the type that just wouldn't lather, and contemplated the scars on his forearms that tore silvery trenches across his skin. The memory of fighting his inner demon on New Year's Eve as Sophie slept in his bed was like a walk in foggy highlands. Surreal and hazy. It felt like it had happened to someone else.

His fingers lingered on the thick scar on his right lower abdominal where the once firm six-pack had vanished under a layer of bloated skin. The scar had stretched; the skin was still numb where he had cut himself and although fading, the ink was still partly visible. Jay shook his head, what had possessed him, he wondered. Dan's voice had been loud and irresistible, and when he had ordered Jay to take the kitchen knife to the tattoo, he hadn't been able to protest. The pain had been excruciating, even under the veil of alcohol, he howled in agony until three layers of raw skin bled into the toilet bowl.

Her inked name bloody and wilted like a reminder of unrequited love on crumpled paper. *Aisha*.

***

Berlin, March 2009 - 1 year before the incident

The weather was still cold for early spring. The tentative green that sprouted from the trees was covered in an early-morning sprinkling of frost. A shy sun hung low above the trees, its feeble rays barely filtering through the canopy. An eerie silence reigned over this remote part of the forest. Gone was the constant droning of Berlin's crowded arteries. Gone the constant hum of thousands and thousands of people talking. People these days never seemed to stop talking. Jay could hear them all constantly; it was exhausting, talking nonsense most of the time.

Now everyone had mobile phones, some even two, which Jay found utterly ridiculous. *Why would you want to have two phones?* And the people continued to talk, everywhere, their phones glued to their heads. Loud, obnoxious, sharing private information nobody cared for in public spaces. He couldn't see much point in being contactable everywhere he went. Didn't people know that phone companies installed microchips in the devices that tracked their every move? He could clearly imagine phone companies being callous enough to track their users' whereabouts, analyse their daily patterns and sell that data on to third-party provider firms. Those in turn would have no qualms in using the information to ensure their product adverts were neatly placed on the consumer's way to work, to the park, and to the gym, their sole aim being to sell more of their products to the unsuspecting mobile phone user. It was a sick world he was living in, too remote from the real things that mattered: eating, sleeping and keeping sane.

Today he had purposely left his cell phone in his flat. Walking with his hands in the pockets of his parka, it was reassuring to feel the empty space only taken up by his car keys. No phone. He had parked his rusty jeep a few kilometres back and walked into the forest. The air was fresh and sweet, full of promise of a spring soon to come and the silence comforted him. The newly grown grass was covered with a sparkling layer of thin frost, a million tiny diamonds that crunched quietly under his feet. He wasn't sure whether he was going the right way. It was a long time since he had been in this part of the wood.

Somewhere the path should take him to a crossroads and then he would have to turn right. The road would open up onto a beach with a view onto the lake.

A wave of nostalgia overcame him as he recognised the path, then the beach. It seemed smaller since the last time, but that was possibly because the waterline had risen during the rainy winter months. The lake reached as far as he could see. Its borders disappeared in the morning mist. On the other side, he recognised the small boathouse and the rickety pier. The small wooden boats had long rotted and sunk to the bottom of the lake, but the wooden island still remained in the middle.

He sat down on one of the rocks by the shore, the sun warmed his face. Absent-mindedly he picked up a small flat pebble. The stone was cold and smooth in his hand. He tossed it across the water with a flick of his wrist, and it bounced on the surface a few times before sinking into the dark muddy waters. Jay wondered if the huge catfish still lurked in the darkness. The place had something about it Jay couldn't quite describe. It was like staring at an old photograph and suddenly stepping into it, discovering that the memory of the place was very different from the actual place. Once lit up by hundreds of candles and decorated with colourful bunting, the boat house now looked empty and desolate. The pier once echoed the many feet bouncing on the weathered wood before the kids jumped into the boats, now every second plank was a gaping hole.

Jay sighed and pulled out a small pill box from the inside pocket of his jacket. He fished out two blue pills and swallowed them. When he had complained to his psychologist about the recurring anxiety attacks, Dr Klein had prescribed him Prozac. He who had been quite skeptical about what he thought were valley-of-the-dolls type uppers or downers, he had listened to the pleas of his mother and finally admitted the pills were helping him rein in the panic attacks. As a welcome secondary effect, it also seemed to quieten the white noise, and Dan's commentaries had died down. He did still sometimes hear him whisper, but it sounded more like being under water while someone shouted at him from the beach. Muffled, distant and most importantly: non-threatening.

The downside was that while the pills quelled his incessant inner turmoil, they also seemed to mute his feelings. Whereas before, he was increasingly overwhelmed by bottled up emotions of anger and extreme joys, followed by soul-crushing lows, now everything felt the same. Detached, as if happening to someone else, he a silent bystander. He was surprised when Sophie once described him as being aloof: inside he was torn by all sorts of conflicting emotions. Now he finally felt that his newfound inner detachment mirrored the way people saw him.

The weeping willow was still there, by the shore, defying time and gravity, its long branches lazily grazing the water. The very same tree under which he had told her he loved her. He smiled at the memory. What a melodramatic teenage fool he had been then, as if he had ever stood a chance. She had been someone else's, as always. As always, there had been another man. But when he saved her from drowning the night of her 18th birthday, their tentative flirt had blossomed into something deeper, they had tied a bond that kept them in each other's life. A bond so tight at times they felt as one. A bond that sometimes stretched over oceans, never breaking. They were meant to be in each other's lives, or so he thought.

He could feel the letter creasing the inside pocket of his flannel shirt, and it forebode nothing good. He had found it in his letter box the night before, having returned from yet another late studio session. He hadn't opened it. The envelope bore her elegant handwriting but somehow there was something different about this letter from all the others he had received from her. It weighed heavy on his heart.

The pills had helped him sleep but his sleep had been superficial. He woke up before the sun rose, downed an espresso and jumped into the car to drive to the only place he knew that held his memories like dried flowers in a scrap book.

He used to like this place; it reminded him of the times he spent here with her. A couple of years after her 18th birthday party, he had returned to the lake with her. He leaned back, stared at the cold sky and remembered. It had been summer. He had picked her up from home and surprised her with a picnic basket and two kids in the backseat of his car.

'I hope you don't mind my two extra special guests this afternoon: Milana and Maxime. Guys, this is my friend Sophie.' The nine-year old twins waved at her like a perfectly synchronised double act. The boy shook his blonde fringe and swept it to one side, pretending to be extremely bored whereas the pretty girl excitedly jumped up, all bobbing ponytail and sparkly eyes, extending a small hand.

'I'm pleased to meet you Sophie', she smiled. Somewhat impressed by her impeccable manners, Sophie had reciprocated her smile and awkwardly shaken the little hand.

'You can call me Pearl, everybody does', Milana smiled. Suddenly shy, she sat back down in her seat and smoothed a crease in her pretty navy and white checked sundress.

'And what's your nickname Maxime?' Sophie turned to the slightly built boy in a matching checked shirt. She didn't get an answer as the boy was completely absorbed in his computer game. His fingers flew over the handheld, his eyes glued to the tiny screen.

'We call him Maxi King, and he's obsessed with his Gameboy', Jay laughed, stowing her rucksack in the boot of the car. She climbed into the jeep. Sliding into the driver's seat, Jay leaned over to give her a light kiss on the cheek.

'Are you sure you don't mind?' He whispered for the kids not to hear. 'I'm sorry to spring this on you at the last minute, but their childminder rang in sick this morning, and I couldn't refuse when the little ones asked me to take them swimming. I hardly see them beyond Christmas and Easter these days', he smiled apologetically.

'Of course not... I mean I don't mind!' Sophie stammered. Jay wondered whether that was a lie as she quickly turned her head to hide her disappointment.

'Don't worry, we'll have fun, you'll see!' Jay smiled, put on his mirrored aviator sunglasses, slipped one of his latest mixtapes in the stereo and put the Jeep into first gear. He had only passed his driving test a couple of months ago, and he still got a kick out of driving the Jeep he had bought off Frank's dad for a few thousand euros. It had been all his savings, everything he had earned working in his dad's company in his school breaks. Closing his fingers around the set of keys, the cold metal cutting into his palm, he had never felt so proud. The car was in excellent condition, and he had loved it from the minute he laid eyes on it. A 1990 Jeep Wrangler. With a soft top. He had always wanted a convertible 4x4 drive.

With the top down and to the sound of a quiet chill-out bass, they drove through the sleepy city, up north in the direction of Tegeler airport. The summer holiday season had begun and judging by the fluid traffic, everybody seemed to have left the city for a break abroad. In no time, they got to the exit leading to Tegeler See. A green jewel nestled in the hills outside of Berlin. The sun was blazing; Jay could feel the rays stinging his neck and readjusted his baseball cap. When he looked over to the girl in the seat next to him, he couldn't help but let his gaze linger a bit longer than the usual furtive glances he stole at her. Sophie's long skinny legs were lightly tanned and her flip-flopped feet lazily rested on the dashboard. She wore the tiniest of denim shorts and for a second Jay felt the urge to put his hand on the warm skin of her thigh. As if reading his thoughts she turned to him and smiled suggestively. *Oh god. She is so incredibly beautiful. That smile.* A rush of heat flooded through him, and he bit his lip.

'Are we there yet?' Milana excitedly slung her arms around her step-brother and the car swerved dangerously towards the hard shoulder.

'Pearl! Get back in your seat!' Jay yelled. He was annoyed; the moment was ruined. Milana quickly sat back down and taken aback by the sharpness in her step brother's voice, looked like she was about to burst into tears. Jay melted at the sight of her trembling lower lip and in a much softer voice continued. 'It's ok, just be careful when I'm driving. And to answer your question, yes we are nearly there. See that parking lot over there? We're going to park the car there, and then we will have to walk for a bit to get to the boathouse. Sound ok?' She nodded obediently. Her brother Maxime didn't seem to take much notice. His eyes still firmly focused on his computer game, he ignored the world around him.

They parked the car in the shade of an old oak tree, unloaded their beach gear and walked down the dusty path leading up to the boathouse. Jay snatched the Gameboy out of his step brother's hand and ignoring his angry protestations, stuffed it in his rucksack. Sulking, Maxime wandered off, trailing behind his sister, who skipped along the path leading deeper into the woods.

Once they arrived at the small beach and found a sunny spot, Sophie unpacked the picnic basket while Jay handed the kids their swimming gear. 'Look at them. They are twins, but they couldn't be more different. I mean physically, they do look alike. Same blue eyes, same blonde hair colour.' Sophie observed them a bit more carefully as they both played on the strip of sand by the water line.

'Indeed they do look alike', Sophie said, 'Although it seems that Max has a slightly different shaped nose, much narrower than his sister's', she noted. Jay nodded.

'But their characters...' Jay continued while the twins squabbled over who got which beach blanket '...seem to develop in opposite directions. It's weird, the more Max becomes loud, aggressive and arrogant, the more Pearl is soft and shy. It's like they're diametrical opposites on the character chart. Isn't that fascinating?'

Maxime had just snatched the navy beach blanket off his sister with a menacing hiss and Milana's internal struggle on whether to cry or protest was apparent on her little face.

'Aren't twins supposed to get on? It doesn't look like they do particularly', Sophie said.

'Most times they don't seem to get along that well. It's mainly Max who is the more assertive one and picks fights. But weirdly when they do get along, they really are one unit. I noticed they have even developed their own language to communicate which each other without anyone else understanding a word they're saying. It's freakishly well-developed. I bet it's hard to have someone so close acting as a direct competitor for everything you learn, you want and need. Like vying for parental attention. But on the other side, they're never alone. They always have each other.'

The sudden sadness in his voice made Sophie look up at him. He stared intensely at his step-siblings who weren't actually related to him. It was a sore point in his life.

'You ok?' she whispered.

'Yeah' he exhaled. 'Right, I think we should stop talking like we're the middle-aged parents of these two little naughty faces', he chuckled. 'Although come to think of it, wouldn't we be ideal parents?' he winked.

'Ha, ha, very funny. You may be, but I don't see myself as a potential mother as of yet. I hate to say it, but I don't warm to the idea of having kids. They make me feel awkward. Besides they're a lot of work. They poo all the time and are always snotty.'

'Really? You don't like kids?' he sounded disappointed.

'Well' she backtracked carefully. 'It's not that I don't like them', furtively glancing at the siblings. 'I just don't know what to say to them.'

'I like kids. I like their simplistic view of the world. Their honesty', Jay smiled.

'Sounds like you could see yourself having some of your own one day', she said quietly.

'I would', he hesitated while looking out on the lake in front of them. 'With the right woman'
Sophie blushed and he knew she understood he meant her. Jay got to his feet and held out his hand for her to grab.

'I think it's time for me to tell you why I've brought you out here to this place today.'

Confusion spread across her face. She had been at the lake before, the last time was for her 18th birthday party two years ago and she hadn't been back since.

'I know you've developed this fear of swimming in the water, and I thought I'd help you get over it.'

'Oh, I didn't expect this trip to become a psychotherapy. When you told me to pack my bikini this morning I assumed we would go to the swimming pool in our neighbourhood.' She laughed as she shifted nervously from one foot to the other.

'But you're right.' She continued. 'Since that night I'm scared of dark waters. I mean I nearly drowned, if it weren't for you saving me. Oh god, that feeling of sinking to the bottom of the lake . It was so dark. So cold. And that water slowly filling my lungs.' she shuddered at the memory.

'As long as I can see the ground, I'm fine. Like in the swimming pool or the shallow waters of the sea in Ibiza, but the dark opaque waters of the lake scares the hell out of me'.

Jay noticed her freckles vanished as she paled. He took her hand.

'Don't worry. I'll be there, we can go in together. I'll stay close, ok? Just trust me.'

She shook her head. Jay looked at her insistingly until she let his green eyes seduce her into stripping out of her denim shorts. As she took off her shirt, he noticed how she looked down at the body he knew she felt so inadequate in and he decided he wouldn't comment on her protruding ribs. He shrugged off his t-shirt in one fluid movement by pulling the collar over his head. He had gained muscle mass since she last saw him in board shorts. Now he was all broad round shoulders, hard pecs and six-packed.

'What are you looking at Soph?' he smiled, as usual completely unaware of the effect he had on the opposite sex. 'You ready?'

She nodded and her embarrassment of getting caught checking out her friend was eclipsed by the panic of entering the green water. He grabbed her hand as they slowly walked into the lake. He liked the way his hand wrapped around hers. It felt natural.

'Pearl, Max listen up. Soph and I are going to swim to the platform over there. You stay here on the beach ok? Don't go wandering off ok? We'll be back in a few minutes.' Pearl nodded and Max's eyes lit up sensing an opportunity to dive into the picnic bag to get the Gameboy.

As the midday summer sun beat down on them the water felt welcomingly fresh. They tiptoed into the deep, trying to ignore the slippery algae under their feet that made their skin crawl, firmly holding onto each other. When the water reached her chin, her nostrils flared and Jay gently pulled her in and protectively folded his arms around her waist.

'You'll be fine ok? This place is so beautiful. Look. The water is so clean you could drink it. This is nature at its best! No chlorine, just wild nature around you. Embrace it.'

'Urrgh...I'm not sure about all the wild nature. What about those ginormous fish at the bottom? The water doesn't look clean and I definitely do not want to drink it. Oh Jay what if the same thing happens again? What if my legs cramp up like they did that time ?' Jay could tell she was starting to hyperventilate. She looked like she was replaying the drowning in her head, picturing herself sinking to the bottom like a stone.

Her breath was ragged and he could see her internal struggle play out in her eyes. The urge to push Jay off her and rush back to the safety of the beach. Then suddenly, without warning, Jay pushed her behind him, shifted her arms around his neck and swam off. Stiff with fear, she held onto his shoulders for dear life. He could feel her chest against his back, his legs kicking the water under her as they swam out towards the platform in the middle of the lake.

They pushed onto the wooden planks and caught their breaths for a few minutes before heading back. Approaching the shoreline, Sophie let go of her friend's shoulders and made her own way back to the beach, safe in the knowledge that with every stroke Jay was next to her, ready to scoop her up in his strong arms. Yet she couldn't help a sigh of relief escaping her mouth when she felt the uneven ground under her feet. Exhilarated, she laughed as they slushed out of the water.

'See? It wasn't that bad, right? How are you feeling?...' Before she could answer, his voice suddenly trailed off and his smile froze.

'Max, Pearl!' he yelled, and rushed over to the side of the beach where the twins had been playing earlier.

Jay grabbed his step-brother by the shoulders and in one sweep yanked him away from his sister. Struggling to regain his balance Maxime fell to his knees in the shallow water while Jay bent over and fished an unconscious Milana out of the lake. Cradling the limp girl in his arms, he ran back to the beach and spread her out on the blanket they had eaten their picnic on earlier. Her chest was flat and her face was turning blue. Jay desperately tried to find a pulse, but his trembling fingers couldn't find the slightest flutter. He felt panic rise as he lifted his hands to her chest to perform an urgent cardiac massage. He pushed deep into her slim chest, pinched her nose shut and breathed into her mouth. Her lungs filled with air. He pressed her torso again. In the intensity of the moment, the world seemed to have ground to a halt. Birds and bees held their breath. The reeds by the water froze as the breeze died down.

'Come on Pearl, don't do this to me', he pleaded, breathing heavily as if to remind her how. But her face remained worryingly immobile. *I can't give up. This can't be happening. Pearl, breathe. Fucking breathe. Please.*

Suddenly the girl's body shuddered, her eyes fluttered and she started coughing, throwing up water. Jay pushed her head gently to the side to open up her airways. She whimpered in agony. Her rasped breath was possibly the most welcoming sound he had ever heard. Only now, he noticed a horrified Sophie sitting next to him, holding a distraught looking Maxime in her arms. Her wet white blonde hair stuck to the side of her face and her eyes flickered with fear, a trembling hand covering her mouth.

'Max, what the hell happened? Did you just try to drown your sister?' Jay yelled at the little boy hiding in Sophie's arms. From his tone it was clear a feeling of concern was overriding the initial anger that had flared up in him. Only mildly aware of the consequences of his actions, Maxime whispered 'I'm sorry', while wiping his nose on his beach towel. His face was closed. Jay wasn't sure whether he really was sorry.

'But why?' Jay couldn't fathom why Max would intentionally hurt his sister.

'We had an argument.' Maxime stared stubbornly at the ground. Judging by the un-repenting look on his face, Jay wasn't convinced his step-brother had any idea of the danger he had put his sister in. Milana sat in Jay's arms and gradually stopped shaking.

'What argument?' Jay pressed on.

The siblings shot a knowing glance at each other, agreed on the unspoken word and shook their heads in unison.

'Nothing', they quickly replied.

Disaster averted and with the twins refusing to breathe a word, Jay decided it was time to pack up and leave for home. Milana was still dizzy and nauseous. Jay helped his step-sister get dressed. She clung onto the towel to climb out of her swimming costume. Still unsteady on her feet, she lost her balance and tripped. The towel slipped uncovering her chest. Black lines criss-crossed her torso as if drawn with a black marker pen. The lines had faded slightly with the water but were still un-mistakenly visible. A line circled the area around the breast that she was yet to develop, then ran down her belly. There were crosses on her ribs and when he turned her around and inspected her bottom, the lines ran across there too.

'What the...Pearl, what is that? Why have you got marker pen lines all over your chest?'

'Nothing.' Milana shot a furtive look at her brother who glowered back at her with dark eyes. She averted her gaze quickly and her lips were white as she pressed them together tightly.

'It looks like those lines surgeons draw on patients before the operations', Sophie remarked, a hint of intrigue in her voice.

They drove back across the city. Having dropped Sophie off at her parents, Jay drove the twins home. They were both sitting in total silence in the back of the Jeep. Both avoided looking at each other, knowing full well they were in trouble. Jay wrestled with himself as to what he was supposed to do about what happened earlier. His step-brother had tried to drown his sister. That was a problem he was going to have to tell his mother about. But if anything he was more confused about the marks on Milana's body. Sophie's words echoed in his mind "Surgeons draw these lines".

Maybe the twins had played a doctor and patient game that morning and Milana had been the patient. Maxime had just marked the areas for surgery. Just like his famous plastic surgeon father did with his patients. When Jay recalled the areas of her body that were circled. Her chest. Her prepubescent chest. Her bottom. Her tummy. Her... He swallowed not wanting to finish that thought. He knew that it was quite normal for kids to explore their bodies at that age, but they were siblings. There was something so creepy about this discovery that he suddenly felt nauseous. From head to toe, a terrible sense of foreboding engulfed him.

***

The cold spring wind rustled the trees. A dog barked in the distance. Jay snapped out of his thoughts, suddenly conscious someone was walking their dog nearby. Jay retreated to the end of the pier and sat on the edge, his legs hovering above the water, the morning mist swirling around his ankles. It was cold and he pushed his head further inside the hood of his parka.

Strangely his mother had not wanted to hear anything. On several occasions, Jay had tried to tell her that there was something wrong with the twins. Milana had kept quiet and the twins went about their usual routine, as if the incident never happened. Jay didn't live with them anymore and all he could do was to urge his mother to keep a close eye on them. She shrugged him off with a stern 'They're just kids, it's part of them growing up. It's all make believe. You're being paranoid'.

But even today, thinking about it again, he couldn't shake the feeling of suspicion. There was something odd about Maxime. It seemed to Jay that the boy was growing up really fast. He was bright, no doubt, for a 18-year-old. Mirroring his father's drive for overachieving, even at a very young age, Maxime revealed himself to be very ambitious. And it felt like he would achieve his goals at any cost. Even at his sister's. Out of them all, he was clearly his stepfather's favourite. On the very rare occasions Caspar took time out from his exploits as a celebrated TV personality, he spent it with his adopted son. Caspar took great pleasure in indoctrinating Maxime on how to become a surgeon. Following these teachings, Maxime would spend hours leafing through Gray's Anatomy, the bible of every student doctor. He enjoyed nothing more than to recite passages he had learned off by heart before going to bed. It was weird how he now not only aped his adoptive father's character traits, but somehow, over the past years, he had also started to look more and more like him. All the more extraordinary, Jay thought, since they had no common DNA. It didn't make any sense. Jay racked his brain for the most rational explanation but still couldn't quite put his finger on it. Maxime's blond hair had darkened and his nose somehow looked slimmer these days. *It was that bike accident and the emergency rhinoplasty. Caspar saved the day and fixed Maxime's nose...*

Escaping his daydreams, emerging back to reality through a thick layer of numbing pharmaceuticals, Jay looked at the lakeside scene around him. At the thought of his step-father he felt a flutter of hatred flicker through him, like a bare electrical wire under water. He pressed his hand on his heart, willing the flood of anxiety to pass. He suddenly became aware of his situation- sitting alone at the end of the pier in the middle of the forest, the man with the dog probably now miles away, a panic attack would probably kill him. He pressed his hand on his heart, willing the flood of anxiety to pass. The paper in his breast pocket creased. He had forgotten about the letter. He looked at it in his hands. It was her handwriting, yes, but somehow the letters conveyed something terribly official and stilted. He took a deep breath and sliced the cover open with his thumb.

After he finished reading it, he paused, his head empty of thoughts. The letter hung limply in his lap. The words crawled over the thick paper ready to jump off the page into the dark waters. Although some part of him had always expected it, he had dreaded this letter since the day he met her, the news still filled him with the deepest sense of regret. She was going to get married but not to him. *Oh Sophie, why?*

end of part two

Part three - Descent into darkness

Jay & Sophie and the others

***

'I'm so happy 'cause today
I've found my friends
They're in my head
I'm so ugly, but that's okay, 'cause so are you
We broke our mirrors
Sunday morning is everyday for all I care
And I'm not scared'

Lithium,
Nirvana

***

CHAPTER 15

Ibiza, December 2011 - 1 year after the incident

The wind blew gently through the silver foliage of the olive trees, and the pale winter sun traced long shadows across the gravel of the cemetery. There was a quiet dignity about the place that soothed the soul. Respectfully silent ravens perched on the cemetery's white walls and stared purposefully into the distance. A stern black cat sat on the newly-erected and unweathered tombstone. Even the colony of ants had diverted their highway to march their soldiers in a tribute battalion at the foot of the freshly-dug grave.

Sophie had expected that on the day she buried her father the weather would reflect the dark despair of a loved-one lost, but the sun was shining mildly, as if to warm her heart. The pain tugged at her. It all felt surreal. She couldn't believe he was gone. Just like that. A last breath and he was torn away, his life light snuffed out like a candle. The emptiness inside her was bottomless. It was like looking into a well of sadness that threatened to swallow her whole, but she knew that at the very bottom, where it was as dark as midnight, there was a flicker of light. It felt like freedom. The ties to the demons of her youth had finally been cut and she was drifting towards the soft light of the pale winter sun.

'Vera?' as she opened her eyes her mother was standing by the tombstone, her hand resting on the cool marble, her gaze firmly locked on the engraving. *Jonathan Francis Liebtreu, Rest in Peace.* The weight of loss sunk her shoulders into her skinny body. She looked so fragile and lost. Like a child, Sophie thought. Her mother's grief-stricken face was hollow and gaunt; Sophie couldn't find the words to comfort her. Instead, she silently wrapped her arms around her vanishing waist. As tears rolled down her mother's face, Sophie gently freed her hands of the small storm light and with infinite care, placed it on the grave. Arm in arm, they stood by the grave, lost in fading memories, in the silent solace of each other's company.

That year they had decided to spend Christmas away from the cold Berlin winter and the whole family had booked a flight to Ibiza. The climate was mild in the winter, and although there was no central heating in the crumbling villa, the fireplaces were sufficient to keep them warm in the December evenings. The giant cactus in the garden had doubled up as a Christmas tree, and their days had been spent walking the cliffs, drinking coffees con leche in quiet bars and lazily lounging on the rugged sun beds in the courtyard, sheltering from the Mediterranean winter wind. Sophie had enjoyed the toned-down atmosphere of an island devoid of tourists, spending her time bonding with the roughly-spoken locals.

Her brother Sam and his girlfriend Janine looked happier than ever. The glow of their newly rekindled love shone a soothing light on everyone. Sophie's daughter Juliet played happily with her little cousin Seth and the mothers shared quiet conversations about the challenges and joys of motherhood while the dads gathered around the winter barbecue. It had been so peaceful.

And then the bubble of their safe haven burst. One morning Frank didn't wake up. The cancer he had kept quiet about had spread aggressively and the medicine had reached its limit of effectiveness. He was gone. 'Don't eat that it will give you cancer' had been his motto for so many years and Sophie knew it had contributed to her eating disorder. *Looks like Cancer won anyway.*

'Now I know what real loss feels like', her mother whispered in a barely audible voice, finally breaking the silence as they stood by the grave. Sophie hugged her tightly, chasing away the memory of the frantic aftermath of the discovery of his cold body.

'I think he would have liked his last resting place. He always loved to come to Santa Inez' Vera continued in a monotonous voice, lost in thoughts and talking to herself. Sophie looked up at the tiny chapel and remembered fondly her wedding a few years back. She had been blissfully happy that day. Her father had got blind drunk as usual, but he had looked content. The only cloud darkening her day had been the argument she had with Jay. She couldn't believe she caught him hitting on her best friend, Camelia. Sophie frowned, shook her head at the thought and smiled sadly. How wrong it all sounded now. How fate was twisted.

***

Ibiza, June 2009 - 1 year before the incident

'¡Senor,despiértese! ¿por favor?'

A hand touched his shoulder.

'¿Senor? ¿Se levanta? no es permitido dormir aquí'

He grunted, swatted the hand away and lifted his head. He blinked, putting his vision into focus and saw the old man staring at him with wrinkled eyes. The naked light bulb dangling from the ceiling blinded him and shot waves of pain through his head. The old man impatiently prodded him with his broomstick and pointed to the door.

'Out mister, out!'

Jay grumbled and, a little unsteady, sat up. How come he didn't wake up in his bed at his father's?

Sophie had married the day before in a small white church with black wooden benches in the picturesque village of Santa Inez. The sun had shone mildly as the guests gathered in front of the church entrance. The small town square had been decorated with white bunting, and the soft pink almond blooms had perfumed the air with a sickly sweet smell that reminded him of the Turkish bakery in his street. She was now going to be called Sophie Liebtreu-Mackenzie.

His tongue felt too big for his mouth, his lips were cracked. He needed water. Damn Lithium, he thought, the drug always made him thirsty. It didn't help that it was hot and dry in this place, and come to think of it that he had ingested copious amounts of alcohol last night. He looked around. It seemed to be an empty storage room full of buckets, brooms and folded up parasols. He peeled his sore limbs out of the bean bag he had fallen asleep in and reluctantly followed the tutting old man down the corridor.

He scratched his head trying to figure out what time it was, where he was and how he got here. The psychedelic swirls on the carpet reminded him of the kid on the tricycle in the corridor scene from The Shining. He half expected little twin girls to appear in front of him, dressed in matching blue dresses. The old man turned around and waved, urging him to hurry up. 'Out out!' were the only words he knew in English.

The old man pushed him into the elevator, pressed the lobby button and with one last disapproving look, went about his cleaning business. Confused, Jay warily crossed the busy lobby and stepped out of the hotel into the hot white sunshine. He covered his eyes and began to fumble in his pockets for his sunglasses. He pulled his Ray-Bans out of his jacket and popped them on.

'That's better', he mumbled. Still desperate for a drink he went through his trouser pockets, pulling out a taxi receipt and a few coins. Enough to buy him a bottle of water at the shop across the street. He looked at the taxi receipt: 90 euros. Seemed a bit excessive. For 90 euros, you could probably cross the whole island. Maybe that was exactly what he did? He wondered. Either that or the taxi driver had ripped him off.

The sign on the wall behind him read 'Hotel Tanit'. He took a deep breath, recognising the place. It was the hotel a beach away from his father's villa. They had been here before, Sophie, Frank and him. On their way back from a night out clubbing. *Was it Amnesia, the club with the foam parties or Privilege, the one with the swimming pool? Yes, the latter one, the one with the retractable roof and the snake charmers, the giant bed and the late night porn show in the swimming pool.*

They had gotten the bus back into town at sunrise and feeling hungry and thirsty they had stumbled into the lobby of the Tanit Hotel. The key had been to be confident, look like you belonged and walk through to the breakfast terrace without hesitating. When the hotel clerk had asked them for their room number, Frank just bellowed '14'. The man nodded, ticked the room of his sheet and showed them a table in the shade of the pine trees. 'The trick is, there never is a room 13, but there's always a 14', Frank had whispered to his two friends.

Proud of their cunningness, they tucked into the buffet like it was their last meal. Jay smiled at the memory. They never felt so much as an ounce of guilt nor did they worry about getting caught. Dressed up for a night out clubbing, with remains of fluorescent makeup smeared on their cheeks and glitter in their hair, they had looked completely out of place, standing out in a sea of middle-class German families in Birkenstocks, white vest tops and Adidas board shorts. He couldn't help but long for those days. Life had seemed so simple back then. Just a series of exciting adventures to be had, the arrogance of youth shielding them from the fear of repercussions.

The hangover wasn't too bad, so he put the lack of memories of the night before down to one of his blackouts. Although still finding them unnerving, he had grown used to them, and so he went through his usual checklist to reconstruct the events of the night before *Where am I?* He looked over the pine trees, the golden beach and the turquoise sea. *Ibiza. Hotel Tanit. I'm on my way to my father's villa, just up the road.*

Why am I here? He remembered the flight he had taken a couple of days ago. Berlin - Ibiza. The nervous anticipation had started on the plane. As so often when he travelled, he very much preferred the journey to actually arriving. He liked looking out of the small window into the vast open skies; it helped him concentrate on the infinite freedom beyond the wings of the aircraft and kept his growing claustrophobia in check. He had always liked traveling. As a kid, his parents would often drive out into the countryside to visit his grandparents. He had loved spending the afternoon sitting in the back of the car, staring into the wide open, listening to his parents sing along to the radio. Traveling was an escape route.

At school he had never really fitted in, his natural shyness and slight foreign accent had quickly made him the target for bullies. He had inherited his Toronto-born mother's lilt and a Canadian passport. His dual nationality had him feeling a foreigner in both countries. Not quite German and not quite Canadian. Traveling had become a cure for his feelings of inadequacy. Being on the road meant not belonging anywhere, it meant that normal daily routines didn't exist, anything went, everything was possible. Sleeping with your clothes on, skipping brushing your teeth, eating sweets for breakfast. Every sight was a discovery, the only worries revolved around the basics: where will we eat and where will I sleep tonight? Traveling gave him a sense of purpose, of movement, just going somewhere, escaping... ultimate freedom.

Only this time round, he didn't want to reach his destination, and he had surprised himself by secretly wishing for the plane to crash.

'Hey Jay!' Sam Liebtreu, Sophie's younger brother emerged from the neighbouring villa carrying a large plastic crate. The champagne glasses clinked loudly as he gently lowered the case to the ground to shake Jay's hand.

'Mate, how are you? Wild night last night huh?' he winked and flashed a knowing smile.

'Mmmm tell me about it.'

'Ha, ha, ha.'

He has her smiling grey eyes. And her carefree smile.

'No, really, tell me about it. I'm not sure I can remember much.'

Sam looked at him slightly surprised but didn't make any comments, maybe he had heard about Jay's blackouts. Their parents had a habit of talking to each other about their kids.

'Well, first of all, thank you for letting me take over the set, it was a great honour. I'm clearly not as good as you, but I don't think the guests noticed that I took over the turntables for a bit. People were rocking it out on the dance floor until we broke off to the club.'

'I let you DJ?'

'Yep, you insisted. I think you wanted to enjoy the party a bit.'

Jay doubted that. There was nothing about that day he had particularly enjoyed. He helped carry the crate to the hired van, then snuck into his father's villa for a quick shower and some clean clothes before helping with the rest of the boxes and champagne bottles. Glad for the company and an extra pair of hands, Sam offered him a ride to the venue. Jay vaguely remembered promising to come to the brunch, but he couldn't remember who he had made the promise to. *A girl? Did I meet someone last night?*

'Dude, you were dancing with a lot of girls last night. You were quite popular, you have to teach me your ways man, it seems the more you ignore the ladies, the more they come flocking to you. Is that it? Treat'm mean to keep'm keen?'

Jay didn't know how to answer that and just smiled vaguely embarrassed. As they arrived at the venue, a beautiful Ibizenco villa with gleaming white walls and an arched entrance, they unloaded the crates and carried them to the large vaulted kitchen to stock an industrial-sized fridge. A fashionable man in his late twenties walked past Jay, his lips pressed into a thin line and his thumbs firmly tucked into his linen waistcoat. He suddenly stopped, turned on his heel and charged back, his finger raised at Jay, his eyes blazing.

'You... you asshole you, you have some nerve to show up and parade your disregard for other people's religions. You Satanist!' he spat at his feet and hurried off mumbling into the distance, leaving Jay wide-eyed, palms raised.

'What was that dude's problem?' Sam asked perplexed.

'I don't know', he shrugged, 'I don't even know this guy. Think I saw him in the church yesterday afternoon but... looks like I've done something to upset him...'

As much as he hated the blackouts, somehow he still found some sort of perverted pleasure in putting together the pieces of the jigsaw. Detective style. He just hoped he hadn't completely fucked up this time and done some irreparable damage. That guy seemed pretty angry.

It was just after 11:00 and Jay decided a beer was going to do for breakfast. They found Frank on the terrace overlooking the garden. In total disregard of the dress code, he wore red shorts and an ugly blue Hawaiian shirt. Jay wasn't sure whether the outfit was meant to be ironic. Frank peered over his wayfarers and greeted him with a wry smile.

'Look who managed to find his way back, the man of a thousand shenanigans. We had bets on whether we'd find you in a prison cell or at the bottom of a Cala', Frank guffawed into his glass of water. Or was that a gin & tonic?

'That bad?'

'What you mean that bad? Ooooh... dude no', Frank hiccupped when he realised. 'You mean, you had one of those nights again?'

Jay nodded 'Afraid so.'

'Oh fuck. And what do you remember? Nothing?'

'Nothing. Woke up in the basement of that Hotel Tanit, a few coins in my pockets and a taxi receipt. No recollection of last night.'

'Man I pity you, you probably had the dirtiest sex and poor sucker you can't even remember it', Frank shook his head at the desolating thought.

'Did you check your wallet?' Sam interjected, dragging a gigantic potted plant from one side of the terrace to the side facing the garden. It was meant to look more festive there, but the pot just left an unattractive mark on the tiles. More and more people trickled in and started cleaning the terrace, fixing paper lanterns to the fig trees and putting bunting up across the garden, chatting excitedly to each other all the while.

Jay pulled his wallet out. He was a little surprised it was still there, but relieved he hadn't lost it again. He had lost his wallet so many times before, he swore he could hear the exasperated sigh of the operator at the bank hotline: 'Again sir? Really? What happened this time?'

A condom wrap fell to the floor at Frank's feet. He swooped it up with a wicked grin.
'Huhu look at this! Guess you didn't get lucky after all.'

Jay didn't react to the jibe; he had found something else. A bill. He stared at it. Looked away and stared at it again. €2,252.57. He swallowed hard and ignored the bead of cold sweat forming on his temples. The heading of the receipt read 'Space'.

'Wow, €2,252 euros! You must have entertained quite a crowd', Frank looked over his shoulder.

'Space opens at what? 7ish? Were you there with me?' he whispered tentatively, desperately racking his brain for some memory. He couldn't find anything, the only thing he remembered was the article he had read on the plane.

Space was the after-party club of choice for celebrities. It opened when the other clubs closed, providing night dwellers and pill poppers a place to continue the night, well after dawn had broken.

'Nope, remember I ... oh no you don't...well I... err well I overdid it a bit. Think that coke was a bit off. Puked my guts out on one of the posh sofas at Pacha's and security banned me from the club. Bastards threw me out on the street. Fuckers.' Frank grimaced at the thought of the two bouncers, built like Soviet tanks, who had manhandled him and didn't react to his feeble attempt at threatening them with a lawsuit. They just said something in Russian to each other and laughed very loudly.

'Ok, so you didn't join me at the after party. Did you Sam?'

Sam walked over balancing a silver tray with Serrano ham, freshly sliced off the leg. Jay stuffed a slice in his mouth. It tasted like heaven, and his stomach growled for more of this salty deliciousness.

'No, I had to go back to the villa. I had no more money left, plus I promised my sister I was going to help organise today's brunch.' An argument erupted in the kitchen, and Sam excused himself and quickly got back to his event management duties.

'So who did I spend that much money with?' Jay pondered. It was getting hot, and he rolled up the sleeves of his shirt to reveal the ink on his forearm.

'What the fuck is that?' asked Frank pointing at the black markings. The marker pen had faded, but the numbers were just about readable.

'Looks like a phone number doesn't it.' Jay had tried to remember who wrote it on his arm since discovering it in the shower.

'I bet it's the chick you banged. Come on let's call it!' Frank thrust his mobile phone in Jay's face. He punched the number in and waited for the dial. It rang for quite a while and Jay was just about to hang up when the line clicked.

'Hello?' A gruff male voice answered the phone.

'Oh hi', he rolled his eyes at Frank's face pulling. Sometimes he wondered if his friend's mental age was above ten. 'Err... I... well I have this number written on my arm and I ...err... figured that I should call. So huh... who are you?'

Jay knew he wasn't making much sense and expected the man to hang up. Why did he have the number of a guy on his arm?

Last night really must have been wild. The man on the line hesitated a moment and then, to Jay's surprise exclaimed:

'Oh yeah, you're that dude from last night right? The one with the amnesia problem, like that guy in the Memento movie yeah? So you told us some dickhead of a friend lost your phone in the club last night, and we were to look for it. And we did. And the good news is that we found it. Wedged in the sofa next to a puddle of vomit. Don't worry the phone's fine. We put it in the safe so feel free to come pick it up. We open the club at around four this afternoon.' The guy hung up and Jay realised that in the space of two minutes he had not only lost his phone but found it again.

Brunch had started, and guests leisurely strolled into the garden, picking their seats in the shade of fragrant fig trees. Waiters brought out trays of tasty tapas and jugs of fruity sangria. The table linen was crisp white, and the cutlery weighed heavy in hand. A subtle lavender aroma hung in the air and just as the day before, the attention to detail was flawless, and the atmosphere was one of laid-back chic. Family and friends embraced the hippie chic dress code and wore white silk and organza tunics and trousers.

Jay was about to tuck into his manchego cheese sandwich when she entered the garden. He froze at the sight of her. Dressed in a long floaty dress, she looked a picture of grace and elegance. Her white blonde hair was tied in a loose bun on the top of her head accentuating her long neck. Last night's excesses did not seem to have left a mark on her, and she smiled a radiant smile. Her confidence and pure joy were infectious, and everyone appeared to gravitate closer to catch a glimpse of her, hoping for some of her happiness to rub off on them. To him, she looked like a goddess.

...Now the beach is deserted except for some kelp
And a piece of an old ship that lies on the shore
You always responded when I needed your help

You gimme a map and a key to your door…

His heart shrunk at the notes of the Bob Dylan song that played in his head, and the stab of longing that pierced through his soul threatened to tear him apart. She was so close he could smell her perfume so familiar to him. He balled his fist around the knife in his hand until his knuckles turned white. The sun caught the freshly cut diamond on her finger and exploded into a rainbow of colour creating a forever impenetrable barrier between them.

During the ceremony, she had put her dainty hand into her future husband's and had smiled that same radiant smile. Pure happiness. Jay had felt dizzy with the desire to jump up and drag the man away from her; the one who was going to become her partner in sickness and in health until death would part them...

He fantasised about swinging a right hook to his chin and smacking the man's head against the cold marble floor in a spatter of blood. In his mind's eye, he could picture himself kneeling next to the lifeless body, wringing his bloodied hands on her virginal wedding gown, begging her to forgive him. Shocked at hearing the voice in his head again, this time suggesting a brutal homicide in a church, he had quickly swallowed a stronger dosage of his anti-anxiety drug. By the end of the ceremony, the drug had started its numbing effect and that strange floaty feeling of sitting underwater had eclipsed his growing anxiety. And so when the guests stood up and walked solemnly to the altar to receive the body and blood of Christ, he had followed them.

Slightly dazed, he looked at the host the priest had gently placed in the palm of his hand. Ignoring the chalice the altar boy held up, he slowly walked back to his seat. Jay took a bite of the wafer-like host. It tasted sweet. He still looked at it wondering what the big deal was and whether the body of Christ was meant to taste sweet when suddenly the young man stood next to him shot him a warning look. Then unable to contain his irritation, the young man leaned over and hissed bitterly:

'How dare you disrespect our traditions. This isn't a macaroon you have with your coffee. This IS the body of Christ.'

Jay shrugged his shoulders nonchalantly which seemed to exasperate the young man even more.

His face was bright red with anger but before he could utter a word, Jay leaned in.

'Go fuck yourself you fanatic', Jay had spoken softly, and although a small smile curled his lips, his eyes were cold as steel. The man had recoiled at the unexpected aggressiveness in his voice and shifted uncomfortably on his bench for the remainder of the ceremony, glaring at him with the hatred of a humiliated man. That red-faced man was the same person he bumped into earlier, and he was now sitting at the newly weds' table. Next to the groom. Jay wanted to slap his forehead. *I offended the overly zealous brother of the groom.*

Suddenly Jay felt a warm hand on his thigh, he looked down on a tanned hand with long silver coated fingernails gently stroking his leg.

'Hey gorgeous', said a raspy voice that sounded like it hadn't recovered from one too many whiskies.

'Camelia - nice to see you', Jay nodded politely. Jay found her pretty in a ferocious kind of way. Her long straight blonde hair was thick and shiny. Her blue eyes piercing. She laughed a 'Nice to see you too', and then whispered hotly in his ear: 'I'm still sore from last night but it was so good. If you wanted to do it again, I'm ready. They have rooms upstairs in the villa', she looked at him with hooded eyes and licked her lower lip suggestively.

Jay nearly dropped his cutlery, quickly shut his mouth and looked over at Frank, who chuckled in his gin and tonic before making an obscene gesture with his hand and mouth.

'Err well Cam. I... umm...about last night. You need to know that...'

'Ah, look I know what you are going to say. I know I'm her best friend, and I know you and her had a history of some sort and I totally understand that you want to keep it discreet for now. So don't worry I won't say a word.'

Jay sighed frustrated. Although one part of him desperately wanted to piece last night's events together, he now wasn't sure he wanted to know the dirty details. *A fling with Sophie's best friend? On her wedding night?* He cringed at the predictability, the tackiness.

Later that day he drove his father's car to the club to pick up his phone. The man at the bar opened the safe and handed it to him with a smile and a stiff Jack Daniels.

'You look like you need one mate', he laughed. Jay reckoned he did need one. He switched his phone on and went through to the photo album. After flicking through a few pictures of graffiti pieces in Berlin, he stumbled onto the photos of the night before. He sighed and downed a gulp of whisky and flicked to the next snapshot. The quality was bad and the lighting all wrong but although the photos were grainy, he could still recognise the faces.

It showed him, sat on a white leather sofa, his arms around three girls on each side, all wearing slinky short tight white dresses. Their limbs long and lean, their skin soft and tanned. Full smiles with big, clean teeth and beach blonde hair, long and tousled. Unsmiling he was raising a middle finger at whoever took the photo. Probably Frank, Jay reckoned. The next picture showed him in a tight embrace with a skinny blonde in a white sequinned mini dress barely covering her pert behind. Jay shook his head and took another sip of his whisky.

The following photo was out of focus; a hand raised against the lens only covering half of the shared kiss. It was Cam he was kissing. *Photographic evidence. Great.*

Jay inhaled sharply. The sight of the next snapshot made his innards melt. Sophie was dancing on a table in the VIP area of the club, a bottle of Bollinger in one hand and the other raised to the sky, smiling victoriously. She had slipped out of her wedding dress into a short sexy blood-red number and stood out against a crowd of guests wearing white. He studied the blurry photo intently and when the barman nudged him to offer another whisky, Jay nodded gratefully.

CHAPTER 16

Solacium, January 2012 - 1 year after the incident

Sophie couldn't believe what she was about to do. She peered through the thick curtain of rain at the gloomy petrol station, checked her watch nervously and slid into the passenger seat. She squeezed out of her flowery dress into something more appropriate, a pair of white jeans and a light-coloured hoodie. She was aware she was putting on a good show; her long, lean legs sprawled across the dashboard, wrangling herself into the tight jeans. The man who tanked up his Mercedes at the next pump nearly doused the place with petrol as he ogled her, open-mouthed.

Her friend Justine had celebrated her newborn's christening in Berlin that morning and Sophie regretted leaving straight after the brunch. She had made her excuses and had taken to the road in her mother's Alfa Romeo. She hated that car. It was too fast and unpredictable. Living in London, she wasn't used to driving anymore, and each car trip now filled her with dread. She cursed and kicked her high heels off and slipped into her trainers. The memory of the conversation she had with Justine's husband was playing in the back of her head like a clip on loop.

'So I heard you are visiting your ...errrm... "friend" today', he had said with a condescending tone, using his fingers to mark the quote. Sophie had bowed her head, trying to disguise the flickering heat in her eyes.

'Yes', she replied, feeling as though she was being pushed into a corner. Sophie knew Justine had told her husband of her plans. And, righteous and straight-laced as he was, the family man, heir to his father's firm and all round self-imbued overachiever, Harald Wachtel couldn't hold back on the judgmental tone.

'Why would anyone want to visit a man like him? Remind me how he did it? With an axe or was it a baseball bat? I read in the newspapers he tortured his victim before murdering him in cold blood', Harald prodded further with narrowed eyes. Sophie glowered back at him, shaking with anger. She disliked him and had done from the minute her friend had introduced them. His thin hair, anally gelled-back, his perfectly-pressed chinos and pastel-coloured Ralph Lauren polos, his world was made of the same certainty as his annual tax return.

'Harald, he is still my friend', she whispered, her voice only thinly disguising her rising anger. 'I've known him for years. He has not had an easy life. The divorce of his parents. The depression. All the pills he had to take. The schizophrenia. He was hearing voices for god sakes, constantly. Voices that told him people were out to kill him. Do you have any idea how terrifying that would've been for him?' Her words sounded defensive, and she hated herself for it.

'Well...' Harald exhaled disapprovingly 'He certainly made his family suffer. And now he's locked up in a cushy loony bin at the taxpayer's expense instead of getting a real sentence. He should have gone to prison if you ask me. Isn't it convenient all these so-called psycho killers plead insanity?'

It took Sophie all her restraint to remain silent and not explode in a fury of rebuttals. *He has no idea. He doesn't understand that schizophrenia is the mental equivalent of having a fractured spine. And he left it untreated for years.*

Frustrated by her silence, Harald continued, pointing at her giggling daughter, busy chasing his Labrador:

'Surely you are not taking Juliet to see your..."friend"?' he emphasised on the word. 'It's not an appropriate environment for a toddler!'

Sophie bit her lip at his patronising tone. *Of course, I'm taking my kid to a fucking asylum! Who wouldn't?* But she reluctantly kept the sarcasm at bay.

Shaking with nerves, Sophie drove at breakneck speed on the Autobahn, conscious that she had no idea where she was going.She felt the envelope crease in the back pocket of her jeans and wondered whether she'd feel brave enough to give it to Jay. She relied on the GPS to guide her through the gloomy rainy country roads. She was still reeling from Harald's words. She wanted to justify herself as to why it was so important she remained friends with the man who she had grown up with. But he would be the last person she would tell the truth to.

***

Berlin, March 2010 - 9 months before the incident

Sophie walked down the street at a fast pace, clutching a photo close to her chest, frantically looking left and right, taking in every person in her vicinity. The man who just walked out the corner shop with a pack of toilet rolls wedged under his arm, the mother trying to appease her crying toddler, the group of moody teenagers sheepishly smoking on the bus shelter bench. The sole thought on her mind was to find him.

She didn't think of what she would say to him when she eventually saw him, she just prayed he was ok. By now she was sure something had happened to him. The phone call with Jay's father had left her worrying about Jay's welfare. He had not replied to any of her emails since the last time she saw him at her wedding in Ibiza. She had tried calling him and left numerous voicemails which he didn't return. Her initial feelings of hurt and disappointment had turned to anger at his indifference. In the end, she resorted to calling his father Henry to find out more about his son's whereabouts. Henry had not said much, but the slight tremor in his voice had betrayed his true feelings. Despite his forced aloofness, he sounded alarmed.

'I haven't seen him in weeks. Actually it's been months now', he confessed quietly. 'In the beginning I thought he was having one of his creative phases, he has locked himself in his studio before and for weeks on end, nobody would really see him. But not this time. I got worried when he started leaving increasingly erratic messages on my phone. Some of it sounded so dreadfully odd, something about people spying on him. Apparently he had found out that his new neighbours were trying to set up...'

He breathed in sharply at the memory of his son's haunted voice '...a brothel.'

'A what?! A brothel?' Sophie asked incredulously, this didn't make any sense. She wondered if he was on drugs. She knew he had some unsavoury characters amongst his hipster friends, who dabbled in illegal substances. The Jay she knew wasn't impartial to smoking marijuana, and perhaps he had given in to more powerful, escapist drugs.

'Yes I know, it doesn't sound right. I tried to return his calls, but he would never pick up. Over the weeks, his messages became more cryptic, he said he knew there was "more to this than what met the eye". That there was "a traitor in our midst". "An evil spirit". Someone he kept calling Dan. I tried to come to his flat to check on him, but he never answered the door. After a while, I noticed a growing pile of unopened mail on the doormat, so I had a locksmith break the front door open. His flat...' his voice trailed off. He coughed and lowered his voice '...his flat was unrecognisable.'

Sophie clearly remembered the clean and stylish interior design of the flat, with its stainless steel kitchen, plush designer sofa and flatscreen TVs. She had admired her friend's eclectic but impeccable taste.

His father continued, 'the screens of his TVs were all smashed. There was food rotting in every corner of every room. He had taped tin foil and cardboard to each window. The air stank of burnt hair and rotting fruit. He had tried to burn his paintings on the terrace. The floor was littered with ashes and strips of canvass. Black and red paint covered most walls, as if he had taken to hurling paint pots at them. '

Sophie suddenly remembered the lacerated wall in his kitchen. 'Were there any marks on the walls?' she asked cautiously.

'Yes how do you know? It looked like...' he paused. 'It looked like someone had stabbed them'

After she hung up, she couldn't shake the nagging sense of dread that sat deep in the pit of her stomach. After she had spoken to her husband, she boarded a flight to Berlin the following day. Now, as she walked the streets of East Berlin, Henry's last words echoed in her head: 'I think he's going insane'.

It seemed no one else knew where he was. She had managed to track Frank down, but he was quite vague about his friend's whereabouts. All she had managed to get out of him, was that they'd had an argument and he had not spoken to him in a while. He did mention that Jay had decided to move out of his flat and move in with some squatters for some reason he didn't understand.

Sophie had pressed on: 'Do you know these guys? Where is the squat?'

He said he didn't know the address. He only knew they hung out somewhere in East Berlin around Kreuzberg. He didn't want to get involved with these people. They were bad news, real bad news, he had insisted. Sophie swallowed hard, coming from a guy like Frank, who probably scored quite high on Hare's Psychopath test, it must have been really bad. She started to fear for Jay's life.

She had called the police, but they could not help. As Jay was over 18 and as he posed no danger to himself or the public, he was free to leave his home for an undetermined time. Although he had a criminal record, his offences had been limited to mild delinquency as a minor. After a reluctant policeman checked their recent records, the only mentionable activity of late had been a verbal warning Jay was given for setting up a tent in the park nearby his home a few months ago.

She called all the hospitals in the vicinity of his apartment, but he was on none of the patient lists, nor had he been in A&E. Feeling increasingly helpless, she focused on the places people would go if suddenly made homeless. Homeless shelters. Soup kitchens. She quickly researched all the charities and homeless shelters in the area. Armed with Jay's photo and a list of addresses, she set off to find her friend.

She hadn't had much luck at the first two shelters she walked into. The people at reception had been rude and unhelpful. The places looked filthy and depressing. Looking at the cockroach infested communal dormitories she really hoped not to find him here. Her shoulders tense and a knot of worry tying her stomach, she continued her search to stop at a small, unassuming shop front: the soup kitchen. She recognised the place from a distant memory. Jay had told her the year they had met that, before Christmas, he had chosen to serve food to the homeless instead of celebrating the day with his mother and the stepfather he so hated. This was the same place; Sophie was sure of it. He had to be around here.

As she opened the door, she was met with a dozen glaring stares and the stench of overcooked Brussels sprouts. She nodded politely and the group of weathered men went back to slurping their noodle soups and gnawing on their stale bread rolls. The fat woman at the soup counter eyed her up suspiciously, and Sophie was suddenly aware that her clean and well-cut clothes outed her as an unwelcome intruder. She mumbled a quick apology, duly ignored by the grim-looking woman, and showed her Jay's photo. Her little pig eyes narrowed, and Sophie felt pins and needles in her arms in nervous anticipation. But to her immense disappointment the fat cook moodily shook her head. Sophie insisted she looked closer at the photo of a young smiling Jay but the woman returned to her pots, ignoring Sophie's pleading look.

'Hey! You!' Someone slurred in her ear with stale wine breath, tapping irritatingly on her shoulder. 'Yes you, lovely lady with the perfume'. The ugly old man leaned over and smelled her hair 'Aaaahhh.... clean and smelling good' He whistled approvingly through a toothless grin. His sailor coat was dull and stiff with dirt. His feet were bare and showed long gnarly black toenails. His straggly beard hid three-quarters of his face. He reeked of urine and alcohol. Sophie found herself backed against the wall with the man's intense eyes glaring at her from underneath a pair of bushy grey eyebrows.

'You're looking for this man, right?' He barked at her, then coughed a loud cough that threatened to tear his lungs apart, regurgitating a black gooey lump that he spat on the floor at her feet. The cook howled in protest in the background. Sophie swallowed her revulsion and nodded meekly.

'I've seen him', the man rasped and then licked his black fingers indicating that this information would cost her money. A glimmer of hope sparked in her eyes and she quickly fished for her wallet in her handbag. He had seen Jay. He was still around somewhere near. She would soon find him. The man took the cash, stuffed it in his hole-ridden underpants and grinned a black gaping hole.

'The musician', he nodded.

'The musician?' Sophie saw her hopes evaporating fast. Maybe the old man was just crazy and hustling her out of her money.

'Yeaaaaah', he exhaled rolling his eyes madly at her. 'The one who plays everything like it's a drum set. Everywhere he goes. Darumm tack tack, darum tack tack. On the park benches and the bins. Some on the street think he is a genius. I think he is a sodding idiot who doesn't know how to use his talent to earn some street money. Poor wanker', he shook his head 'His cluelessness is surely going to kill him out here.'

'Do you know where I can find him?' she whispered, stuck with an image in her head of her friend sleeping on lonely park benches.

'Why would you want to find him? Are you his girl? Didn't know the poor sod would have a girl this pretty', he said mockingly, and she knew he was trying to get more money out of her. Sophie thought about his question for a second. Why was she trying to find him and, more importantly, what was she going to tell him once she got to him? She shook her head, she just wanted to know he was safe.

'Look, here's another note, now just tell me where he is, alright?' She snarled at him. The old man stepped back, snatched the money out of her hand and pointed at the apartment blocks by the river.

'He was sleeping around there lately, so yeah, your best bet will be around those flats. Good luck lovely lady. God bless you.'

The tramp limped out of the soup kitchen with a toothless grin. No doubt Sophie had made his day and he walked straight into the liquor store across the street. That night the man would probably see himself refused entry at the shelter after failing the alcohol breath test and would be forced to sleep on a park bench by the river. He probably wouldn't survive the night.

Sophie ran to the apartment block a few hundred meters down the road from the soup kitchen. She crisscrossed the narrow alleyways. No sign off Jay. Again she walked the blocks from the other side. After a couple of hours, she stopped by the river, exhausted and disappointed, cold panic rising. *What happened to him, where is he?* She couldn't understand it, he had seemed fine the last time she had seen him, at her wedding. As usual he had been distant and quiet but he appeared to have had fun. Cam had confided in her and had told her the details of her one-night stand with Jay.

Cam had sheepishly admitted that it had been the best one-night stand of her life and, with a determined glint in her eye, she affirmed that she wanted this to be the start of a relationship. To Sophie's horror she had even described him as being of potential 'the one' material. Sophie didn't know how to react, she had just gotten married to the man she thought she was going to love for the rest of her life. The kind and funny Mr Mackenzie. The copper-haired, fair skinned investment banker she had met at a black-tie work event. The man who loved her so much he let her spend a few months in Berlin while he stayed in London when she was made redundant from her analyst job. The man who turned a blind eye at her strange relationship with Jay.

She knew Jay and her were supposed to be just friends – so why shouldn't Jay be happy with her friend? Why not? She had swallowed her hurt and had given Camelia her blessing and wished them good luck. But still that didn't explain why Jay hadn't replied to her emails. She had mentioned that she knew what had happened but told him she wished him all the best anyway.

She walked back to the bus stop as the sun slowly started to set. It was getting late. A man sat on the steps of the apartment block on the opposite side of the street, his head buried deep into his hood, rolling a cigarette. She casually looked over.

The hood covered half of his face but as he looked up to light his cigarette she looked into a pair of bright green eyes. She sucked in her breath.

'Jay', she whispered, her heart started beating frenetically. His steely stare bore into her with cold disaffection until he recognised her and his eyes widened in surprise.

'Sophie?' The cigarette fell to the floor and quietly burnt down to the filter before dying out.

Running, she crossed the street without checking the traffic and stopped at his feet, breathless. For a moment that felt like an eternity they just stood there, staring at each other. The stains on his trousers and the dirt on his boots contrasted sharply with her prim designer jacket and heeled boots. Finally, she broke the silence with a sob. Tears of relief streamed down her face and as she held out her hand, his photo slipped onto the dusty street. He stood up and removed the hood to reveal a shaggy mop of hair. He hugged her awkwardly and quickly let go. He invited her to sit down next to him on the steps.

'Jay, what happened? You need to tell me, I need to know. I'm worried about you' she whispered, wiping the tears with the back of her shaking hand.

The last of the day's sun warmed their faces and as he passed her his thermos flask, he started to talk. The coffee was cold and tasted bitter. He told her about the new neighbours who moved into the flat above his. The first thing he noticed was that they would always ignore his polite greetings, which had irked him slightly, but he had put it down to bad education. Then he started hearing the nightly tapping on the ceiling and the walls. The clicking of heels on the wooden flooring woke him at night.

'I'd look out of the door spy and see these men loitering in the corridor. They wore dark leather coats and looked hungry. They looked like animals.' Sophie shifted uncomfortably at the cold tone of his voice, but he took no notice and continued. 'They would come late at night and queue outside the door of the flat. It was one in and one out. Sometimes they would go in groups. It was creepy.' He went through the pocket of his jumper and pulled out a small tin box. He flicked open the lid and picked out some tobacco and Rizlas.

'It started with nightmares and then I stopped being able to go to sleep. I have had bouts of insomnia before but nothing like this. I was lying in bed for hours and hours, listening to the noises in the flat above. The clicking of the heels, the men in the corridor sniffing in excitement, the rhythmic tapping against the wall...'

He finished rolling his cigarette and offered it to her. Sophie shook her head, no thanks she mouthed. He shrugged his shoulders and slid the cigarette between his lips. She studied him. He had grown a beard and his hair was shaggy and probably in need of a good scrub, but otherwise he looked fine. Tanned even, as if he had spent the last weeks basking in the spring sun. It was the look in his eyes that unnerved her. A slightly vacant look. Unaware of her scrutiny, he carried on.

'Soon I started listening to music all night. I started wearing my headphones all the time. The music was a barrier to drown out the voices. I would sleep during the day when the men had gone, and the flat was empty. But I couldn't help thinking about it and soon I could hear their voices in the corridor even with the headphones on, I could hear them speak about what they were going to do in that apartment. And then I understood. The clicking heels. There were girls. The tapping against the wall. They were having sex. I felt sick with disgust. I started to observe them. I thought before I could go to the police I needed to gather evidence. I started to track when they would show up and when they would leave. I even tried to draw sketches of their faces.'

'After a while I started hearing this girl crying. She was crying every night at dawn when the men left. I could hear her sobbing through the walls. It was fucking heartbreaking. And I just sat there unable to do anything.'

'Did you not go up and check on her? Like knock on the door?' Sophie asked, wondering how much of his story was true and what was paranoia.

'No, I was too scared. As I said, I was gathering intel. I needed proof before going to the police. I had called them previously and they came around but when they rang the doorbell this old woman opened the door. Probably a cover up.'

'One evening I was observing them through the spy hole on my door and as I put my eye against the glass, someone looked back at me, on the other side. I ducked immediately - Fuck - it scared the shit out of me. A big red eye. It just stared at me. As I sat on the floor, my heart pounding in my chest I knew they knew that I knew about them and their dirty business. Since that day, I started taking more precautions.'

Sophie thought about the tin foil and cardboard panelling on his windows.

'And then one evening, while I was on watch, I had set up a look-out flap and I saw him walk by. HIM.'

She looked at him expectantly. 'Who?'

'Caspar'

'What?! Your stepfather?' she hadn't expected that.

He nodded with dark eyes and continued.

'I thought at first that he was coming for me, and I was planning to ignore him as I usually would. But he talked to the men in the corridor and then he walked into the flat. He is part of their ring. That week I saw the girl at the grocer's in our street. She looked so young. I'm sure she is not a day older than 16.'

'Oh my god Jay.' She shook her head. His stepfather Caspar, visiting a child prostitute, in Jay's building? This sounded too crazy but then again, she grabbed her head, could it be true? What if this really was true? She really didn't know where reality ended and paranoid delusions started.

'I wasn't as surprised as you. He's a creepy asshole and I knew it. Remember that time Milana was showering and he just walked into her bathroom?'

'But Jay didn't your mum say it was to check the boiler?'

'Yeah sure, the 'boiler'…' he air quoted. 'He just wanted to see her naked…The sick bastard…'

She put her hand on his arm. 'Jay...Jay, listen to me.'

He stopped rocking back and forth and looked at her as if he'd only just realised her presence. 'I'm going to ask this, but please don't be offended, I just... I'm just trying to understand, ok?'

He nodded hesitantly.

'Are you taking any drugs?'

He looked at her exasperated.

'Fuck, why does everyone keep asking me this. No!'

Frustrated, he violently flicked the cigarette butt on the pavement. A lonely passer-by skipped over it and looked offended. It was getting dark. The sun had set and the capital's sky lit up in shades of purple. The neon light above their heads started flickering to life and bathed the place in an all-encompassing glare. Sophie started wondering if they should move to a more crowded place. She suddenly wanted to have people around them.

'Maybe that's the problem.'

'What?!?'

'Look, your dad told me about the anti-depressants and the anxiety attacks. Maybe this is related, maybe if you are no longer taking these drugs, it makes you more...' – she didn't want to use the word paranoid – '...astute to your surroundings. Do you still smoke, I mean weed?'

'Yeah well sometimes. But what's that got to do with it?'

'It makes you paranoid.' There was no other word for it.

'You don't believe me? You don't believe this is true? The flat, the men, the crying girl, you think I made that up?' He shouted at her. She sadly shook her head.

'I don't know Jay. I want to believe you but... look I just want you to be ok. Is this the reason why you left your flat?' She quickly changed the subject.

'Yes, I couldn't live there anymore. I feared for my life so I went to stay with friends, but didn't stay long. Then I took my tent to the park until the police asked me to move. My tent was confiscated so I moved into this squat I had heard of from a friend of a friend. I stopped doing live events. I just couldn't stand the crowds anymore. I needed a break from the studio and the radio. It was just too much. Life on the streets was very simple. It gave me anonymity. I became an observer. I could roam the city and felt invisible, no one pays any attention to the homeless guy. Sleeping under the stars at night, I felt almost free. Fortunately, we had a short winter and a sunny spring. It made it easier.'

Suddenly the entrance door to the building opened and a young man stepped out to walk his dog. The dog sniffed Jay's hoodie and barked. Jay got up, picked up his rucksack and grabbed Sophie by the arm. They started walking down the street towards the riverbank. The air was fresh and dry. The city hummed quietly only disturbed by a distant sound of ambulance sirens. The sound of a capital city. They stopped at a small cafe and sat down for a cup of coffee. Sophie was aware of the other guests staring. They did make an unlikely couple. A shaggy-haired man with a beard and dirty trainers sitting with a skinny girl, clad in designer clothes.

'We are quite the couple aren't we?' Jay joked as if reading her thoughts.

'Yes we are', she chuckled. 'Tell me more about your time on the streets. Isn't it dangerous? What do you live off? Where do you sleep? What do you do all day?'

Jay looked at her pensively as if to evaluate how much he could tell without shocking her.

'The squat was never going to be a long-term solution. The people I lived with were not ideal flatmates. You never knew who was going to share the mattress with you that night. There were five toothbrushes in the bathroom, but we must have been 10 sleeping on the floor on some nights. The house itself wasn't in too bad a condition. We didn't have any electricity as the energy company had cut off the power after one too many unpaid bills. However, we had running water. Cold water. Everyone seemed to have an interest in music and most of the time we would sit together for impromptu jam sessions.

Unfortunately, some of the guys were into drugs. Real badass drugs. Crack and heroin. Their antics soon made it unliveable. I slept with one eye open every night, my passport and wallet stuffed under my makeshift pillow. I had been robbed of some of my stuff, like my iPod and some books, but when one night, I woke up to one of the guys holding a knife to my throat for some spare change I decided to leave the house.'

'I tried my luck at getting a place at the homeless shelter but the people there were in a really bad way. You were basically given a spot on the floor of a filthy dormitory to share with 20 smelly rejects of society. The old man next to me snored so loud the whole floor trembled. He would wake up every hour grunting, to pick up a pen and write random number sequences on a sheet of paper he kept rolled up in a vial around his neck. Another guy couldn't stop farting and reeked of vodka. I left after the first night and decided not to come back. These guys were just too disturbingly fucked up. So I chose to sleep in the door entrance of a warehouse by the river. Sometimes I would sleep on the roof of the boat-house right next to the river-bank. That's my favourite spot. I can just look up and watch the stars.'

'I spent most of my days walking around the city observing people. Sometimes I would get coffee and sit on the steps of the art museum. It gave me solace. The library was another great place to hang out. But it was the books I was interested in. I just finished 'The Catcher in the Rye'. What a powerful book.'

Sophie nodded, she had found JD Salinger's book haunting and uncomfortable. Promoting lying and drinking and reversing moral codes. It was the book that Mark Chapman, John Lennon's murderer, was found with after he had committed his crime.

'The internet proved to be a good time waster,' he said.

'You never replied to my emails though?' she asked anxiously.

'I know and I'm sorry. I just didn't know what to tell you. You're married and I'm homeless. There was nothing for me to be proud of and nothing I could say to you.'

'What about Cam? I thought you guys hit it off?' she couldn't help but feel a pang of jealously at the thought of them being close.

'Ah Cam. Yeah, that didn't work out. She's a great girl but...' but she's not you, he thought. 'Anyway, Frank looked after her and I think they're dating now.' He shrugged his shoulders to signal he didn't care, but Sophie thought about her conversation with Frank and how the two of them hadn't spoken in a while. That must have been the reason.

The waitress brought two plates of lasagne and Jay licked his lips hungrily. A welcomed change from the tasteless broth at the shelter or the McDonald's bins he was used to going through, looking for cold cheeseburgers and fries.

'Jay, but surely you don't have any money problems?' As far as she knew he made an excellent living. He replied that he didn't want to use his credit cards for fear to becoming traceable so he lived off a one time cash withdrawal that he had hidden in a box, buried in the park and tried to make it last for as long as he could. Sophie looked at him, incredulous, and they finished eating in silence.

'It's getting late Jay. I don't want you to sleep outside tonight. I'm staying at this little bed and breakfast in Kreuzberg and I want you to stay with me tonight.' Jay shook his head 'Please?' she pleaded. He looked at her beautiful grey eyes wide with concern and nodded slowly... 'ok'.

'Is this all your stuff?' she asked, pointing at his rucksack.

'I have some spare clothes and some bits and pieces in a locker at the train station but have a spare set of clothes in the rucksack, I just picked that up from the launderette earlier this afternoon.'

'Ok then let's go.'

Sophie paid and they walked out into the night. As they crossed the road to the nearest underground station, Sophie tripped and when she grabbed his hand to steady herself it felt warm and safe. She just held on as they walked on. It felt good. It felt right.

She didn't want to let him go.

CHAPTER 17

Solacium, January 2012 - 1 year after the incident

Jay paced in his bedroom in a heightened state of anxiety. His heart was beating wildly in his chest. He stopped by the mirror and smoothed his jaw-length hair behind his ears. He wondered nervously whether he should have gone to the hairdresser who came once a month to cut the inmates' hair. But a quick military buzz cut seemed to be the only choice and Jay hadn't been too keen to look like a jarhead.

He put on his thick-rimmed glasses and looked at himself critically. Everybody in here thought he looked like American filmmaker Michael Moore, and Jay thought that was quite an insult. Sure enough, he had still some way to go to regain his trim figure but he hoped that regular gym sessions would further get his overall weight down. If only those pills would stop piling on the pounds. His metabolism had slowed and even if he rarely ate more than a child's portion, his weight only marginally decreased.

He sighed in frustration and looked at the photograph Sophie had brought him on her last visit. A beaming couple smiled into the camera with bright eyes and shiny white teeth. The photo had been taken in a club on Ibiza; Jay wasn't sure if it had been Amnesia or Pacha. The medication had deconstructed his long-term memory. More and more often he found himself struggling to remember details of his memories. They had looked so happy, their eyes shining with mischief, the future was bright, their world full of opportunities waiting to be snared. As much as he loved that photo, sometimes he had to take it from his nightstand and lock it in his locker as the sight of her beautiful innocent face filled him with a sense of sadness so intense he needed to take her out of his sight.

His roommates had initially tried to provoke him and had taunted him about the photo of the random couple, not realising it was picturing a young Jay, handsome and tanned with chiselled features and piercing green eyes. He looked nothing like that photo anymore. He gently stroked Sophie's white blonde hair and delicately placed the frame in his locker.

He made sure he had showered that morning. Twice. Once before breakfast and once after lunch. That was one thing he felt compulsive about. He needed to smell of soap at all times; it had become a slight obsession, but he didn't care. The faint perfume of soap reminded him of the laundry his nanny would leave on his bed every Thursday evening after she had cleaned the rest of his parent's house, and the smell comforted him. It reminded him of happier times.

He paced around his bedroom waiting for the knock to come. He felt a panic attack trying to break through the wall of medication, but he could only feel the faint tremor. The drugs held fort. He wasn't going to freak out. Those days were over. What was he going to say to her? And even more worryingly, what questions would she have for him to answer? He knew he was going to be challenged to explain why he had done it. *She will want to know.* He had rehearsed a narrative that he hoped was taking into account that in her view he was a violent murderer while explaining the duress under which he had acted. But now with the anxiety coursing through his brain he didn't remember anything.

The knock on the door startled him and with one last look in the mirror, desperately trying to steady his shallow breathing, smoothing his hair one last time, he walked out of his bedroom to greet, for the first time since his incarceration, the woman who sat in the visitors room. She was wearing pair of white jeans and a light-coloured hoodie. Her long blonde hair knotted in a bun, she wrung her hands in her lap. 'Sophie' he whispered, and she looked up at him with wide eyes.

***

Ibiza, June 2010 - 5 months before the incident

It was a late afternoon and Jay had walked down to the beach. It was unseasonably hot and muggy. The weather forecast had predicted thunderstorms coming up from the coast. As he looked to the horizon, big leaden clouds rolled menacingly into view. He climbed across the rocks to his favourite nook, just in between the two bays, overlooking the sea and sheltered from view. He sat down, his legs dangled over the edge, and he lit up the first of many cigarettes. He wondered why he was here. His father had talked him into joining him on a 'spa retreat' break. He knew his father meant well, and he made an effort at this pathetic attempt to bond and said yes, an answer he regretted the second he hung up the phone. All, he wanted to do was return to his room, close the door and listen to music. Shut the world out and the voices in his head.

The three months stint in the psychiatric ward didn't seem to have helped much. Indeed he had plenty of supply of the drugs they'd given him, but they had mostly ended up flushed down the toilet. He hated the pills. They made him sluggish and slow, as if his brain was wrapped in cotton wool and like a boy with a butterfly net, he constantly chased an idea and never seemed to catch it. It was exhausting to hold a conversation now. The side effects were brutal, and the sudden weight gain was very visible. He hated it. People stared at him in the street, and it wasn't because they recognised him as the DJ from one of the top 10 MTV video clips. His fame days were over. People stopped and stared and behind his back, they pointed and giggled. When he looked in the mirror, the man, who stared back at him with vacant eyes was a stranger. A fat ugly stranger with man boobs. Gone were the sculptured abs and the firmly toned torso. He shivered in horror. Man boobs. Nothing screamed desperation more than man boobs.

On most days, he felt too depressed to face his reflection, and so he covered every mirror in the house with blankets and towels. It drove his father nuts.

'What is this? A refugee camp? As long as you are staying under my roof you will stop this nonsense. Just go to the gym. Walk it off, for god sakes.'

Good riddance, Jay thought as he flushed the pills down the toilet. He decided he was going to walk that tight-rope between sanity and schizophrenia. Reducing the dosage to a minimum, just enough to keep the hallucinations at bay and allowing him to have a clear enough mind to hold a proper conversation and get off the sofa.

He looked down at the swirling water, waves gurgling beneath the rocks, and stubbed out his cigarette. He instantly longed for another one. His tobacco cravings had spun out of control. It was either that or eating. And he didn't want to eat. He was going to shed that weight. But then he sagged his shoulders in defeat and wondered if there was any point. That wasn't going to bring Sophie back. A slimmer version of him would not get her back. He had to accept the fact that he was never going to see her again. She had been quite clear that morning when they checked out of the bed and breakfast. She had barely looked at him when she turned to the concierge to hand over her key.

He lit another cigarette.

***

Sophie and Jay walked through the dark streets of Berlin back to the bed and breakfast in Kreuzberg. Although well into spring, the nights were still a little chilly. It was late. They had taken their time to walk back, stopped for a drink in a bar and a kebab at the corner shop. They had talked and laughed. And if it weren't for his slight unkempt style, they looked like any other young couple searching for an adventure on a Thursday night.

The check-in desk was unmanned, but Sophie had the night key. It was a small boutique hotel, no more than ten rooms. It was simple, modern and, most importantly, clean. As soon as they stepped into the lift a blanket of awkwardness engulfed them. As much as the conversation had flowed all night easily, all of a sudden they were just too aware of their proximity. Sophie had let go of his hand a long while ago and yet somehow the palm of her hand was still burning from where his skin had touched hers. To escape the awkward moment, she wondered for a second if she should check her phone for messages. She thought of her husband and guiltily pushed her phone deeper into her handbag.

After what seemed like an eternity, the lift door finally pinged open, and she breathed in. They'd had a few drinks, and she was feeling a bit light-headed as she failed to insert the key in the slot.

She steadied herself against the wall with an apologetic smile as Jay opened the door for her. They stumbled inside, and Sophie headed to the mini bar. A drink would be good. It would steady the sudden nerves and would make her feel less awkward. She reached for two mini-bar sized whisky bottles. Giving the place a cursory glance, she stopped thinking that him sleeping in this room, was a good idea. It seemed terribly small; the bed was in particular quite narrow. But now she had finally found him, she wasn't going to let him sleep another night on the streets. She was going to convince him to seek professional help, with the right medication she was sure his mind could be mended. *All will be alright. He'll be fine... we'll be fine.*

'I'm going to take a shower', he mumbled as he pursued to lift his jumper over his head, lifting the t-shirt beneath to reveal a ripped six-pack. Sophie quickly turned her head away, embarrassed, and nipped at her glass. As the amber liquid burnt down her throat, she thought about how much she hated whisky. It made her stomach churn. She poured one for Jay and turned to him. His jeans hung low on his hips and showed off his toned lower abs. She couldn't help but stare.

'What's this?' she pointed at the thick scar below his belly button.

'A long story' he nodded grimly. His hands flitted over the white skin of what had once been Aisha's name. The 'h' and the 'a' were still faintly visible. Even spurned on by Dan's insistent whispers, he hadn't managed to stand the pain to cut out the last two letters but at least now he didn't have to be reminded of the sting of her betrayal each time he got dressed.

She noticed the hurt in his eyes and refrained from asking further questions. She ached to run her fingers on his taut stomach. She blushed at the thought, and her heart skipped a beat when his fingers touched hers as he grabbed the glass.

As the noise of the shower filled her head, tossing images of broad shoulders and strong arms, she flicked on the TV, desperate for distraction. *What the hell am I thinking? What is happening to me?* Quickly she flicked through the romantic scene of a dumb Hollywood movie to the channel with the satellite filming the earth and the trance chill out music. She breathed in slowly. She liked that program, Space Night. She remembered quite a few nights when they were younger, coming home from parties, they would smoke a spliff and quietly discuss the events of the night, Space Night's soundtrack playing in the background.

'Incredible right? They still play this after broadcasting time, after all these years. Isn't that quite extraordinary?' he walked into the room, rubbing his wet hair with a towel. She choked on her sip of whisky as he walked around the room with only a towel wrapped around his waist.

She took another sip to suppress her embarrassed cough. What was happening to her? This wasn't how she felt a few hours ago. How did he morph from someone she thought needed her help into someone she started to feel a whole different need for? This was insane. Was it his ripped body?

'How did you keep that fit living on the street?' she mumbled, feeling the heat of the alcohol on her tongue.

'I had all the time in the world so I went to the outdoor gyms, or for a run or even a swim in the nearby lakes. Plus, you know I didn't eat that much. So it was kind of easy to stay trim...' he laughed.

Having pulled on a pair of fresh jeans, he sat down on the velvet sofa next to her, extended his legs onto the small coffee table and swirled the whisky in his glass.

Or was it his eyes? His intense, slightly haunted look? The luminous green of his pupils? The way he looked at her as if she was the only woman he had ever laid eyes on? Only for his gaze to darken seconds later, like a dark cloud covering the sun on a tentative spring day. There was something urgently wild and untamed about him. The way he moved across the room like every object in it was his and owed its existence to him, a commandeering silent force. Something mildly rebellious and devastatingly troubled. A mysterious place within him full of unspoken thoughts she knew she would never reach. He kept her on her guard; one moment seemingly close enough for their souls to touch. Close enough to spill all secrets. Only for him to retreat back into a dark corner, miles away from her. Although she was afraid of what she may uncover, she wished he would let her in.

She looked at his hands. They were big and strong. She wanted his arm around her shoulder, to feel the weight push her down. He picked a cigarette from the packet on the table and lit it. Plumes of blue smoke escaped through the balcony window. Alongside the alcohol burning in her stomach there was something else, which she could no longer ignore. A dark, primitive longing that sat deep in the pit of her belly.

'What is it? What are you looking at? You can tell me, you know,' he said in a low voice. His question startled her. What was he referring to? That she was attracted to him? That she was married and damned to burn in seven hells because all she could think of was how it would feel to kiss those lips again? The memory of the lighthouse kiss in Formentera popped into her head, and she bit her lip. That was such a lifetime ago. Everything had changed. Everything had become so complicated. Her breathing turned ragged. But hadn't their brief romance always felt like unfinished business? She knew she was on the brink of doing something so regretful she would bear the consequence of her actions for the rest of her life.

She needed some air and jumped up to walk out onto the balcony. She looked down on the quiet city, its night lights twinkling like stars in a distant galaxy. She thought of her trusting husband back in London, who patiently awaited her return. The man who had been so good to her. A pang of guilt threatened to rip her apart, a foreboding of sins she yet had to commit.

When his hand slowly caressed her shoulder, she shivered. All her carefully constructed walls broke down, stone by stone. The self she had so carefully put together, the image of the trusting wife, the smiling career woman, the perfect mother she wanted to become, all dissolved under the touch of his hand. The hunger grew, reckless and dangerous. An all-consuming fire. A rage. A lust. She wanted him blindly, not caring about the consequences. A lifetime of repressed desire for a man she knew she could never see a future with, but who was so deeply anchored in her being. So unconditionally part of her past. Who had saved her life and shared so many memories. Some good and some not so good.

She turned around to face him and looked straight into his eyes. Ignoring his look of surprise, she lifted her hands to his freshly-shaven face and gently pulled him down to her. His lips were warm and tasted of whisky. He kissed her back slowly and buried his hand in her long soft hair to pull her in closer. Their kissing, weighed down with a lifetime of crushing lust, was breathless and urgent. He lifted her up and pushed her against the wall, her slender legs wrapped around his waist. Her skin felt soft and warm. She whispered in his ear a hot and impatient 'I want you'.

***

Jay shifted uncomfortably. The dark, thunderous clouds were advancing slowly and inexorably, already half way through the pale sky. The memory of their night together pained him, like a thousand needles piercing his skin.

A cold wind had risen. The waves had grown bolder, spilled over the rocks and licked his bare feet. He balled his hands to tight fists and looked down into the waves. A headache was brewing. One of those headaches.

Time for a pill, he thought, but instead of reaching into his breast pocket he lit another cigarette. The tip of his fingers had a dirty yellow tinge. He didn't care whether he was risking losing control over his rational thoughts. He was ready to give in to the fear and let the hallucinations guide him.

He had wanted her too. He loved everything about her. Her smell. The fine white hairs at the base of her neck. The smiling crinkle at the corner of her eyes. He wanted to melt into her and never let her go.

Anger and passion coursed through him. He hated her for not choosing him. For choosing a stable and sane husband, who had a boring job, who had money and was able to give her the life she wanted. The white picket fence, the Labrador and the Range Rover. Two kids. Smiley cute little blonde kids. As a happy, shiny family, they would wear Barbour jackets on the weekend and run through the New Forest in mud-spattered Wellington boots. They would gaily saunter through life, looking slim and healthy, smiling pearly-white smiles while pressing a coin into the homeless guy's hand, full of their righteousness. Their Facebook account would show reels of photos of them at glamorous parties, on elegant weekend breaks with their cute offspring. People would admire them and like them too much to feel jealousy. They would organise themed dinner parties and secret Santas. They would travel the world, climb glaciers and trip through the desert on camel's backs. They would grow old and sit on a weathered old couch holding hands while watching TV.

He sucked in the smoke and exhaled slowly; the seething anger made way for a deep-rooted sadness. It wasn't that guy's fault; Sophie's husband had given it his best shot. He had wooed her. He was tall and handsome, healthy and sane. His genes were good. He was going to take care of her children. And she deserved it. She had always had this happy-go-lucky attitude. Carefree and brave, hungry for adventures and new perspectives. She was a good person, she deserved to be happy and cared for by someone who would ensure she would get everything she wished for in life. Jay had to let it go. It was time he gave up piecing together a fantasy where his story had a happy ending. He was broken beyond repair, and he couldn't keep hiding it from her, he couldn't dupe her into thinking he was going to be ok.

When they parted the morning after, she had looked at him with sad eyes 'I'm sorry, but this can't be. I've made my choice.' And that was to return to London leaving him with the faint smell of her skin on his and the memory of a life they could have had if only... he had been normal.

...I've really, really been the best of fools, I did what I could, 'cause I love you, baby, How I love you, darling, How I love you, baby, How I love you, girl, little girl, but baby, since I've been loving you, I'm about to lose my worried mind...

The Led Zeppelin song echoed in his head.

He flicked another cigarette butt into the dark, angry waves. He would never be in a position to rival that man Sophie had chosen to marry. There was no blame, no jealousy. Just a feeling of emptiness. Whatever broke Jay's mind had done an excellent job. The headache was strong, and its spidery tentacles crawled to the front of his mind. Jay braced himself to hear his voice again.

This is the end my friend. She is gone. There is nothing left. Dan's whisper was faint and distant.

Is there nothing left?

Don't be a fool. Your friends? They abandoned you a long time ago. Since you became 'unmanageable'. Did they come looking for you when you were on the streets?

They hadn't. When he had tried and tried to explain why he couldn't leave his flat anymore, that he was on a mission to uncover a paedophile ring in his building, his friends had first shown consternation and disbelief. They even offered their help. However, they soon had turned deceptive and had obstructed his intel-gathering. They had told him he was paranoid and should stop smoking and start taking his medicine. He had driven them away.

Even your family has turned their back on you. They are ashamed of you. You are the chink in their perfect world. You ruined everything.

Dan's voice grew stronger and louder in his head. Jay knew he was right. His mother had not listened when he told her about his stepfather. She had never believed him and always, without fail, backed her husband. She had laughed off his suspicions of having an affair with his girlfriend Aisha. She had grown angry and defensive when he tried to warn her about him being involved in the raping of a child. He had seen him, in his building. In that corridor. He didn't have irrefutable proof, but he had seen him. And she chose not to believe him. She accused him of being paranoid and delusional. Her fights had ended with her calling a psychiatrist, a family friend. A stern older woman with piercing eyes and large thick glasses. Dr Klein. She had prescribed some more of those pills which made him as responsive as a slug.

They made him quit his flat and move in with his father. They were trying to gain access to his bank account to dispose freely of the money 'to pay medical bills' they said. But when his stepfather tried to convince his mother to have him sign a form that declared him handicapped, Jay flew into a rage. They told him he would receive state benefits and would be considered for special needs jobs. He was beside himself with anger. Caspar had gotten very smart. This was quite a clever ploy to get rid of him. To neutralise and belittle him. But they were mistaken, even though the drugs made him slow he was not going to sign some nonsense piece of paper, go on record and declare himself too insane to function.

Dan was right. They had turned their back on him. They were ashamed and had started to exclude him from the family. When they all flew to Canada for Christmas to visit his grandparents, his mother told him that he wasn't invited. She tried to make him believe it was for his sake, that a family trip was just going to cause more friction. Jay knew his stepfather was pulling the strings. Jay wanted to get rid of them, escape the family, start afresh, but they had a tight grip on him, and his passport was carefully guarded. His father had locked it in his safe. Jay was under surveillance. He wished death would take them, his father, his stepfather, his mother, all of them... and free him.

He wished he could do something about it. Tightening his fingers around their necks as they slept. Pressing his fingers down on their soft old-people's skin. And press. Until their windpipes squashed under his grip like overripe bananas. Freed.

Ignoring the rising fear in his core, he looked down into the water. His vision was slightly distorted from the headache, but he saw their faces under the surface. Their dead black eyes looked up at him. Their mouths open in silent accusations. He slid down the rocks into the cold water. His feet touched the sandy ground. Waves lapped at his torso and sprayed his face. He tasted salt on his lips as he slowly marched away from land into the vast open waters. He could feel their cold limbs brushing against his legs. Their long cold fingers clawing at him. He shivered and wondered how he had killed them this time. Probably drowned them. His stepfather's corpse floated next to him, his black mouth whispering:

You can't just walk away. You can't kill us off. Your life is ruined. We tried to warn you. We gave you everything to succeed. And you were too lazy. Too stupid.

Their dead bodies stank of sulfur, their rotting insides picked on by hundreds of hungry little silver fish. He stumbled over his feet, pushing the corpses away from him in terror and started swimming. Away from them and towards the horizon. It had begun to rain, and the warm raindrops ran down his face and washed away his tears. His arms were aching, the muscles burned in protest and his lungs screamed, but he ignored the pain and continued swimming in the open waters. Waves crashed on his face. He didn't care anymore. He was going to swim until his body gave up and then he would slowly surrender himself to the sea. He welcomed the fear of his death. He knew it was going to be painless. Alongside the death of his parents and that of his stepfather, he had fantasised enough about his own. With every stroke, his arms pained. The muscles cramped up as the salt rusted his bones. His eyes burned, and he coughed up another wave that glugged down his throat as his lungs protested in agony.

The bottomless sea spread out below him, its darkness hiding more cadavers of his thoughts. More evil enemies luring him down to join them. He could feel them drawing him in, yanking at his legs, sucking him into their dark kingdom. Away from the sun, life and love. Into perpetual gloom. He had spent most of the last years feeling like he was sitting at the bottom of a swimming pool, disconnected, trying to communicate with the outside world but only getting distorted noises
through the forever undulating waters. Considering how long he had spent swimming back to the surface only to be dragged back down to the bottom, he found it only appropriate to surrender to the element, only this time there was no bottom. He would drift down into the darkness of the watery womb of the mother who had never wanted him. Cold and unwelcoming. No umbilical cord to the surface. No lifeline.

He stopped swimming. The coast had disappeared in the mist of the storm. His head bobbed up and down in the waves, his body rose and sunk, his arms and legs tugged and tossed around like a rag doll. An appropriate metaphor for his life, he thought as he slowly exhaled and closed his eyes. He breathed in the water. It was cold and alien. It ran up his nostrils and slowly filled his lungs. Fireworks went off behind the lids of his eyes which quickly transformed into one blinding white light in which, in its midst a face appeared. An ethereal beauty. Translucent skin. Wide eyes with purple shimmering pupils. White blonde hair floating like a halo framing her face. His guardian angel smiled invitingly, and he suddenly felt all the terror seep from his body.

The fear vanished. He was going to be ok and when she extended her hand he reached out.

CHAPTER 18

Solacium, January 2012 - 1 year after the incident

The clinic had been fairly easy to find but when she drove into the compound, Sophie was shaking with nerves. She was facing him for the first time in four years and had no idea how she was going to react. Although they regularly spoke on the phone, she didn't know what to expect from him. It was over three years since *it* happened. She glanced at her watch, 5 minutes to two, against her expectations, she had made it on time.

It had been raining all day without stopping but somehow the gloomy overcast sky gave Sophie some form of solace. Bright sunshine would have not felt right. This wasn't going to be a joyous 'bring out the bunting and the cupcakes' reunion and the grim weather felt like a fitting backdrop to illustrate the Greek tragedy she was about to meet.

The trees in the park adjacent to the stern-looking building were heavy with rain and a low mist was rising towards the shadowy towers of the 19th-century hospital. Sophie was surprised by the eery quaintness of the place, the white-washed walls of the buildings contrasting with the black slated rooftops. Not what she had expected, but then she wasn't quite sure what she had expected, a Shawshank Redemption-like state prison from the fifties? The psychiatric institution of One Flew Over the Cuckoo's nest or a more sinister place like in Silence of the

Lambs? She didn't know, and the uncertainty of what awaited her made her lightheaded with dread. She looked up at the tall windows and its iron bars and shivered at the sight of the five-meter high fences, the electronic locks and the barbed wires.

As Sophie was buzzed in, she walked through the armoured entrance, her heart beating so fast in nervous anticipation that she thought she was going to faint. By the time she was taken through passport control, had an airport style security check performed on her and shakily waited to be buzzed into the next chamber, she couldn't look the wardens in the eye for fear of bursting into tears.She stubbornly stared at her feet while she was escorted up the stairs to the first floor. She discreetly patted the back pocket of her jeans, making sure it was still there. The envelope creased under her touch and she sighed.

They had to pause every ten meters for the two wardens to unlock the bullet-proof double glazed doors separating each chamber. As they advanced deeper and deeper into the bowels of the building, a heavy blanket of despair descended upon Sophie, getting heavier with each step she took. *This place is where dreams come to die.* She wiped a tear from her eye with a trembling hand and suppressed the urge to turn on her heel and run away.

He has changed, physically and psychologically. Don't expect him to look anything like the last time you saw him. Be prepared to be shocked. Henry's words insistently echoed in her head. Jay's father had looked at her with the haunted eyes of a broken man and she had quietly listened to him knowing that there were no words she could say to bring solace to the father who had brought up a killer.

The pungent smell of disinfectant lingered in the air as Sophie waited as instructed, awkwardly standing in the corridor outside the visitor's room. The tick-tack of the clock on the white wall resonated in her head like a drum. Each minute passing seemed like an hour.

She heard him before she saw him. A low-pitched voice echoed in the sterile corridor; the voice Sophie recognised from the phone, the same voice he had when she last saw him. But nothing Henry had warned her about had prepared her for what she saw as he appeared in the corridor. He was so tall and had put on so much weight, Sophie felt her mouth drop open as she gasped for air. He looked like a giant. He was wearing thick-rimmed glasses and his features had distorted, as if the bones under his skin had shifted and moved forward. It was like seeing him through the looking glass, a grotesque caricature of himself.

The wardens stopped him, leaving a two meter distance between him and Sophie and proceeded to unlock his hand and foot shackles, during which Jay calmly stared at her with assessing eyes. Sophie swallowed hard; he looked every inch the schizophrenic murderer. Her instincts cried out to back against the wall, inch over to the door and slam the panic button.

'Sophie' he whispered, standing completely still, his hands folded in front of him. His voice was thick with emotion.

Sophie's heart broke and the lump in her throat swelled as she recognised the look of sheer relief on his face. It was as if he had just realised the voice on the phone had really been Sophie's and not a figment of his imagination. She had kept her promise; she was here to see him.

Suddenly Jay smiled. A happy-to-see-you smile so honest and warm it reached his green eyes and lit up his face. Completely taken by surprise by his beautiful smile, something snapped in her and melted her fears. Suddenly letting her guard down, she ran to him and threw her arms around his neck with a heart-wrenching sob. The wardens nervously reached for the tasers on their belt, but Sophie didn't pay them any attention. Tip toeing, her skinny arms wrapped around his shoulders, she buried her head in his neck and breathed a sigh of relief at the smell of fresh washing powder. His clean jaw-length hair brushed softly against her cheek. His huge hands held her tiny frame with such care she felt like a butterfly in a steel cage. She was aware he could crush her and break every bone in her body with one breath, but she didn't care.

Underneath the terrifying exterior, it was still him, her friend, her Jay. She knew it.

***

Berlin, October 2010 - 30 days before the incident

'I don't care, just get the fuck over here!' Frank Stahl yelled into his mobile before hanging up and stomping over to the PR girl at the entrance. The pretty redhead was holding a clipboard and was going through a list of names. Attendees for tonight's press event. He had insisted she called every art journalist at every national newspaper and trade publication to be here tonight or risk missing out. He wanted this to be a success; a news story splashed across the stands. He had worked so hard to set this up; he wasn't going to have a lily-livered artist like his friend ruin his big opening night. *Friend*. He stumbled over the thought. He wasn't quite sure if he could still describe him as a friend. He was a stubborn idiot, but he was a talented stubborn idiot, there was no doubt about that and Frank was convinced he had found the right artist to represent. Jay was undeniably the star of the show.

Frank had set up the art collective 'ARTificium' and had recruited quite a few artists and musicians to his team. Tonight was going to be the pinnacle of his work over the past years. It was going to be the night he was to unveil his secret weapon. His most tortured artist. The most eccentric and talented painter he had in his band of dysfunctional friends and acquaintances. He looked over the redhead's shoulder and nodded approvingly at the list of journalists.

Yes, he thought confidently; they were all going to show up. Happy with the names on the list and giving his PR a stern 'don't mess this up' look, he patted her bum. He ignored the murderous look she shot him and stalked off to the bar area. He wasn't sure about the lighting; it was still too bright in here. In his mind's eye, he had imagined the place would feel intimate and intellectual. He wanted people to converse holding thick crystal tumblers of premium whisky, surrounded by shelves of vintage books reaching the ceilings. He wanted battered old leather armchairs to disappear in blue clouds of cigar smoke.

Unfortunately, it appeared the organisers had not heard him. He called the events girl, a sexy blonde; he forgot her name, *Anne Marie? Anneli? Amelie? Something like that.* She had also told him that even though he did not think cigars were technically classed as cigarettes, they would still break the smoking ban. There would be no blue smoke circling the intellectual bar area. Frank cursed under his breath as he wiped his upper lip. He was getting hot and sweaty. The suit he had got specially made for tonight was perfectly fitted. He had filled out over the years, and many hours in the gym had given him a tall and robust frame that the tailor-made suit underlined perfectly. It had cost him an arm and a leg, but it was worth it. He had loved the expensive midnight blue fabric which, according to his girlfriend Camelia, 'made his ice blue eyes all the more piercing', but now the high thread count made him sweat. He longed for a drink and some fresh air. He eased the knot of his pale blue tie a bit and nervously ran his hand through his freshly styled hair. He cursed again as he felt the expensive hair gel dissolve under his greasy fingers. Naturally white blonde, he knew he looked intriguing. A man whose age you couldn't really guess. He liked and cultivated that mystery. He had been to the tanning salon, and his usual deathly pale skin shone a healthy glow. He grinned at himself passing the white baroque wall mirror. His freshly whitened teeth gleamed.

The events girl apologised profusely and went on to sort out the light. 'More lamps, less neon' he snapped through clenched jaws. She nodded so eagerly her ponytail quivered before quickly disappearing through the back corridor and into the bowels of the warehouse. He looked around the space he had made the gallery area, and he nodded, content. He had found the perfect place. The old print factory was spacious and had an unmistakably urban feel to it. Its exposed brick walls and apparent piping fitted the street-art inspired exhibition. It was dark and stripped bare, back to its roots and exactly what Frank had looked for when he went venue scouting. He had ordered for the concrete floor to be coated in black paint with fluorescent arrows guiding guests through the exhibition. 243 objects of various shapes and sizes. Local artists from Berlin, Amsterdam and London. This was going to be his night. He was going to cement his reputation as a gallerist and urban art dealer tonight. Fame and fortune awaited him, of that he was certain.

His phone buzzed interrupting his moment of self-congratulation. As he fished it out of his pocket, he couldn't help his heart skip a beat in expectation of a last minute cock up. He checked the screen. *Fuck. Jay. Again.*

'Mate? Where the hell are you?' He rolled his eyes in exasperation as he walked over to the first of Jay's paintings suspended from the ceiling on a thick wire. It was his favourite, a giant canvass, dripping in neon yellow and grey tones. A warped vision of the tower blocks of East Berlin, it captured the restlessness of the city.

'What do you mean 'at home'? What part of 'get the fuck over here' did you not understand?' Frank felt nervous now. He touched the edge of the painting. It was probably one of his best, if not the best. Frank knew he could sell it for a good 25,000 euros, if not more. Maybe 30,000 if Jay showed up and did his schizophrenic spiel. No doubt he was his main artist, but he needed him to be here, showered and looking halfway presentable. Frank refrained from lashing out at him, which he knew would only make things worse. Jay was likely to retreat back into his shell and vanish as he had done many times before. So Frank changed tactics and went for the guilt trip.

'Listen man, you're my best friend', he didn't flinch at the lie. Since the one-night stand with Cam developed into his first serious relationship, Frank knew that his friendship with Jay wasn't worth much anymore. But 'Hey shit happens' was his attitude, and she did choose him over his paranoid friend. It wasn't Frank's fault. If anything he probably did them both a favour, particularly Cam, saving her from a doomed relationship with a schizophrenic.

'I have a lot riding on this event tonight and I need you to be here. You're my main guy, and there are some people here I want you to meet. Potential buyers and gallerists' Omitting the bit about the press conference, Frank decided that he would brief Jay once he was here, rather than scare him off now.

Following his worst paranoid episodes, during which he was convinced he had uncovered a paedophile ring in his building, and even after a stint in a psychiatric ward and being prescribed some heavy-duty psychopharmaceuticals, Jay had become extremely cagey and avoided talking to strangers. He even had trouble trusting his family and friends, including Frank.

'Jay? You still there? Good. Ok, this is what I want you to do: get off your sofa. Are you showered? Yes? Can you run a comb through the bird's nest that his your sorry excuse for hair and get dressed... I don't care, something that screams fucked up artist. I'll get a car to pick you up in 15 min. You hear me? You got 15 min to get ready. Good boy.' He snapped his phone shut and started pacing around the gallery heading for the bar. A drink would calm his nerves.

Around 45 min and another few phone calls later, his tortured artist finally walked through the door looking positively scruffy, wearing a black hooded jumper, navy jeans and a pair of worn out Red Wing boots. Frank wondered if Jay had ever worn anything else his entire life. The trousers were a night sky of paint splats and even the skin of his hand, when he extended it to shake Frank's hand, shone grey with faded paint.

A crowd had gathered around them and an excited whisper buzzed as people recognised Jay Adler – the posh, controversial, tortured artist, son of entrepreneur Henry Adler and socialite Elizabeth von Schoenefeldt and stepson of celebrity plastic surgeon Caspar von Schoenefeldt. Jay's slightly wayward ways in the past years were widely reported in gossip columns, and he attracted quite a following. His notoriety had hit mainstream when his stepfather appealed for his safe return on national TV.

'How embarrassing.' Jay had made a series of caustic remarks whenever Frank had tried to breach the topic with him. His stepfather had become a well-known public figure, who enjoyed nothing more than to bask in the spotlight and his involvement had extended the fame to his stepson. The difference being Jay loathed being famous as much as he hated being linked to his stepfather in any way.

Jay had become extremely awkward around people. Frank initially had put it down to arrogance, an aloofness which Frank had tried to copy when they were younger but that had somehow, over time, morphed into an awkward distance, particularly in social situations. Jay permanently seemed absent, unable to look people in the eye, hiding behind a pair of thick dark-rimmed glasses. Frank breathed a sigh of relief as he noticed Jay had made an effort. He had trimmed his beard. His hair looked healthily floppy.

The photographers started circling like a hungry pack of wolves and snapped away. Guests grew braver and drew closer, eager to get a good look at the cowering man trying to hide under his hood. A scrum of journalists materialised and started shouting questions at him.

'Is it true that you suffer from depression and schizophrenia?';
'Is your mental illness inspiring you to paint?'; 'Once you got off
the streets, where did you go?'; 'What statement are you
making?';'When did you come out of rehab?'; 'How would you
describe your relationship with your stepfather?'; Jay flinched
and raised his hands to his face as Frank protectively jumped in
to push the crowd back into their ranks. He could hear Jay's
heavy breathing and Frank hoped he wasn't going to have a
panic attack. 'Stay with me Jay. It's all good. Stay with me man',
he shouted above the noise. Jay broke away and pushed his way
through the crowd, running towards the exit.

There he ran. His artist. Frank balled his fists tightly and felt like
punching a hole in the wall. Damn it, he thought. *I should have
told him the press would be here; I should have prepped him.* Now he
was gone, and Frank knew the man would never be persuaded
again. What a waste, thought Frank as he downed his second
whiskey, then turned around, flashed a white-toothed smile and
faced the journalists' questions.

***

Berlin, October 2010 - 14 days before the incident

Nervously clutching a white envelope in his hand, Henry Adler
stopped outside the closed bedroom door. He hesitated for a few
seconds and listened. It was silent behind the door, but he knew
his son was inside. The breakfast tray on the floor had remained
untouched. The banana had blackened, the milk in the tea had
clotted. Henry let out a resigned sigh, rapped on the door and
walked into the room without waiting for an answer.

Jay was lying on his bed, on top of the duvet, fully dressed and
with his headphones screwed on. He seemed fast asleep buried
in the hood of his jumper. Again, Henry suppressed a shot of
anger. It was like having a bloody teenager in the house who
barricaded himself in his bedroom and communicated in grunts,
never letting go of his headphones.

A cursory glance around the bedroom revealed it to be surprisingly tidy. All the pencils were neatly stacked on top of his black moleskins on the tiny desk. The floor was devoid of dirty socks and food debris. Suspicious, Henry quickly checked the closet. The few clothes Jay had brought with him were tidily hanging off their hangers. He closed the wardrobe and wondered whether he should check his son's trouser pockets for clues. Nothing but a few coins and a strip of chewing gum as it turned out. Jay seemed to have quit smoking, which was encouraging. Henry continued his search and hastily rattled the bottles in the medicine cabinet in the en-suite bathroom. The bottles were all half full. Henry nodded approvingly; Jay seemed to remember taking his pills. Satisfied with the results of his investigation, Henry sighed, relieved. Pensively he glanced over at his sleeping son.

Jay had gained more weight recently and the grey cashmere jumper his grandmother gave him for Christmas last year now looked tight around the waist. Henry's frustration grew at the sight of him. His son used to be so handsome. His ex-wife had been obsessed with dressing him in designer clothes since he was a toddler. Designer scarves and socks, baby cashmere and assorted outfits for every day of the week, nothing was too expensive. Elisabeth had dragged Jay from castings to photo shoots, desperate for the world to see her perfect child. Henry wondered whether he should have stopped her. 'Too much pressure on the lil'one' his mother had repeatedly warned them.

Nowadays all his son did was sleep and eat. *Why didn't he just get up and stay awake long enough to go for a run?* Henry didn't get it. A great sports enthusiast himself, he couldn't fathom why his only son was such a couch potato. He could barely admit this to himself, but he was embarrassed. People were talking behind his back. He couldn't stand the look of pity in their eyes and awkwardness when they enquired about Jay's 'state'. They wouldn't even say the words 'mental illness'. The only person, he felt he could remotely confide in was his best friend, John Liebtreu. But jealousy was a strong feeling and every time he thought of his friend's daughter the pain was overwhelming. Sophie was happily married and apparently expecting her first child. Sophie was all that Henry had wished his son to become. Successful and happy. These days Henry avoided talking about him altogether.

Jay stirred in his sleep and a pang of guilt chased the painful comparison away. Henry sat down at his desk, pushed the white envelope in front of him and stared at it for a little while, his heart heavy with the decision he had made. He wished he could somehow make peace with the fact that his son was schizophrenic and that without his medicine he was a danger to himself. Ibiza last year was the proof. Keen to lock the paining memory away, he looked out of the window into the garden. A warm October sun bathed the ochre leaves of the apple orchard in a golden light. Henry noticed the hedges needed trimming. He made a mental note to call the gardener to come round next week.

Only by sheer coincidence he had noticed that Jay had jumped off the cliff and started swimming out at sea. He had come down to the beach to ask him for the keys of the villa, when he realised that his son was struggling to stay afloat in the waves. He yelled at Jay to come back to shore, but the wind had been too strong and drowned out his voice. In blind panic, he ran back to the beach and shouted for help. A neighbour came to the rescue and untowed his Zodiac dinghy. When they reached the spot where they had last seen him battling to stay afloat, Jay had already gone under. Henry had flung his shoes off and jumped in after him. He had struggled to find him in the murky waters and had to surface for more air before going back down.

Panic ringing in his ears, after agonising minutes searching through stinging eyes, he eventually spotted a blurred shadow slowly drifting towards the darkness. His arm in a tight grip, Henry hauled his unconscious son onto the boat and praying silently he had looked on as his neighbour Stefan von Kempen performed an urgent cardio massage. His lungs burned, and his sight blurred, he held his son's cold blue hand willing him to breathe again. Again and again the man pounded Jay's chest. It had been the longest five minutes of Henry's life. And just as Stefan slowed down his pace, and Henry's desperate heart sunk, Jay's eyelids fluttered open and he started coughing up seawater onto the bottom of the inflatable.

Henry had put him on the next plane home and signed him straight back into the psychiatric ward. He was a practical, no nonsense kind of man, used to making painful yet necessary decisions. That's how he had gotten to run his father's publishing empire, but what he was about to announce was, even by his standards, going to be tough.

'Dad? What are you doing here?' Henry hadn't noticed his son had woken up.

'I need to talk to you...' He answered quickly, feeling uncomfortable. A feeling he had a lot around his son lately. There was something in the way Jay looked at him that was vacant as if he listened to someone else talking to him at the same time. The doctor had said that was probably the case. The diagnosis had revealed he had paranoid schizophrenia, and one of the symptoms was hearing voices. Multiple voices. Henry assumed his son wore the headphones so the constant music would drown out the noise. The psychiatrists were still experimenting on the right dosage of the drugs. Sometimes Jay was fine for a few weeks, could hold someone's gaze for more than a minute and have a normal conversation. But then he would suddenly relapse into a catatonic state where all he would do was lie in bed. Like now. He had been like this for days, since the opening night of the gallery. Although his dramatic exit had fuelled the speculations of his mental instability, it also contributed to the popularity of his work. *What a waste of talent.* Henry hung his head.

'I don't want to get up', Jay groaned and turned away from him to face the wall.

'Come on, you have to', Henry tried again a little more irritated.

He was supposed to be at a meeting with the principal stakeholders of the firm. Looking at his overweight schizophrenic 30-year-old son it pained him to know he would never be the heir he had wanted him to be, the company he spent building all his life would have to be sold. But not just that. At 30, Jay was still living in his house. That irritated him the most. He was constantly there, a permanent reminder of his failure as a parent. He had tried to convince Jay to move to his mother's who had a ten-bedroom mansion in the countryside, but she had refused to take him in. She feared him, she had said.

'Jay listen to me.' He touched his shoulder. Jay flinched, shrugged him off and sat up straight.

'Don't touch me. Don't ever touch me again,' he hissed, alarmed. Henry backed off somewhat shocked by the unexpected intensity in his voice.

'We need to talk,' Henry repeated, this time more firmly. Refusing to acknowledge him, Jay stared holes in the ceiling. There was a steely stubbornness to his attitude way beyond the teenager sulks his father was used to.

'I've spoken to your mother and your stepfather. We are all concerned about your recent... err... behaviour. It looks like the symptoms are ...err... worsening'. Henry was finding this conversation excruciating. After all these years, he still hated his ex-wife for always leaving him to deal with his son's troubles and delivering the uncomfortable truth. He braced himself for what he was about to say, shifting nervously in his chair.

'Your behaviour has been erratic again over the past months, and we have taken the decision to...' He paused breathed in for courage '...to look after your finances for you.' Jay didn't move.

His eyes were now fixed on an invisible dot on the white wall in front of him.

'Jay, we need you to sign this paper.' He opened the white envelope and held it out. Jay slowly took the official looking document and for the first time in weeks, looked his father in the eyes. A questioning look.

'What is this?'

Henry wiped his forehead with a monogrammed handkerchief.

'It's a precaution; it's in your best interest,' he mumbled.

Jay glared at the legal document. The heading read 'Application for Lasting Power of Attorney'. It had a yellow sticker marking the blank space where his signature was missing. Henry didn't look him in the eye when he handed him his silver fountain pen.

'It says here that I hereby relinquish all responsibility for my finances to Caspar von Schoenefeldt.'

Henry nodded slowly, he didn't agree with his ex-wife on this point but the law stated that the power of attorney couldn't be a direct relative and Caspar's fox of a lawyer had managed to shoehorn him in the process. Jay read on, his brow furrowed in confusion.

'This includes the trust-fund money and my current accounts?' Henry nodded again. 'It also says here that I'm mentally incapacitated. Mentally incapacitated?!? Father, I thought we had agreed...not to...is this a joke?'

'Sadly not.' With a slightly trembling hand, he smoothed his silk Hermes tie. He always did that when he was nervous. Today it was little yellow giraffes he stroked.

'Look, I know this sounds worse than it is. It's legal jargon ok? It's just semantics. The bottom line here is', he checked his Rolex, he was going to be late if he didn't leave in the next 10 minutes. A quick look out the window confirmed that his driver was waiting in the driveway, 'that you are having difficulties managing your money lately. At first we thought it was one of your odd arty projects, but then you bought 500 kg worth of eggs and had them delivered here and stored in my garage for two weeks!'

'I told you father; it was for an art project.' He insisted, mumbling each word dripping with a contained resentment as he remembered the stink of the rotten eggs he hurled them onto a giant canvass with great liberation. Henry ignored him and continued.

'And what about the vintage black cab you auctioned on the internet? The one you had shipped from London at great cost only to leave it to rust at your mother's?'

'Well, there wasn't enough space in your garage, with all the eggs' he shrugged his shoulders defiantly. They'd had this conversation before.

'And now this, the bunker?' Jay rolled his eyes. 'Don't roll your eyes at me! Jay, you bought a bunker? What do you think you are doing? Preparing for doomsday? Are the voices telling you to do this? Is this related to your paranoia about the paedophile ring again? Or is this about Milana?' Jay's obsession with paedophiles and child prostitution was disturbing but not as disturbing as his burgeoning conviction that the relationship between Caspar and his adopted daughter was somewhat suspicious.

Henry didn't want to think about it. He had found out about the bunker when the surveyors had called for additional information to complete the paperwork. He had answered the phone and discovered his son had put in an offer to buy a bunker. 140,000 euros for a 100 square meter second world war bunker, a ruin to be more precise, lost somewhere in the deep dark woods, in the countryside outside of Berlin. Henry nearly fainted.

'I wanted to use the space as an art workshop', Jay tried to explain but his father wasn't listening. Henry nodded and thought about the entry in Jay's diary he had read, about how he considered living in there too and that he was concerned about the damp-proofing of the underground rooms.

'Nonsense, I've had enough of this' Henry checked his watch again. 'We all have had enough of your obsessions. Just stick to taking your pills, lose some weight and try to become healthy again for Christ sakes! Now sign the bloody papers!' he was losing his patience, he checked his watch again. He needed to go now if he were to make the meeting on time. Jay pushed his jaw out and with a deft wrist movement, ripped the document to shreds. He threw the remains in his father's face, like confetti at a wedding.

'Fuck you! I will not sign this crap. How dare you say I'm mentally incapacitated. I was depressed! My girlfriend cheated on me! With Caspar!' Jay's eyes glowered with hatred at the painful memory. 'Have you forgotten? After he fucked my girlfriend, he made her abort the child. He destroyed our relationship. Who wouldn't get depressed after that?! And you want me to hand over my right to decide over my money to... him?' He yelled, eyes bulging, as he got up from the bed, his massive frame towering over his father.

'The same man who visited the flat where these men raped a child? Of course, he denied ever having set foot in the building', his laugh was dripping with sarcasm. 'BUT I SAW HIM. What about Milana? Have you seen how he LOOKS at her? And now he wants to gag me financially. Take away my freedom, control me. Why? BECAUSE I KNOW TOO MUCH' He shouted in his father's face, and Henry backtracked, shaking, to the door, intimidated by the sudden burst of anger.

By now Jay was seething, his burning eyes holding Henry's increasingly scared gaze. He was not finished; there was so much more to say. There was a whole tsunami of feelings threatening to break down the dam he had carefully constructed with the help of the drugs. But like the little Dutch boy who stuck his finger in the crack, he knew that if he withdrew his finger the dyke would burst open, and the dark, cold water would engulf everything. He lifted his fist to his father's face, ready to punch but instead he lashed out at the TV screen next to him. Blinded by his escalating rage, he repeatedly hit the screen until it shattered. He crunched over the remains, snatched his headphones off the bed, grabbed his parka and slammed the door behind him.

***

Berlin, October 2010 - 5 days before the incident

The constant humming was annoying, but not as annoying as the interspersing cackle of laughter that burst through the walls of his study room. Maxime sighed and pushed his pen into the fold of the leather bound tome he had borrowed from his dad, while he considered moving his revisions to his bedroom. Jay and Milana were playing that stupid game on the console again. Some inane racing game with pimped up cars. He shrugged his shoulders with the greatest contempt he could muster. They were so childish. He didn't care much for these type of games. Not that he never played himself, but he rarely had the time these days as he spent every free minute he had pouring over his anatomy manuals. And when he did have the time he preferred to play in the privacy of his bedroom rather than the gaming room. He got a thrill from playing ego shooters. He scribbled a quick 'check Call of Duty - Black Ops release date' on a post-it note, before returning to the section on skin grafting on a lower leg trauma injury.

His sister's strident laugh echoed through the hall. God she annoyed him sometimes. He always thought of her as a lesser version of himself. Instead of wanting to become a surgeon like him, she wanted to become a nurse. She always opted for the path of least resistance. The easy way. It wasn't just her lack of ambition that got to him; he also loathed her appearance. He automatically ran his finger along the straight bridge of his nose. Sometimes he could feel the cartilage crackle under the fine skin. Whereas his twin sister still had her original large flat nose, after the rhinoplasty work, the surgeon had narrowed his upper lateral cartilage and reduced the nasal bone. He now had a straight nose he was extremely proud of. In family photos he looked very much like his father, side-parted blonde hair and sparkling blue eyes, whereas his twin still sported the look of a war-torn country. She reminded him of the miserable life they only just escaped every time he looked at her.

He often wondered about just how different him and his sister were and how twins were supposed to have a special in-utero developed bond that he failed to see. He had made it a rule never to think about the mother who carried them in her womb, before delivering them into eastern European poverty and the horror of a third-world orphanage. He refused to think about her, the mother who abandoned them – he really had no thought to spare for her. He clapped the book shut, annoyed, and rolled his sleeves up to reveal an inked right forearm. The number 88 in an old Germanic font. The 8th letter of the alphabet, H. Double H. Heil Hitler. Since 7th grade, he had loved history classes and had developed a keen interest in World War II and its main protagonists. He had been particularly impressed with Dr Josef Mengele, nicknamed 'The angel of death'; a doctor who had conducted human experiments on war prisoners. One of his studies had been to analyse the bond between twins, and some of his cruel experiments had researched how to separate Siamese twins, foregoing general anaesthetic and rawly sawing limbs and organs together with a zero survival rate of his 'patients'. Despite the evident madness of the man and the rudimentary methods he employed, as a twin and aspiring doctor Maxime could understand the man's motivations to push the boundaries of humanity in the interests of furthering science. There was something to be learned, Maxime thought, and looking idly at the felt tip tattoo on his arm, he played with the thought to have it inked for life. 88. A winning number.

Maxime crossed the hall in a few long strides and kicked the gaming room door open with a bang. Undisturbed, Jay and Milana didn't look up from their gaming consoles, their eyes glued to the screen, their pupils reflecting the shiny cars of the racing game, their mouths slightly ajar in concentration. Sitting cross-legged on the sofa, Milana looked like a skinny child in her oversized marl-grey University of Toronto sweatshirt, a present from her step-brother. Her long blonde hair was scraped back in a tight ponytail, and she nervously bit her lower lip while swerving the console pad in front of her. Jay looked like a giant next to her. His hands were so big, the console pad seemed to disappear between his fingers.

Maxime frowned. He got along fine with his stepbrother, and he found his deteriorating mental health fascinating to observe. It was quite entertaining to witness the latest developments of Jay's paranoiac delusions. Often while listening to Jay's delusional accounts of yet another strange conviction, Maxime wondered if the schizophrenia diagnosis was correct as he was certain Jay would also score quite high on Dr Robert Hare's psychopathy checklist. The lack of empathy was one of the characteristics Maxime admired the most and secretly vowed to develop himself. Jay had many interesting theories about prostitution and paedophile rings, but he also came up with reality-distorting stories. Stories Maxime found far-fetched, but nonetheless amusing. Like the theory Jay had about his nose. Jay was convinced that his father Caspar had instigated the accident.

According to Jay, he had witnessed his stepfather kick the back-tyre of the bicycle Maxime rode around the driveway so Maxime would topple over and smack his head against the pavement. An excuse for Caspar to perform cosmetic surgery on his adopted son, to remodel the nose so it would look just like his.

'Do you mean my father broke my nose ON PURPOSE? To surgically enhance it to look like his? So we'd look like father and son?' Maxime had laughed the crazy allegations off. 'In any case Jay, he did me a favour! I could still look like my sister!' Maxime couldn't remember the accident in much detail, but he would never forget the feeling of his teeth cutting through his upper lip and his nose bursting open like a blood-filled balloon.

Jay was very protective of his step-sister which Maxime found mildly annoying. The two seemed to have a stronger bond than him and his sister would ever have. Some form of mutual understanding. Maxime remembered vividly how Jay went berserk that day at the lake when he discovered the pen marks he had drawn on his sister's body. Maxime had later tried to explain it had been for research purposes and that he was only pointing out the various surgical procedures he had learned from his father. He was convinced there was nothing creepy about that, but Jay made him apologise to his sister and promise never to touch her inappropriately ever again. He had become more cautious and found other less visible ways to continue with his research. He was all too aware of Jay's suspicious glances every time he let his gaze linger too long.

Maxime observed them playing another round on the console and when the 'Start New Race' sign flashed up on the screen, he opened his mouth to yell at them to keep the bloody noise down. But he never got to utter a word. Jay suddenly tossed the console pad to one side.

The coke bottle on the floor swerved and fizzed the sugary brown liquid all over the thick cream carpet. Jay jumped up and grabbed Milana under her armpits and in one quick swerve pinned her against the wall. The family portrait shook as great grandfather von Schoenefeldt trembled in his frame looking onto the scene unfolding next to him.

'What did you just say?' Jay shouted at her. His eyes were wide with anger and rolled wildly in its sockets. Milana's mouth dropped open in shocked protest. The racing cars crashed against the road block and came to a humming halt as the video game went into 'Game Over' mode.

'What did you just say? Milana darling, you can tell me! You have to tell me! Is that what he's done to you?'

Spit foamed at the corner of his mouth as he fired questions at her. She tried to wriggle herself out of his steely grip, but he was too strong, pushing his full body weight against her, crushing her ribcage.

'Jay!' she squealed, panic rising. 'Let go!'

'He did, didn't he? That asshole! That son of a bitch. I knew it. All these times he let his hand linger on your thigh. I knew it, that fucking scumbag!' He wailed in agony, holding her so tight his knuckles turned white. Maxime finally snapped out of his stupor, grabbed his stepbrother by the shoulders and tried to pull him back with all his might, away from his twin sister. But Jay was too strong, too tall.

Milana burst into tears. 'Let go!' she screamed at the top of her voice. Suddenly, as quick as the burst of anger had engulfed him, Jay calmed down. Milana slowly slid to the ground, a sobbing heap. Jay shrugged his brother off and with one shoulder swing flung him on the sofa where he remained, gobsmacked. Milana looked up at her stepbrother towering over her. Jay smoothed his long fringe behind his ear. With a trembling hand he wiped the spit from his lips. A look of fierce protection in his angry eyes, he stared at her for a while. When he finally spoke his voice was deep and measured.

'Thank you for finally telling me. You confirmed my suspicion. I'll take action. I'll restore justice. That animal, how could he! He'll never touch you again. I promise.'

A chill crept up Maxime's spine as he watched Jay walk out of the room.

'What the fuck was that?' Maxime whispered at Milana, who wiped the snot from her nose with the back of her trembling hand.

'I don't know', she hiccupped. 'I swear, I didn't say anything!' They stared at each other for a moment, both trying to make sense of what just happened.

'Oh God, Max, this isn't right. We need to tell mum, I think he is having an episode again. Shit. I'm worried about him. Do you think he is off his meds again? Do you think he's hearing voices again?'

Maxime nodded. Jay had recently displayed increasingly erratic behaviour and their mother had warned them both to stay away from him. But Milana couldn't do this. She loved him too much and wanted to help, to be there for him when he felt lonely. She was convinced she could find a connection. Help his deteriorating brain to find a way out to normality and no matter how strange and far-fetched his delusions were, she stood by him. Until now.

'This has gone too far', said Maxime, pointing to her arms where angry purple bruises were blossoming like morbid flowers. Milana nodded.

***

Berlin, October 2010- 3 days before the incident

'Hi my name is Torsten, how can I be of assistance today?' he asked with a fake friendly voice. He called it his 'I'm your bitch' voice, the syrupy sweet tone which dripped with sales intentions. He sighed internally while smiling broadly. He hated his job. His boss had pulled him up a couple of times on how he spoke to customers. Apparently he sounded 'uninviting' and 'uninspiring', when in fact they wanted him to give the client an 'unforgettable experience'. *Ridiculous.* Buying tennis rackets and golf clubs was never going to be the 'experience' people craved for. *A helicopter trip around Machu Picchu, yeah maybe that would qualify as an 'experience'. But buying a new pair of sweatbands? Mmmm.* Torsten had his doubts. When he had shrugged his shoulders his boss threw a hissy fit, taken him aside at the weekly staff meeting and told him off good and proper.

In a patronising tone he was asked whether he had read the customer value proposition. Of course he had, Torsten protested, which was a lie so big even he didn't buy it. His boss raised a plucked eyebrow. He got away with a warning and a promise to learn the customer experience charter off by heart. He was going to be tested on it in detail the next day. 'I'm disappointed, you're wasting so much great potential.' Torsten thanked him with a smile that reached from one ear to the other, taking full advantage of the knowledge that his boss fancied him.

Seeing him standing by the men's tennis sportswear bargain basket, Torsten had just wanted to raise two middle fingers at his stick-thin frame and tell him to shove his shitty handbook up his... *The faggot.* He had nothing against gays but just because the boss loved cock didn't mean he had to act like a bitch... Torsten swallowed his frustration and inched his smile further up. Like a bloody toothpaste ad.

'Huh?' unaware of the cashier's heated internal dialogue, the man in front of him slowly raised his head. Torsten noted the greasy long hair strands curling up behind the ears of the man, the field of dandruff flakes on his shoulders and the dark rim of his shirt collar. Being the type of guy who would take a shower before and after the gym, Torsten had a thing for personal hygiene, and he suppressed a desire to grimace in disgust as he froze his smile. That man looked like a shower was long overdue.

'How can I help you Sir?' he repeated, politely pointing at the bat in the man's hand. 'Do you wish to purchase this?'

'Mmmm.' The man twisted the bat in his hand as if to check its weight. He swerved it slowly to the ground and back up again. Testing its velocity Torsten assumed. He wasn't a big fan of the sport himself, actually if he was truthful to himself, he didn't even know the rules to the game. It was a yank game. His sport was football. The whole hitting a tiny ball with a bat. *Nope*. Not for him.

That man was going to be one of those monosyllabic customers. His favourite. The sort that didn't give a damn about customer service, that would just walk into the shop, pick the bat they liked, swing it around a couple of times and then would push the cash onto the till and disappear. No exchange of words necessary. His kind of client. Unfortunately, it was not going to be enough. In the corner of his eye Torsten could see his boss circling the kid's football boots section, picking up shoes at random and putting them back on the shelf all the while shooting him side glances with eyes that said last chance saloon. Ok then, time to up the ante, thought Torsten.

'Sir, may I?' Torsten had to prize the bat off the customer's hands. 'This wooden baseball bat is made of natural wood. It's an exceptional product. See here? The bat is varnished with a transparent varnish that leaves a solid top-coat. The grip of the bat is left unvarnished intentionally because otherwise the wood would be unable to soak up the moisture and sweat, and that all creates a better grip.'

The man didn't look at him. He shifted nervously from one foot to the other. Torsten ignored him; he was going to prove to his poofter boss that he was a goddamn excellent salesman and would keep the job long enough to buy his neighbour's VW Golf. He had to. He was planning on visiting his girlfriend who studied in Amsterdam, and he needed a car.

'Do you play Sir?'

The man nervously ran his hand through his greasy hair. Sweat beaded his brow. He looked shady but maybe that was because of his beard. Torsten hated facial hair. Even if that meant going through the hassle of wet shaving every day, frazzled long beard hairs looked dirty.

'No', the man whispered tonelessly.

'So this is for your kid then I assume.' Torsten was on a roll. 'Well let me see'. He expertly twirled the bat around '80cm. That's what I thought'

The man looked like he was going to bolt for the door. Maybe he was a bum off the street, who he had interrupted shoplifting but on second look, Torsten decided that the checked, although stained, cashmere scarf and the, although worn, fur-rimmed parka both looked expensive. His shoes were caked in paint and grime, but he recognised them being Redwings, a boot he knew retailed at around 250 euros, a steep price for him, let alone for a bum.

'Pardon me?' The man asked with a gruff voice.

'How old is your son? This bat might be too big for him. You see, this is the adult version. We have a 70cm for 8 to 10-year-olds and a 75cm for 10 to 12.'

His boss seemed pleased with Torsten's new found levels of dedication to customer satisfaction and slinked out of sight to sort the basketballs.

'It's for myself', the man murmured fingering the collar of his shirt nervously. He seemed hot and uncomfortable. Now that he was off the hook, Torsten was going to release the poor bastard.

'Oh ok, great. Anything else you need? A pair of gloves maybe? No? Ok then, that'll be 49.99, please. Would you like to pay cash or card?'

'Cash.' The man's face was ashen as he pulled out a wad of cash held together by a rubber band he snapped open and started counting. The tip of his fingers were stained with black and red paint. His fingernails were dirty. Torsten couldn't help but purse his lips as he grabbed the cash off him.

'Well, thank you for shopping at Sportsarena. I hope your experience with us has been a pleasant one, and we hope to welcome you back with us soon.' Torsten delivered the script with haste while slipping the notes into the till. *Now move along Beardy, move along.*

'I don't think they'll ever let me come back after this.'

For the first time, the man looked straight into Torsten's eyes, with a bone chilling stare. His green eyes pierced into the cashier's skull with such intensity that Torsten's offence at the remark vanished. Torsten felt a primal fear rise inside of him. *This man. There is something incredibly odd about him.* He watched the man shove the bat under his arm and shuffle out into the busy street where he disappeared amongst hundreds of late-afternoon shoppers.

***

Berlin, October 2010 - 24 hours before the incident

Sam Liebtreu figured his friend looked odd these days. He wondered if the overweight man with the long unwashed hair sitting opposite him, listlessly picking at his jerk chicken could even be called his friend. It was true they hung out sometimes but mostly at the request of his sister Sophie.

'My darling brother', she had said. 'Since I'm in London and very pregnant, can I ask you for a favour.'

'Anything?' he ventured, he loved his sister. She was his inspiration, so very driven and career oriented, nothing like him in that way. He who worked in a coffee shop for a measly minimum wage, after getting kicked out of cooking school. Poor attendance and drug abuse. That was a bit lame. Everybody smoked weed these days. He was young, only 21 years old; he had plenty of time to figure out what he wanted to do in life.

'Can you keep an eye on Jay?' she begged him. 'I worry about him. He's had it tough over the past few years, and I don't want him to...' she had choked back tears '...hurt himself.'

The pregnancy hormones were heavy on her, and he had to promise her over and over that he would look after her friend. He didn't even have to force himself that much. He did admire Jay. He always had since he was a kid. There was something so inherently cool and edgy about this man. A Tarantinoesque nonchalance. Sam looked up at Jay as he poured them another glass of wine. An aloofness that masked seething anger bubbling under the surface, like red hot magma ready to erupt. Sam admired his talent. Everything the man touched turned into art. He played the drums like he lived the music in all its pain and glory. He produced music that made him ache with melancholy and painted extraordinarily grim renditions of the gloominess of existence. He was a talented tortured soul. A real one.

'So how is she?'

Sam cocked his head. How was she, he thought avoiding Jay's cold green stare. He took a sip to buy some time to put together his answer. The truth was Sophie was well, big and bloated, and ready to give birth any time now. She was past her due date so anytime now was indeed very probable. He looked at Jay's pained expression and decided to not tell him about Sophie's impending newborn. He wasn't sure whether she had told him that she was expecting a baby, and he had a feeling, knowing the history of the two, that Jay didn't want to know.

'She is doing just fine Jay.' With his tone he had really said 'let it go mate, don't dig at this', and Jay didn't. He just nodded in silence and continued picking at the chicken bone with huge hands.

'What about you? How are you doing? I heard your exhibition was quite a success', Sam ventured cautiously.

'It seems it got some traction, yes. Frank will be happy with this; he got himself some commission money there.' He smiled sadly. The press had made the most of his short appearance and the published articles had generated a flurry of interest from agents and buyers. Then suddenly he tossed the remains of his chicken onto the white tablecloth and excused himself. He took so long to come back that Sam debated whether he should take a look at the men's restroom to ensure he was ok. But before he had finished his thought, Jay came back to the table. Pale and sweaty. He wiped his mouth with the back of his hand. He looked unwell. His eyes were bloodshot and his skin deathly white.

'Huh, wow...what in fuck's name happened to you man? You don't look so good bro...'

'Yeah...I'm not sure... maybe the chicken. I feel quite hum... uncomfortable. It is hot in here, right? I'm not making this up, right?' He rambled. Sam had trouble understanding him as he talked into his hands.

'Can we go?' Jay whispered.

Sam paid for dinner, and as they walked out of the restaurant, Jay said:

'Look I'm feeling better now. Let's stay. Let's have a drink somewhere.' He seemed agitated.

'Sorry. I'd love to dude, but man I gotta get up tomorrow to get to my bloody useless job and that starts at 6:30am. Yep, that early. So I'm off to get some sleep. I think you should do the same. It's a school night, after all.'

'Listen. Whisky's on me, ok?' he insisted. Sam shook his head. His girlfriend Jasmine was probably waiting at his flat.

'Sam, I need to be with someone sane tonight. You're reasonable and sane. Stay with me. Dan's coming back. I can feel him taking over. I can't control him anymore you see.' Jay continued to whisper intensely, his eyes wide open.

Sam stared blankly at him. *Dan? Who the hell is that?* When he put his hand on Jay's shoulder and apologised, Jay shrugged him off irritably, muttered under his breath something that Sam wanted to ignore but sounded awfully like "You're abandoning me, just like your sister", and walked off. A lonely silhouette in a black parka and a blue hooded jumper.

It had started to rain. Sam pulled over the hood of his coat, and as he walked to the bus station, he made a note to give Jay a call in the morning. Maybe they could arrange to go out, after all it was Halloween tomorrow night.

***

Berlin, Halloween 2010 - 2:30am - Schoenefeldt residence

'Ok then, see you shortly. And son...' Elisabeth von Schoenefeldt waited for him to respond '...drive safely.'

He had slurred his words and she was worried he had been drinking again. As she put the receiver back on its base, she looked at the kitchen wall clock, 2:30 am, and a terrible sense of foreboding engulfed her. Nothing good could come out at this time of the night. She tapped her fingers nervously on the gleaming worktop surface. Although she had given up years ago, as soon as she noticed her upper lip had the appearance of wrinkled crepe paper, she was now itching for a cigarette. She had quickly arranged for the wrinkles to be zapped with botox and decided it was time to ditch the terrible habit. But ever since she could feel a latent craving that would become untenable each time she felt anxious. She rifled through the jars in the top cupboard looking for the emergency cigarettes she hid in the coffee tin. Sure enough, the packet was still there. The tobacco was dry and threatened to disintegrate before she could light it, but it did the trick. Leaning against the industrial-sized fridge, the old lady inhaled deeply. Blue smoke hung low in the air as she tasted the stale tobacco on her tongue.

Elisabeth tried to recall Jay's exact words but the conversation was a blur. The primary cause for concern was the panic in his voice. Possibly the start of another paranoid episode. He had spoken too fast – in short, incoherent sentences, choking back tears. And he mentioned Dan again. Elisabeth shivered in her silk dressing gown. There was something different this time; she could feel it, a new sense of urgency. Only a few days ago he had confronted her with the disturbing accusation that her husband had sexually abused his stepdaughter Milana. After the first wave of shock had washed through her, she reminded herself that this was just another one of Jay's paranoid theories about his stepfather. She trembled at the painful memory of the ensuing fight.

He had screamed at her for closing her eyes to a most disgusting crime happening right under her nose. But she couldn't believe him. Over the years he had come to her with increasingly paranoid thoughts about his stepfather, they ranged from the more anodyne, like Caspar favouring his step brother over him, grooming Maxime for succession despite being ten years his junior, to the more serious allegations that he had seduced Jay's girlfriend and not only impregnated her but also forced her to abort the child.

There was a time her son had accused him of using her as a guinea pig for unlicensed botox injections and all sorts of new plastic surgery procedures. Then there was the paranoid idea that his neighbours operated a child prostitution ring that Caspar headed up. What horrible nonsense. And the list went on and on. She shook her head in desperation. Caspar was, in his eyes, the root of all evil. Their relationship had started with the traumatic event the day he had walked in on her and Caspar at the tennis club and Elisabeth knew that she had a big part to play in the twisted power plays between the two that followed.

After years of counselling, Dr Klein, her son's psychiatrist, established Jay suffered from a paranoid schizophrenic induced obsession with his stepfather, rooted in this particular incident 20 years ago. He not only saw the man as the reason his parents divorced, but was also reminded daily of his insufferable guilt for telling on his mother. The fights that ensued had been terrible, Elisabeth winced at the painful memory. Plates had flown across the kitchen. Doors were slammed. Her 10-year old son had screamed hysterically and had barricaded himself in his room. He wouldn't come out from under the bed and had refused the food the nanny would leave on the floor for him. By the next day, her ex-husband had to lift the bed up while she grabbed her screaming and kicking child by his legs and dragged him to the bathroom to wash him. He had soiled himself; the excrements had caked his legs and back. He was feral. A biting and seething animal. The next day she had booked an appointment with the child psychologist Caspar had recommended. Shortly after, her 10-year old son had been put on a mild dosage of antidepressants to balance out his mood swings. In the following months, he had become mute and withdrawn.

Elisabeth stubbed out the cigarette and felt restless. She started unloading the dishwasher. *All I ever wanted was for our family to be happy.* She slid the stainless steel knives into their block; one by one the shimmering Japanese blades disappeared into the wooden slit with a menacing hiss. She wondered whether the psychiatrist was wrong about the trigger of her son's mental illness. She was convinced it had been the months following the birth of her son that caused the irreparable damage. The birth itself had been long and arduous. Her baby was born with a tongue stuck to his palate, a defect that had not been spotted by the doctors until the baby had been turned in, half-starved after three days, unable to take any milk. He was kept in the special care unit for a week. Elisabeth's eyes welled up at the memory, still fresh after all those years of her tiny son, only a week old, his legs no larger than her husband's finger, fed by tubes in a sterile cot. He had pulled through, but the emotional shock had left a dark mark on Elisabeth. As a mother, she had failed to spot the danger quick enough. She blamed herself and the realisation that her son's well-being was her responsibility for the rest of her life had sent her into a postnatal depression so severe, she had to be taken away from her son for fear of harming him.

After the electroconvulsive therapy, she suffered emotional detachment and loss of her short-term memory. She had felt history repeating itself, her growing distance with her son mirroring the strained relationship with her mother.

'Mental illness is hereditary', her husband Henry had said, his voice thick with resentment. The passionate fights with him resumed over the years and their inability to understand and cope with their young child's needs fanned the flames of the growing hatred between them. Slowly she realised that, despite the initial attraction, their whirlwind romance had bottomed out, and it started to dawn on them that their personalities were incompatible. Then one day when she woke up with yet another bruise to hide, she packed her bags and slammed the door on the debris of her marriage to rebuild her life with her lover.

She poured herself a tumbler of whisky and lit up another cigarette. She thought of the pack of temazepam on her bedside table. *I could use a tranquillizer.* She looked up at the clock. Her son was going to be here shortly. She shook her head; she didn't know how to feel about him anymore. Desperate and powerless, she had dragged him, over the years, from psychologists to psychiatrists, from cognitive to occupational therapies. She had fed him anti-depressants and mood stabilisers. She had tried the strict parental approach and had ruled her son's life like a prison warden. When he ignored her and went on a hunger strike so effective it sent him to A&E, she went for the opposite approach and left him entirely to his own devices. Nothing had quelled her constant fear of being a failure as a mother, as he went on to being arrested for illegal event organising, breaking and entering into government owned premises, drug possession, public disturbance, destruction of public property and so on. It had been a constant struggle to keep him in school. He had no academic drive and fled reality with music and art. However not in an Ecole des Beaux Arts style – she could have lived with that – her son's art was illegal street art, destructive and insane.

Her eyes welled up. Her handsome boy for whom she had dreamed up a successful life, heir to her ex-husband's publishing empire, a successful marriage and grandchildren. Her dream had died a long time ago, the night she had answered the first of many late-night phone calls from her son. Panting down the phone, his voice was thick with tears and panic.

'Elisabeth?' She looked up as Caspar walked into the kitchen in his checked pyjamas, looking alarmed. 'What's wrong?'

She sobbed faintly as she talked.

'Elisabeth, please hear me. He needs help. Professional help. He needs to be in care. Permanently. This whole situation, it's killing you'. He spoke reassuringly.

As she studied the worry lines on his handsome face, she knew as so often was the case that he was right.

'I know you don't want to hear it but I think it's time to talk to Dr Klein again. Jay needs to be interned. Solacium is the right place. He will be well looked after', he whispered in her ear, hugging her tightly. 'Go to bed. I'll handle this ok? I'll speak to Jay and get him to sleep in the guest room. I'll talk him out of whatever delusion is plaguing him. And tomorrow we will make an appointment with Dr Klein. Ok?'

After the incident with Milana earlier in the week, she had hesitated to call the police. She felt her son was heading down a very dangerous and aggressive path. Although his father assured her of the opposite, she was convinced Jay had stopped taking his medicines. It had only been the call with the psychiatrist that calmed her down. In his current unstable state, he will not excessively express his frustration. He will only take his anger out on objects. He will never hurt a human being; the certified psychiatrist had said to them.

Elisabeth wasn't sure whether Caspar was the right person to catch her son in a downward spiral of delusion. Caspar would only aggravate him. She, his mother, should talk to him, she knew she could talk him out of whatever paranoia plagued him. Suddenly she felt exhausted, of her son, of her worries, of everything. She just wanted to go upstairs and swallow a couple of tranquillizers and sleep. She nodded slowly and gently kissed her beloved husband goodnight.

***

Berlin, Halloween 2010 - 2:55am - Schoenefeldt residence

When the door bell rang, half an hour later, Caspar von Schoenefeldt opened the door. He flinched at the short flickering of hatred in Jay's dark eyes. His hair, wet with sweat, stuck to his fat face. His skin was ghostly white in the faint light of the corridor, highlighting the dark circles under his eyes. He looked like he hadn't slept in days, and he reeked of alcohol.

'Caspar. Just the person I was looking for tonight', he hissed through clenched jaws in a tone so glacial it sent shivers up Caspar's spine.

As Jay silently followed him into the kitchen, Caspar forced himself to remain calm and fought the urge to glance over his shoulder. *That kid is so lost. It is time to get rid of him.* He had enough of the problems he was causing him. It was about time that his wife got a bit of rest. He needed to protect Milana and Maxime from Jay's violent outbursts. It was time his family started having a life again.

While he fixed them a cup of tea, he silently rehearsed what he was about to tell his stepson. *Solacium is a mental institution with an excellent reputation. No, better not use the term 'mental institution, it sounds too...maybe...I should call it rehab.*

Jay sat down at the breakfast table and stared at the knife block in front of him. He didn't move or say a word. Caspar fleetingly glared at him, wondering whether it was worth calling the police. He shook his head. He was not going to panic. He got this. It was only Jay. He could handle him. He had always been able to. The water hissed in its pot, and he dropped two chamomile tea bags in the mugs. As he placed the cups on the kitchen worktop, Jay stared at him, with unblinking eyes, casually playing with the kitchen knives. He slid them in and out of the wooden block, one by one, transfixed by the sound of the Japanese blade scraping against the wood. The light bounced off the stainless steel blade. Caspar suddenly broke into a sweat.

Quick as lightening and surprisingly deft on his feet despite his weight, Jay jumped up, brandishing the largest of the knives. In one swift motion, he pushed his shocked stepfather against the wall and drove the knife through the palm of his hand and pinned him to the wall. Blood sprayed against the eggshell white. Caspar's mouth hung open; his face frozen into a mask of terror. Before he could howl out in pain, Jay gagged him with a tea towel. Caspar's eyes rolled wildly in its sockets as he bit down on the fabric, the pain so unbearable the scream died in his throat. Jay smiled a cold smile that didn't reach his burning eyes, holding the gag in place.

'Ssssh. Now keep quiet. Listen to me. I'm far from done Caspar. You will pay. Don't worry you will pay. For every single wrongdoing. Aisha, my unborn baby, my mother and Milana. You will pay'. His voice sounded distorted, like someone else was talking in his place.

Caspar's eyes were tearing as he desperately tried to yank the knife out with his free hand. Blood ran over his forearm into his silk pyjamas. He didn't see the second knife coming as it crashed through his other wrist and slammed into the wall. Caspar coughed, choking on his gag and his body slacked.

'I won't be a moment Caspar', Jay promised, his eyes glinting in the bright kitchen light. Alight with primal hatred, the evil smile still spread across his face. 'I have another surprise for you. Don't go anywhere.' He chuckled at his joke as he looked over to his stepfather, arms spread wide, crucified against the wall, his face a mask of pain, blood dripping onto the expensive black and white tiles.

When Caspar, dizzy with fear and torn with pain, managed to look up again, he saw his stepson standing in the doorway, gently tapping a baseball bat in his hands. His eyes glowered darkly, possessed by hatred. Caspar felt a warm flow spreading in between his legs as a foreboding terror took hold of him. He looked at the pool of urine forming at his feet when the thick wood crashed against his left foot, and he instantly knew that not only his foot was broken but also that he would never walk again.

**

London, Halloween 2010 - 3:30am - London Chelsea Hospital

'Aaaaaaaaaarrrrrr.' She screamed in agony as a hot blinding pain stabbed through her, threatening her innards to explode. The pain was cruel and overwhelming, a pain she had never experienced before. She had feared and anticipated it for nine months, but none of the worrying and the pregnancy books had prepared her for this. The excruciating pain eclipsed her mind, and she no longer was a woman, she was a growling animal, overtaken by the instinct of survival. She was going to get through this, no matter what. The pain ebbed away as quickly as it had appeared, and she breathed in, her body trembling from the sudden absence of pain and steeling itself for the next wave.

And sure enough like a London Tube train thundering into its station, the pain flooded in and took hold of her shuddering body, leaving her howling like a dog, her bitten fingernails clawing the bed sheets. It was untenable. *Where. Are. The. Fucking. Drugs. This. Has. To. Stop.* Her mind stopped resisting. As her innards were bubbling like a volcano ready to erupt, gone were the good intentions of her birth plan 'au naturel'. She needed the fucking drugs and lots of them.

As soon as the needle pierced the skin on her spine, the morphine released in her body, and she could feel the cold drug diluting in her blood. Soon, with a sigh, the pain started vanishing into a distant fog.

'Are you ok Miss?' the surgeon asked from behind his green mask, a look of concern in his bright blue eyes. Sophie nodded feebly, slowly loosening a grip that left angry red marks on the pale skin of the man's arm. She wasn't sure whether it was the bright lights of the operating theatre or the epidural that blurred her vision, but as the surgeon gently pushed her back into the sweat-soaked sheets and switched the headlamp on, she knew there was no turning back. She was about to become a mother and the thought filled her equally with terror and exhilaration.

Blinded by the flooding light, she blinked and turned her head to find her husband sitting next to her. She had forgotten about him. Somebody pushed her numb legs into a gelled casing, and a belt was zipped tightly around her swollen torso. Panic rose inside her. They were about to cut her open. *With a scalpel.* Her breathing accelerated, and her heart bounced in her chest. One of the assistant surgeons whispered something in her husband's ear, he nodded, looking concerned and out of his depth but determined. Martin bowed down to her, taking her cold hand in his.

'Darling, look at me. It's important, listen to me now. This isn't going to hurt, but you'll have to stay with me, ok? Don't faint. It'll all be over in fifteen minutes.'

Sophie looked up at her husband, the loving expression on his trusting face was marked with the frustrated realisation that she was in charge now and that he was sidelined to the role of the passive supporter. He held her hand tightly. He hadn't left her side for the past eighteen hours.

'When this is over, I promise, I'll book us a holiday. Wherever you want to go.'

'The Caribbean?' she whispered, her eyelids fluttering with exhaustion and her mind numbed by the drugs pumped into her spine.

'Yes, think of white sandy beaches and palm trees and us three happily strolling into the sea.'

She smiled feebly as her head swam. The drugs were effective, and a strange sense of euphoria coated her brain in cotton wool. She barely noticed the team of doctors rushing around the operating theatre, passing trays with bloody towels and scalpels. She concentrated on her husband's blue eyes looking down at her with love and admiration. Martin looked pale and tired; the freckles of his skin had faded, and as he ran a trembling hand through his copper hair she noticed a strand of grey.

Suddenly an unwelcome thought pierced through the fog. *What if...what if the baby doesn't have blue eyes...* She didn't finish the thought as suddenly a weight lifted from her stomach and instantly she felt an overwhelming feeling of loss. *No don't take it away*, she screamed in her head, unable to move a finger.

'It's a girl! Congratulations Mom and Dad, she's a beauty!' The distant voice of the surgeon echoed in the room was followed by an angry scream that rang in Sophie's head like an alarm. She could barely make out a tiny bloodied leg dangling above the screen as the doctor held up her daughter before she fainted.

She awoke as the midwife, gently lay the small bundle on her chest. Sophie's arms flew up to hold her, and she looked into her daughter's little face with utter amazement. *Finally, she is here, my little Juliet.* The baby's eyelids fluttered, and Juliet slowly stared back at her mother. Sophie held her breath and her heart bounced against her ribcage. *She is beautiful.* Sophie looked up at Martin, at his tired face lit up with wonder and pride, tears of joy streaming down his cheeks at the miracle they had never expected to happen. Despite all his tests confirming his sterility, his wife had become pregnant. His eyes shone with pure, untainted love and unable to hide her emotions, tears rolled down her cheeks. Sophie looked back at her daughter. *Big, dark-green eyes and dark brown hair.* The realisation stabbed her like a knife to her heart. Deep down she had known the minute the blue line appeared on the pregnancy test and there and then, clutching the tiny bundle close to her heart and feeling the reassuring hand of her loving husband on her shoulder, she vowed to take her secret to her grave.

EPILOGUE

Ibiza, January 2012 - 1 year after the incident

The late afternoon sun shone on her legs as she looked out of the bay at the turquoise sea. It felt good to be back on the island, if only for a short while. Seeing her mother, even for a weekend, had its challenges but overall she was pleased to have her daughter spend some time with her. Plus, living in London, the sun was a rare commodity she couldn't get enough of. It felt strange staying at their villa; it was as if time had stood still on the island and everything remained the same. The yellowing framed family photos on the wall, the dusty hardbacks in the library and the smells that brought up so many memories. Sophie loved the spicy fragrance of the lavender bushes and the humid salty air.

She reclined in her deckchair, confident that her mother was entertaining her granddaughter Juliet building sand castles, and her thoughts trailed off. It felt strange being in Ibiza without Jay. Everything reminded her of him and the time they spent together. The smell of the pine trees at dusk when they used to walk to the bar up the road. The warm breeze on their skin as they sat on the rooftop looking up at the starry night sky. The hammock by the barbecue they had so often cuddled up in, feet dangling, reading their favourite novels. She sighed as she sifted through her memories like sorting a box of old polaroids. Until the harsh neon light of reality shone through the golden haze of her memories and highlighted that nothing was the same and everything had changed.

The haunted villa had been sold and transformed into an oligarch's playground with its ghosts walled in the basement gym. The swimming pool of their first kiss had been sold with its house, to a Swiss architect who had padlocked the entrance and raised the walls. In her mind's eye Jay's beautiful, youthful face, with his disarming smile, tanned with haystack hair, morphed into the bespectacled, overweight man with guarded eyes she met at the mental institution.

She thought of Henry, Jay's father and her heart shrunk with sadness. In their last conversation he had mentioned how bereft he felt of his son, how shame and loss now dictated his life. How he admitted to sometimes wishing he hadn't born a child into this world who would cause so much grief and heartache and that he blamed himself for not hearing the cries of help in time. How, to this day he didn't know what happened, and what had gone on in his son's head. Sophie couldn't even fathom the depths of the man's sorrow and didn't attempt to give him any words of wisdom for fear of sounding condescending.

Sophie often thought back to that gloomy afternoon she had spent with Jay at the Solacium clinic. He had responded to her hug with a light smile and had awkwardly patted her on her back. As they sat down in the sterile visitors room, on opposite chairs with only a small table separating them, Sophie was nervous if not a little panicked that the wardens had left them alone. She couldn't help but discreetly scan the room for possible objects he could harm her with in a violent episode. The chairs, the table, even the water bottle was a potential weapon in his hands. Then she looked at his hands; they were those of a giant, if he wanted to hurt her he could do so with his bare hands. He wasn't handcuffed. The rain drummed against the double-glazed windows and through the iron bars she could make out the blurred shape of the tall trees in the dark.

He spoke softly, and his head bowed, he stared at his hands.

'I got us some water. They normally don't allow any drinks up here, but I thought we would get thirsty.'

Ever the gentleman and regardless of the predicament he was in, he was her host and he was going to make her feel welcome and cared for. She noticed the bottle and the glasses were made of plastic. Of course, they wouldn't allow glass in here. But he had a way of handling the plastic cups with as much delicacy as if they were his grandmother's 18th-century crystal flutes and the sparkling water, the most exquisite of champagnes. Trying to ignore the odd sight and quelling the rising fear with a waxen smile, she nodded politely. She pointedly avoided looking at the blood red panic button on the wall behind him, a constant reminder that the man sitting across the table was a violent schizophrenic murderer.

The conversation, at first hesitant and slightly stilted, slowly started flowing and soon, like slipping out of their suits into their favourite sweatpants, they slipped into their childhood friends comfort zone, trying to reconnect the dots where they left off.

It was frighteningly easy to forget the thick walls, the bars on the window, the very reason for his internment and instead laugh at his sarcastic comments about the irrational behaviour of his fellow inmates. Just as she started feeling relaxed, legs folded on the chair, swigging nonchalantly from her plastic cup, he shot her a bone-chilling look over the rim of his glasses and froze her mid-laugh.

'Jay, don't look at me like that. You scare me!' she breathed nervously, pushing a stray hair strand behind her ear with a slightly shaky hand.

'Sorry, I didn't mean to. It's just … I can't believe you're here. You're seeing me like this, in here, and you're still talking to me. I just can't believe you're here', he repeated as he reached over the table and grabbed her hand. She resisted the urge to withdraw it. His hand was warm and dry.

'Look at you, you look amazing, like an angel bringing light into this godforsaken place.'

He let go of her hand to scratch the stubble on his jaw. Her hand felt cold and abandoned, longing for his warm touch. He smiled and told her his beard had been so long it touched his chest, but he had shaved earlier that week, for her.

'I was a frightful sight. I wanted to make this reunion as civilised as possible and not to scare you. Too much that is.'

A shy smile curled his lip. His straight teeth were poster-boy white. For the first time, she dared a closer look, the perfect arch of his eyebrow, the exotic green of his eyes, the soft light brown hair, and she recognised him. Underneath the terrifying exterior, he was still the Jay she knew and loved.

'You know, my life is just a succession of failures. Each one more dramatic than the other. I don't want to sound overly intense, but you know, it's the truth. There is only one life, and I kind of fucked it up, badly. I sometimes lie in bed at night, listening to my roommates snoring, knowing that the next day is going to be just as hopeless as today was, and I really wish I'd done things differently…' Jay paused.

Sophie shifted uncomfortably on the chair trying to rid her left leg from the painful pins and needles.

'I wish I'd realised earlier that I was ill, that my brain worked differently from everyone else's. I should have known…' The emotion strangled him as he sighed heavily into his hands.

'But you didn't know. That's the tragedy of this illness, Jay. Schizophrenia prevents you from distinguishing between reality and the paranoid fiction conjured by the sick brain.' She was aware that he knew that better than her, but it reassured her to say it out loud, like an absolution it reinforced her own efforts of conviction. He remained silent for a few seconds, his hands flat on the table.

'I did know Sophie.' He eventually spoke. 'Somewhere deep down I knew something wasn't right. It runs in the family you know. My mother went psychotic. She suffered from a postnatal depression so severe they had her on electroconvulsive therapy. It's a family curse. I don't think I have ever told you this Sophie, but my grandmother was convinced for most of her life that her neighbour was a spy. From the Stasi. She believed they had bugged her apartment and listened to her phone calls. She felt followed and persecuted for most of her life. Until one day she snapped, walked over to her neighbour's garage and emptied a petrol canister over his car. Then she waited patiently until he got in, ready to drive off to work, and she lit up a match. The car went up in flames. Tragically she had accidentally doused herself in petrol, and she screamed so loud it alerted the whole neighbour hood as the flames burned her flesh. They said she screamed for the devil to take her, that she was ready to trade one hell for another.'

Sophie reeled at the horrifying story. *It runs in the family.* The words echoed in her head.

Jay continued, his voice breathless as he talked faster.

'I know I shouldn't be saying this, but somehow Aisha had every right to abort our child. The curse is hereditary. But now it stops with me.'

Sophie swallowed hard. *Oh god. The curse is hereditary. The curse stops with him.*

'Look, it might not be hereditary; it's not entirely proven. The drugs and the divorce trauma are just as much triggers as genetics...' She was clutching at straws. *His grandmother set herself on fire. Oh god.*

'Sophie everybody does fucking drugs! Everybody's parents divorce! But not everybody turns into a...' In his anger he struggled for the word. '...Monster', he finally whispered, defeated.

She got up the chair and nervously paced around the visitor's room. She thought of her husband Martin looking after her daughter while she was in here and how he had no idea her conversation with Jay was going to change everything. She looked out of the window, and the forest of Solacium unfolded in front of her. She breathed in slowly, readying herself. She bit her lip and closed her eyes, willing her voice to be steady. For the first time since their first phone call, she plucked up enough courage to ask him the question she had burned to ask him.

'Do you feel any guilt for what you have done?' she whispered without looking at him. She needed to know whether she could forgive him, accept the causes for his crime and try to move on.

He paused again, this time for what seemed an eternity. Sophie bit hard on the nail of her thumb. When he finally spoke his voice was slightly shaking. Sophie was still staring out of the window.

'It's difficult to feel guilt for something I believe someone else has done.' His voice sounded muffled as if he was speaking into his hands. 'I know it was me who committed you-know-what, but it feels like it was someone else. A warped other version of me. But, to be honest, I want to feel guilty, I want to ask for forgiveness. But... it's hard. It's like ten tons of steel crushing me. Taking the responsibility for my actions will be my undoing.'

'I don't think so, I think it will be the beginning of your healing. I think it is time for you to admit it', she whispered. A raven circled the pine trees and settled on a branch with a squawk. A heavy silence hung over them, full of expectations. Minutes passed. She worried he was going to walk out and turned around to face him.

'... I...killed...him...' he whispered hauntingly staring at his hands '...with so much hatred. It was like a red veil in front of my eyes. There was so much blood. I wanted him to suffer for the sins I thought he committed. That sound the bat made when I crushed his skull in a final blow. It haunts me. Every night.'

Silence. Sophie bit the nail of her thumb until she tasted the blood.

'But why, Jay, why did you do it?' Her voice was anxious.

'I hated him SO much. He abused my sister. My sweet innocent little sister. He raped her.' His voice was barely audible. The ugly word hung in the air. Sophie sat back down on her chair facing him.

'Jay did you imagine that or was that true?' The shock of the revelation flipped her stomach, and her words rasped against her swollen throat like gravels under a sole.

'I don't know... I don't think so...no.' He hesitated. 'But sometimes, very selfishly, I wished it was true. Because that was my reason, the motivation for my actions. I ... just wanted to protect those I loved. I was so convinced they needed my help, my mother and my darling sister.' His voice was as flat as a hum but Sophie heard him loud and clear.

'Do you feel guilty?' She repeated gently.

His head hung low as he whispered his answer. She could barely hear the words, but she knew he said them. Those two words she had longed him to say for so long. In such a different context. 'I do'.

'I do' His breathing was ragged. He thought about the family he had destroyed. The insurmountable pain he had inflicted on his mother by not only depriving her of marital happiness but by taking away the son she, despite all, couldn't help but love. The disappointment he had subjected his once proud father to, time and time again. The shame and constant sadness his siblings experienced when taunted by their peers. The consequences of his actions had rippled through his family, leaving all involved feeling bereft and all hope for a happy ending snuffed out like a candle. 'I do' Two little words that bore the power to change everything. Two little words that could be his atonement. He was crying.

'Jay?' she said very gently, extending a hand to touch his.

A soft sob.

'It's going to be ok. You're a good person.' It sounded like she was convincing herself. Or at least trying. She didn't know if they were going to be ok, but she knew in her heart that he was a good person. Deep down she knew that given a different path in life he would have been everything his family had hoped him to become. A successful young businessman, a loving husband and a good father.

'Sophie?'

'Yes?'

'I love you.'

Her soul tore apart at the words she had longed to hear from him for so many years. The knot in her stomach wound tighter. She could feel the tears building up at the back of her throat.

'I know,' she whispered, wiping a hot tear from her cheek.

'It should have been us two…' His voice was full of regret as he gripped her hand tighter.

'I know.' There wasn't much else she could have said as they both thought about the life they could have had together if fate hadn't dealt them such cruel cards. They thought back to the night of the illegal rave party where unbeknownst to each other they could have turned the wheels of fortune in their favour. If only they had grasped the chance to talk to each other about their real feelings, their life could have been so different.

'Jay?' She softly broke the contemplative silence.

'I love you too,' and the words were liberating. She reached into the pocket of her jeans with a trembling hand and slowly pulled out the envelope that she slid over the table in front of Jay. He looked at it with a question mark in his eyes. She nodded and he proceeded to rip it open. He turned the photograph and his mouth dropped open in surprise.

'Her name is Juliet' Her head numb with thoughts of regret and hope, Sophie pointed at the smiling toddler on the photo, her innocent little face bearing none of the fears her mother harboured since she first had laid eyes on the tiny blue strip on the pregnancy test upon her return from Berlin.

'She was born on the 31st of October last year' Sophie whispered, the same night Jay had murdered his stepfather. A life for a life.

'Is she…?' He spoke with a voice thick with emotion and pointed at his chest as the words failed him.

'Yes' Sophie nodded feebly, tears rolling down her face. Jay looked up at her and a smile slowly curled his lips as he started to understand the magnitude of the revelation.

Sophie closed her eyes and said a silent prayer for their baby's fate not to follow that of her father's.

The End

ABOUT THE AUTHOR

SJ de Lagarde is half Dutch, half German, was born in France and has been living in London for over 10 years.

She is fluent in four languages and holds a masters in European cultural studies and translation as well as a baccalaureate in literature and philosophy. She works in international communications and is a regular guest lecturer at ESCP Europe and London School of Economics. She is a mental health advocate and a certified mental health first aider.

She has been a passionate reader and storyteller since childhood and 'Solacium' is her first published book, a contemporary coming-of-age novel about friendship, murder and schizophrenia, based on a true story.

She is currently working on her next novel.

Printed in Great Britain
by Amazon